AF332077

FEMEN

The Story of the Two Founders
of the International Feminist Movement

Olivier Goujon

FEMEN

The Story of the Two Founders
of the International Feminist Movement

Max Milo

© Max Milo Editions, Paris, 2023
www.maxmilo.com
ISBN : 978-2-31501-141-4

Foreword

In this story, there are blondes to die for, Russian spies in Montmartre, kidnappings, beatings and corrupt politicians, real and fake escapes, fascists, Islamists, embezzled money, a complacent administration, hungry media. And then there are lies, hatred and indifference.

It is the story of a betrayal, and of a revolution not lost to everyone. The very human story of a stolen passion.

This is the story of Anna, Sacha, Oxana, Inna and the others. The sincere story of Femen.

A wave and roots

> "You would think that only extraordinary
> or abnormal people could have endured all these
> hardships, but no, they were day-old schoolgirls,
> students, girls who had never left
> their homes before."
> Svetlana Alexievitch,
> *La guerre n'a pas un visage de femme*,
> in *Œuvres*, Actes Sud, 2015.

Odessa, Pushkin café, 10:30 p.m., April 3, 2011

"Femen is the fourth wave of global feminism[1]."
I have no doubt.
After a week spent running around Ukraine, Kiev, Donetsk, Odessa..., fleeing from the police, sleeping in trains and poor hotels, meeting journalists in secret, running

---

1. Unless otherwise noted, all quotes in the book are from interviews conducted by the author between November 2009 and September 2016.

from secret meeting to improvised demonstration, I am exhausted. But I am sure of what I have just experienced: Femen is an effervescent movement that will mark the history of women forever, like the English suffragettes, Black feminism or the MLF.

Odessa is still cold in April, and the wind from the Black Sea freezes the trees and the blue benches of Brochnoiavska Square. Two blocks away, the grand staircase of the Potemkin was the scene, a few hours earlier, of an impressive demonstration by Femen. I photographed, as if on a stormy sea, three girls screaming that their country is not a brothel and their bodies not for sale. Naked and painted breasts. Jostled by a squadron of violent police and a horde of conservative journalists, they were also booed by the crowd of passers-by. But the three blond children with raised arms emanated a power that only the cold and perfect conscience of the revolt sometimes offers. A conviction pegged to the body and the brain. And glittering eyes that say, "I defy you."

Four hours later - three of them spent at the police station - I can hardly recognize the well-behaved girls sitting in front of me in this cozy downtown bar. Inna and Sasha have traded flower crowns, thongs and graffiti for ordinary young women's outfits: turtlenecks, warm boots and fashionable jeans. They leaf through a magazine and joke about a singer who is divorced once again; they seem to have the carefree attitude of the young people from the big families of the former *nomenklatura* who still occupy the Italian dachas in the Moldavanka district. Around us, students are commenting on a course they have just taken at Metchnikov University. Life is sweet.

I have been following the Femen action for almost two years. It all began in the early summer of 2009 with a short article in *the* Italian daily newspaper *Repubblica*: "Young women demonstrate in the streets against prostitution in Ukraine. A few minutes later, I discovered on the Internet that the girls were called "Femen". They have a Myspace page where they publish photos of their demonstrations. The images are crude and dull. They come from small cell phones, but you can see pretty angry blondes, a summer sky and cops sometimes amused, sometimes frankly annoyed. I obviously smell a good subject. The page was recently created and, despite a thorough search, I can't find any reference in the French, German or Italian press, apart from the *Repubblica articoletto*.

I send a rather short message to the "Contact" section of their web page: *"French reporter, interested by making a report about Femen action. Can I meet you in Kiev? When*[2]*?"*

I had long forgotten this message when I received an email one Saturday night in November from a certain Anna Hutsol: *"You can come on monday we make assault Ukrainian parliament dressed like prostitutes*[3]*."*

---

2. "French journalist would like to do a report on the action of Femen. Can I meet you in Kiev? When?"

3. "You can come on Monday, we will storm the Ukrainian parliament, disguised as prostitutes."

The time to cancel my appointments of the week, to find a flight for the next day, and I am in Kiev at 1 am. At 7 o'clock, I meet Anna and Sacha. The story begins.

Back in France, I will publish a small article in the German press. The Polaris agency, in the United States, will also distribute some pictures. But it was *VSD* that published the first real photo report on the Femen. *VSD* will order a sequel...

I think of this in Odessa, two years later, watching Sasha massaging her frail arms abused by two clumsy policewomen who have pinned her against the granite robe of the statue of the Duke of Richelieu, at the top of the stairs that a stroller is rolling down in Eisenstein's film.[4]

The cops are getting meaner and meaner," sighs Inna, "one day they will put us in jail for a long time. Sacha smiles gravely: "Our only chance to get out alive is for people to talk about us all over the world. We must internationalize the movement!"

For me, it's very clear, France is the place to start. And I explain the French context, the concept of secularism so close to Femen's convictions, the freedom of expression, the possibility of spreading from a solid base...

"Germany too...", intervenes Sacha.

"No, France," retorts Inna.

---

4. *The Battleship Potemkin*, 1925. Serguei Eisenstein's film tells the story of the mutiny of the sailors of the *Potemkin* in 1905 in the port of Odessa. It is both a communist propaganda film and a monument of Russian cinema.

Paris, five years later

Femen is almost as well known as the Pope or Cristiano Ronaldo. I hear about it from one end of the planet to the other, in a Guatemalan newspaper, on an Australian TV. In Mexico City, I meet an artist who paints murals in honor of Femen. At the Venice Film Festival, I meet Sacha and Inna who have come to present a film[5]. Everywhere, in the magazines and on the screens, I see yellow and blue circles, blond hair and flower crowns that inspire fashion and cinema... Femen has become a "brand", an American-style *brand*. It is also a "movement", a non-physical place where sympathizers, activists, artists, politicians, journalists... Like surrealism in the 1930s, pop art in the 1960s or Al Qaeda in the 2000s[6].

But where are the warriors I discovered in Kiev or Donetsk? What happened to Sasha, Anna and Oxana? Why was Viktor ejected from the movement? Why did Amina, Safia or Eloise slam the door? Who manages the money, now that it is flowing? How did Inna build her network? How did Inna build up her network?

I saw Femen born and raised in the slums of the Kiev suburbs, I see today a movement linked to fashion, contemporary art and the Paris City Hall.

---

5. *Ukraine Is Not a Brothel*, Kitty Green, Noise & Light, 2013.

6. Inna frequently uses this provocative image to talk about Femen, most notably in the *Guardian* article of November 8, 2013, "Femen leader Inna: I'm for any form of feminism."

Has the fourth wave of feminism become a pearl between
the cobblestones of the system it wanted to shake?
I call Sacha.

Sacha, exile is his kingdom

"In the months following David's death,
solitude had provided a precious refuge;
it was not a state, it was a place."
Donato Carrisi,
The Tribunal of Souls, Calmann-Lévy, 2012.

**Paris, January 31, 2016,
in the aquarium of a café in Belleville**

The weather is fine. The boulevard of Belleville is swarming with an animation of end of market. Stalls pack up, water jets chase the relief. The café is filled with bearded bruncheurs. Some have old cameras slung over their shoulders, others have wicker baskets and short pants. The bruncheurs have bikes that they park within sight and vintage sweaters.

I am waiting for Sacha.

I am less interested in what the movement has become in the last few months. I don't understand much about it anymore. I have seen French feminists, Osez le féminisme, Ni putes ni soumises, etc., get enthusiastic about Femen, then move away. I have seen Inna on the covers of books and magazines, I have seen her at Frédéric Taddeï's, at Antoine de Caunes', at Laurent Ruquier's, at Thierry Ardisson's...

And then I heard French names: Pauline, Marguerite, Safia, Elvire...

And I didn't hear about Oxana or Sasha anymore.

Then I realized that something was going on and I wanted to know.

Sacha arrives. She has a grey wool coat, a hat and big white sneakers.

In my strongest memory, Sacha is an elusive creeper that threads between the big legs of borrowed policemen. She was unbound, I see her slender and yet slumped, a little. Her blond hair tight behind her head stretches her pale gaze. But she smiles. And orders a black tea.

"I would like to tell the story of Femen."

She looks down and says that no one is interested in Femen anymore. Not even her. I say yes. She says no. Then: "You've known Femen since the very beginning, you don't need Oxana or me to tell it[7]."

My last report on Femen dates back to March 2012 and the action in burqa, on the square of Human Rights in Paris, against the Islamic veil and in support of Aliaa Magda

---

7. Unless otherwise noted, quotes are from interviews conducted by the author between November 2009 and September 2016.

Elmahdy[8], Egyptian feminist activist threatened with death. In 2012, place du Trocadero, Sacha was a tank with blue eyes; in 2016, in Belleville, I find a wounded animal.

We talk a little about his life. "I like the cafes in Paris, with heated terraces, you can see people living."

Sasha married Dimitri, the Russian journalist kidnapped and beaten with her in July 2013 by the Russian secret services in the center of Kiev. Torture creates bonds. They live together in a studio in Montmartre. Dimitri works for independent Russian news agencies very critical of Putin and also some American newspapers. This summer, they followed the Tour de France. Sacha visited France, loved the Millau viaduct, the Livarot and the lakes of the Pyrenees.

"It was quiet."

Calm? Is Sacha "calm" now?

She smiles again, "Okay, what do you want us to say?"

Let's start with the real story of Femen...

---

8. Aliaa Magda Elmahdy publishes, on October 23, 2011, a naked photo of herself on her blog "A Rebel's diary" to protest against "a society of violence, racism, sexism, sexual harassment and hypocrisy." Threatened with death, the young woman found political asylum in Sweden.

In Khmelnytskyï,
where everything begins...

> "Women are not at all wrong when they refuse
> the rules of life that are introduced to the world,
> especially since it is men who have made them
> without them."
> Michel de Montaigne, *Essays*, Book III,
> chapter 5, 1595.

It is necessary to imagine Khmelnytskyï happy... even if it is difficult.

In the west of Ukraine, wedged between the wheat plains of Eastern Europe and the first villages of Galicia, the Podolia plateau is cold and flat. It rolls, unimpeded from the mountains of Moldova, an icy wind that whistles through meandering valleys. In the center of the plateau nestle peasant villages cut off from the world at the first snows. Winter is endless and dark. From March to November, it doesn't rain much, but the sky is often heavy and the sun livid. Short summer, few visitors. 264,000 inhabitants huddle around a ruined medieval castle. They have long worked for the Russian railroads, which arrived in 1822, the first attempt to open up the city. The other historical provider of jobs was the Russian army - which occupied several local garrisons - both hated and indispensable to the economic life of the villages of the Khmelnytskyï *oblast*[9].

Today, the whole *region* is devastated, Khmelnytskyites are unemployed, "and most often alcoholics too[10]", adds Anna.

Khmelnytskyï is a land of Cossacks. These nomads plunderers of the steppes and enemies of the least bidder, often of the Russian and the Tatar. They settled down around the river Boug which crosses the city born with wooden houses. In 1648, it was the Polish-Lithuanian occupier of the Republic of the Two Nations[11] that the Zaporogues Cossacks drove out, led by a certain Bohdan... Khmelnytskyï. The revolt is violent and lasts eight years, before the occupier finally retreats beyond the banks of the Dnieper, to the west and towards the Lithuanian strongholds of the north.

Moldavian, Cossack, Lithuanian, Polish, Ashkenazi... the land of Khmelnytskyï has undergone multiple influences over the centuries, but the enemy has most often been the Turk to the south and the Russian to the east. Even today,

---

9. Administrative region.

10. Unless otherwise noted, quotes are from interviews conducted by the author between November 2009 and September 2016.

11. Federal aristocratic republic formed in 1569 from the Kingdom of Poland and the Grand Duchy of Lithuania. It lasted until the third partition of Poland in 1795.

it is the most Western European region of Ukraine in terms of affinities, "but it is mainly due to geographical proximity," says Anna, "for the rest, the patriarchal way of life is directly adjacent to that of the Russians.

Anna's mother, a country child, is approached by a Carpathian giant at a village party. At the time, it doesn't take much in central Ukraine to decide on a marriage. But Mr. Hutsol was unemployed. He answered a classified ad from a company based on the shores of the White Sea, in the far north of Russia. He is recruited and the young mother-to-be decides to follow him. And here is the little crew on their way to the Russian Great North, where a secure job as a truck driver in an iron mine and a heated apartment are waiting for them, in Murmansk. It is there that the couple will get married and that Anna will be born in October 1984, then her little sister, one year later.

"I saw my father as a living god, able to drive huge trucks, I admired him," confides Anna to Galia Ackerman[12]. She was disappointed when the couple had to return to Ukraine at the end of the Soviet Union. Dad Hutsol, depressive and violent, will not let go of the potato alcohol that is secretly made in the barns of Podolia.

This was the time when Anna became closer to her mother. "My father had quit, he was unapproachable, in every sense of the word." She participates in the work of the small farm where her grandmother took them in. The

---

12. Galia Ackerman helped the Femen to tell their story in *Femen*, Calmann-Lévy, 2013.

new Ukrainian state assigns the abandoned wing of a former kolkhoz to the little Hutsol family. They cultivate a plot of land. They raise a few animals.

The young girl begins to nourish her revolt by becoming aware of the division of tasks in the hamlet where they have failed: the women take care of the farmyard and the vegetable garden, "while the men drink or fight instead of looking for work. Her father, however, decided to go and look for work... in Siberia and to abandon his family. The child is deeply marked by the divorce of her parents. "Even though I was happy that my father was leaving. It is Anna who pushes her mother to get out of the grip of this evil man who beat his wife and children before sinking into an alcoholic coma. The character of the future soul of Femen is revealed: while her mother postpones the divorce, Anna runs away. She moved in with her grandmother for several weeks. Refusing to return home before the divorce is finalized, she confronts her mother with a difficult choice: "It was essential, it would have led the whole family into its decline.

Anna's father now lives in Moscow and has taken care of himself; the young woman still refuses to see him. From time to time she returns to her mother, who has given her half of the family plot of land. But the life of the founder of Femen is elsewhere...

The other major event in Anna's childhood was the end of communism. "The men of the Khmelnytskyi *oblast* lost their jobs when the Russian army left. It was the women who took charge and ensured the survival of the villages in the region. They did not mind being beaten by the men who beat them. They did not rebel. This is the Russian soul!

When she was old enough to go to high school, Anna went to the more lively streets of the center of Khmelnytskyï. There she met a mischievous blond boy with whom she smoked her first cigarettes. Viktor and Anna are the same age, 14 years old. Anna also made a few friends, but "it was harder with the girls, again because of the submissive side of Ukrainian women, they only thought of finding a husband, without any desire to question the patriarchal system and to move forward by themselves. Anna did.

Anna's heart is a little wary. I remember one day, sitting on a bench in front of the marriage registration office in Khmelnytskyi, watching the couples coming out. The girls were about 16 years old, I thought they looked sad, as if they had just imprisoned themselves for many years... and I believe that this is what had just happened to them."

If Anna refuses the path of marriage and family, it means that she has to support herself, because her mother is poor and her father's flight, with the few family savings, has not helped.

At 16 years old, Anna works in the markets, loading and unloading boxes at dawn, in the cold, for a salary given from hand to hand: "Khmelnytskyï is a hub of food trafficking in the region, its market is huge."

She obtained her certificate of completion - the equivalent of the baccalaureate - and enrolled in college. She promised her mother in exchange for accepting the divorce. Anna will study accounting and management. "Nothing exciting, what interested me at the time was reading." Her mother thought that it was the business that would keep her out of trouble. Anna attended classes with difficulty and indiscipline, but eventually graduated.

Anna the rebel discovers political philosophy and Russian literature. Tolstoy she does not like, "too long", Dostoyevsky, "too hard", and Gogol, "a Ukrainian, not a Russian". *Dead Souls* - for what the book gives to see of the character of Russians and Ukrainians, made of revolt and renunciation, joy and sadness - is an essential work in the formation of the young woman.

But first, Anna was interested in great ideas: Karl Marx, Friedrich Engels, Rosa Luxemburg. It was above all August Bebel, the former president of the German Social Democratic Party (SPD), whose major work, *Woman and Socialism* (1883), she read several times and which inspired and structured her thinking. Anna organized reading committees and exchange meetings on the theme of the place of women in Eastern European society. "It is a central book in my training, it is through Bebel that I was able to theorize, to understand things that I felt without being able to put them into words.

This is the time when she gets even closer to Viktor, who goes from being a friend to a boyfriend. Together they build a political path, read, go to clubs, attend conferences.

The young woman with red hair, already short - "it's also a gesture of revolt" -, is struck by the savagery of Western capitalism that arrived in Ukraine in the early 1990s. Her father is nothing, her mother is exhausted to grow three carrots, "while under the Soviet regime, they had a status, a place. Many young intellectuals note the decline of Ukrainian workers, whose training is no longer adapted to the new economic model. It is a malaise that will continue to grow until the Orange Revolution of 2004, and even after.

A few hundred meters away, Sacha's parents are experiencing the same descent into hell. A little further away, Oxana's family is getting poorer by the day. The revolt of the three friends is fueled by this downgrading even before being feminist. However, they will quickly understand that their condition as women is the first obstacle on the way to a better world.

Anna believes in this better world. Her friends and family are amused by it, then wonder. It will be some time before she is taken seriously. But the road is marked out. Anna will never deviate from it.

Together with Viktor, she runs a small philosophical circle in a courtyard of a building on Dubov Street, the "Center of Perspectives". Looking back, Anna is amused: "It was amazing to found a political philosophy circle at the age of 18, people were watching us, sitting in a circle, commenting on Marx and Bebel, I can see them leaning out of the windows..."

Like her peers, Anna had been going to Mass since childhood. At the age of 14, she decided, to the despair of her grandmother, that she would no longer go. "I quickly freed myself from religion, I understood that it was primarily a tool of oppression."

In Khmelnytskyï, where everything begins...

With Viktor... and August Bebel, Anna discovered that women are the weakest link in the capitalist chain, but that this situation ultimately gives them a dominant position, since the power of a chain cannot be greater than that of its weakest link... In other words, "we understood that if women decided to oppose social injustices, the machine would seize up at all levels", she explained to me during our first meeting in Kiev in November 2009.

The woman is the grain of sand of the capitalist system.

Anna met Sasha and Oxana at a meeting of the Center for Perspectives on August Bebel. "Oxana came first, she made herself available to make signs, demonstration materials, then Sasha joined us a few weeks later." They are 17 years old. They are full of energy and passion. Their feminist concerns are emerging. Anna gathers around her determined girls and tries to convince Viktor, who thinks that the cause of women has no future: "I had to fight to bring him on this ground.

Within a few months of graduating with an accounting degree, Anna found a job, lost it and decided to leave. "I was a secretary in an auditing company. My boss ran for office, lost and fired me." Political meetings take up her time. She even managed to get a few grants from the town hall. The Center for Perspectives, the first structure she created in 2005, became "Nouvelle Éthique" in 2006. It will become Femen in mid-2008. But "the framework of Khmelnytskyï was too small, it was necessary to go to Kiev, especially if we wanted to speak about liberation and equality between men and women". Through a relation of her former boss, Anna found a job in Kiev in a public relations agency. "That's where I discovered how to create an event and how much people can care about the color of a star's panties!"

In the fall of 2007, Anna packed her bags. To change the world. To try.

Sacha, the tastes of the wise child

"Beauty is told even less than happiness."
Simone de Beauvoir,
La Force de l'âge, Gallimard, 1960.

Sacha is fragile. Her health is fragile because her character has the obstinacy of Churchill, the constancy of Mandela and the quiet strength of Gandhi. Even today, Sacha has to take care of her lungs and bronchi. This is the last straw for a girl who spent most of her youth with her breasts exposed in all kinds of weather.

Sacha is also one of the most beautiful women I have ever met. Her beauty is paradoxically important in her feminist story.

Sacha is even more than the others the symbol of the message that Femen wants to send: "We will use the desexed weapons of femininity in the service of feminism." Making people forget her beauty is not easy. But, in fact, when she appears with a straight chest, a serious look, a bare chest and a raised fist on a church square, in the middle of the smoke of a demonstration, or when she struggles like a devil horizontally, grabbed by a squad of left-handed rednecks, almost nobody notices her plastic before her determination. She does not use the emotional categories of posture, smile or tenderness too often attached to feminine charm. Sasha is first and foremost beautiful because of what inexorably emanates from her: will and courage.

Mr. Dad is a military man. Like Inna's. But Sacha does not look like his father, unlike Inna. Sacha spent his childhood between Ukraine and East Germany, where the captain was stationed before the fall of the Berlin Wall. The end of communism marked the repatriation of the family to Khmelnytskyï and the beginning of a long sullenness. Mr. Shevchenko will never get rid of the bitter-sweet nostalgia of an ordeal he experienced as a humiliation, like many soldiers at the time. Sasha sees this as one of the issues in the current conflict with Russia: "The liquidation of the army has deeply marked the Ukrainian soldiers, they will see in the conflict against Russia in 2014 a way to revive this pride, for themselves[13]."

In Ukraine, Sacha and his parents live with Alioushka, Sacha's maternal grandmother. Sacha's childhood was ordinary, between a father who was often absent for "business" which the young woman still ignores, and a worried and attentive mother, still today.

---

13. Unless otherwise noted, quotes are from interviews conducted by the author between November 2009 and September 2016.

At school, Sacha does not bond easily. She is shy and distrustful. For a few weeks, she was the victim of racketeering and persecution by a gang of petty criminals from the technical high school. This is not anecdotal: "I told myself at that point that no one would ever coerce me again."

Duly noted.

Like many Ukrainians of his generation, Sacha opened up to the outside world with the beginnings of the Orange Revolution, in 2003-2004. It was his political birth. The tendency in Khmelnytskyï is rather reformist and the liberal professors of the public school where Sacha is in first grade close an eye when the pupils desert the rickety benches of the cold rooms of the Moldavian prefabricated building to go and taste the heat of "what we thought was a wind of freedom". Sacha is obviously infatuated with Yulia Timoshenko[14], the *pasionaria* with braided pigtails. "The disappointment will be as great as the hope raised. Immense.

To something, disappointment is good... Because at the end of 2005, it was the period when Sacha met Anna, Viktor and Oxana: "A friend in college had told me about a group, the Center of Perspectives, I went to a meeting, it was a discussion, Anna and Viktor were leading it, we were sitting in a circle around them, I was next to Oxana, that's it...". This is how great stories are born.

---

14. A businesswoman and member of parliament, Yulia Tymoshenko was Prime Minister from January to September 2005, then from December 2007 to March 2010. Implicated in a scandal of gas contracts between Russia and Ukraine, she will be imprisoned for seven years.

Sacha, the tastes of the wise child

The four friends will become aware of the world in Marxist philosophy circles. In the middle of a park in the summer, in the back of a hollow-walled room with a stove and a Formica table in the winter, Sacha finally puts words to the injustice she feels.

But the unease can only grow.

The young girl and her parents often talk about their own youth in the Komsomol, the Leninist Youth, whose limitations Solzhenitsyn will emphasize without ever denying its greatness and enthusiasm. Sasha perceives both the nostalgia of her parents and the superficiality of her time. She regrets the loss of ideal that accompanies the entry of Ukraine in the concert of the "frequentable" nations. A few years later, the thinker and mediologist Régis Debray would speak of the fall of communism as the "disappearance of a sacred[15]". This link that stretched a people towards a common goal. Sacha does not find in the advent of the market the spiritual nourishment she is starving for. Her need for an ideal is such that she will be, like Oxana, tempted by religion. "For three months, on the advice of a teacher, I was part of a sectarian religious group; I quickly understood what place was reserved for women in these communities!"

In this mess of economic uncertainty, coupled with a political identity crisis, in which the Ukraine of the 2000's finds itself, Mr. and Mrs. Shevchenko have a very clear idea in mind: they have to put Sacha in a home.

---

15. Régis Debray, *Jeunesse du sacré*, Gallimard, 2012.

And for Mrs. Shevchenko, this means the university of economics where Sacha must register. This is not the choice of the young girl, she has more of a taste for history and religion... as if to better understand what she already suspects is the enemy. But her parents have made an implacable mathematical calculation: the opening of the country to the venerated capitalist economy will create fortunes in Ukraine. Oligarchs will spring up by the dozen from tar, wheat or mines to become the new masters of the country - like Abramovich, Chernoi or Pugachev in Russia - who will then invest in the Western European stock exchanges. These oligarchs are still in gestation in Ukraine. And where better than at the University of Management and Economics will their Sasha be in the front row to get hold of one of these future caciques? And who better than their blonde and beautiful child to seduce one of them? Sacha will study economics because she needs to find a husband! "In Ukraine, everything revolves around this for girls: find a husband, rather rich, and if possible a foreigner. Or an oligarch.

For Sacha, this is unacceptable.

However, the young girl knows that she does not leave boys indifferent. Since she was 14 years old, she has been the object of interested attentions, seduction attempts, honest and not so honest propositions... Her naivety and the prospect of earning a little pocket money will even lead her to play the supermodel during a discotheque fashion show. It is necessary to put on a ridiculous costume and to circulate between the tables where are sat mature and drunk men. The humiliating reflections of the boors cured

Sacha, the tastes of the wise child

her forever... Sacha refused, with disdain and constancy, the offers of fashion, cinema and modeling that came at the time of Femen's fame, and even at the bottom of the wave, when she arrived in Paris, when she sometimes had only a handful of euros in front of her.

It is an understatement to say that Sacha has values and that she sticks to them.

Yet she enrolled in college because it was the only way to acquire the knowledge that she was convinced would be necessary in the struggle she foresaw. She skips the economics courses, where the sons of oligarchs are to be found, and prefers those devoted to the humanities and political sciences.

In Sacha's destiny, May 9, 2007 is an important date. It is traditionally the day of the Victory over Nazism for the countries of the Soviet space, the equivalent of May 8 in France. On this day, contests, parades and demonstrations take place all over Ukraine. Sacha, Anna and Oxana walk at the head of a column of about thirty girls. Some of them are from the Center for Perspectives and New Ethics; they have recruited and convinced the others in the street. Already! They marched under different banners, demanding more social justice from the government that had just emerged from the Orange Revolution. "We were organized, beautiful, willing, we became aware that we could be a female force," says Sasha.

The time for individual advocacy came a few weeks later, in the fall, following an injustice discovered in the local newspaper. A medical error, probably due to a doctor's

alcoholism, caused the death of two patients. Sacha calls
Oxana. The two friends are moved. Something must be
done. This day remains in their memory as the day of a
second essential realization. "I knew about misery, I saw a
lot of it around me, but there I understood that we had to
change things, or at least try. Sasha and Oxana camp out
in the freezing cold, in front of the hospital where the two
women who were victims of reckless transfusions by the
accused doctor had just died. Covered with bloody sheets,
the two young activists spend long hours under the falling
snow, holding a simple sign "Whose turn is it?", which is
addressed to negligent doctors, especially when it comes to
treating poor people. At the end of the day, the governor
and a medical examiner ask them to stop their claims and
promise to take action. The offending staff, two doctors and
a nurse, will be fired.

This first success galvanized them. It was time to found
Femen. Anna left for Kiev several weeks ago. She is waiting
for them there.

Oxana, childhood of art

"Woman contains everything, or everything contains only her. It is the same wonder that hovers over a sublime mountain or a cherished brow, that drowns melancholy and deliciously in skies or in eyes, and in lakes like skies and eyes."
André Gide, *Nouveaux Prétextes*, Gallimard 1911.

Paris, November 22, 2015

"The only true art is the revolution[16]."

There is the implacable nostalgia of Slavic passions in Oxana's eyes. Her large, bewildered eyes tell before her voice what Femen should have been and how it was forgotten. They confess what the prisons of Russia and the truncheons of Ukraine failed to accomplish and what her ex-friend Inna succeeded in doing: her breaking.

---

16. Unless otherwise noted, quotes are from interviews conducted by the author between November 2009 and September 2016.

I find her in the Marais. She has come to visit Azad Asifovich, the curator of a group exhibition in which the young artist is participating with painters from all over the world. It is a tribute to Anna Guenrikhovna, a Russian film-maker from the 1950s who was censored by the regime.

The child prodigy of Khmelnytskyï lent a magnificent "hijacked icon" which represents three angels haloed, smoking and drinking around a table. Mysterious, erotic, provocative. The angels have a tender and lowered look... Perhaps the melancholy of a lost fight. They think, no doubt.

I see it as a dream betrayed.

The wind is fresh and the sun is shining a little. It is the end of autumn. Oxana says that she is "no longer Femen". Rather, she is "Femen forever", but she has been dismissed from the movement, like Sacha. Dispossessed.

And yet, "Femen is Sacha and me, more than any other... And it's Anna too, at the beginning".

Oxana comes from Khmelnytskyï. Her family history is as dull as that of her friends. Almost a cliché: a brave mother, a resigned and alcoholic father. "This is also what brought us together with Sasha and Anna, our family stories that are similar." Oxana's mother works at the market, selling what she finds, often what she grows in a small vegetable garden, which she also buys from a wholesale dealer in Kiev and offers on the Main Square of Khmelnytskyï to a penniless crowd. Oxana and her little brother, Lyosha, wait for their mother at home and sometimes accompany her to escape the violence of their drunken father.

Oxana does not meet art - "art has always been present in me" - but the possibility to express herself is offered to her. The child already feels almost a mission. She puts meaning in everything and does nothing by halves. "That's my major point in common with Sacha, we are excessive. Inna, on the contrary, is perfectly thoughtful."

The possibility of art comes to Oxana through the installation in Khmelnytskyï of a workshop of iconography. Her mother enrolled her because she had too much work and not enough time.

Oxana is 6 years old and a revelation.

The hyperactive little girl, who has trouble staying focused for more than a few moments, discovers the patience of an angel. She spends hours on a detail, as if fascinated by her blank sheet of paper or her canvas. Her teachers are more than enthusiastic. A few years later, they propel her, at less than 10 years old, in a course reserved for adults. Her talent bursts into the open. The first orders arrived. They were weddings: "In Ukraine, icons are often made for important occasions in life, especially in religious life, of course. Imagining colors, atmospheres and contexts, Oxana paints "to measure". She invariably twists the religious scenes she paints "into ideas in her head. "I imagined more provocative situations, Christs and Madonnas that are no longer in their original function." Here and there, Oxana introduces uchronic details into her small canvases. "It was hard to spot because people didn't want that of course, but I would put a cigarette in one hand, a sexual form... I don't think I ever had faith, but I gained my atheistic certainties as I developed my art."

Oxana, childhood of art

At the time of the Femen revolution, it was Oxana who came up with the idea of using toplessness for actions. This is not a coincidence. Oxana feels the world before she sees it. She rants without always having the words to express what she perceives. This sometimes makes her angry.

As we entered the art gallery in the Marais, my genius smiled and recalled the moment in his adolescence when the idea of entering the orders came to him. Religious? "It was because of the orthodox iconography, or rather for it. What is certain is that I chose God for the love of his image, for the artistic beauty that he had aroused in men, without asking myself whether one could walk on water." The fad will remain a fad: "Soon after, I found the answer to the question of walking on water," she laughs, "it is impossible!"

Fortunately for art and for feminism.

While her artistic soul was still awakening, Oxana was learning about politics and philosophy. At the age of 17, she and Sasha join the Center of Perspectives, the philosophical and political think tank that will be their destiny. Her thirst for learning is matched only by the power of her rebellion.

Oxana reads Marx and dresses punk.

She writes poetry and shouts in the street.

She is thirsty for beer and freedom.

From that "already ancient" time when she met Anna "in the park where philosophical meetings were held", Oxana retains the frenzy and enthusiasm that accompanied her political discovery and that of her two friends. Oxana is the most instinctive of the three; Viktor and Anna's speeches on Marxist dialectics applied to feminism bore her. Not that she refuses to learn from the great intellectuals, but her method of learning is experimental, sensitive, carnal. Oxana does not try to conform her action to a theoretical model, she is content to follow her life path in the street and to learn from it.

This frenzy of action and reflection, "which animated part of the youth of the 2000s", has given way to the uncertainty of the 2010s in a country that has not recovered from two revolutions and a Russian invasion.

Nostaglia.

Azad, the curator of the exhibition, interrupts us. He tells Oxana how much he loves the nostalgia of her icons, "the contrast between the sweetness and the violence that emanates from them," and suggests that she organize a solo exhibition for the spring: "We would need at least thirty works." Will Oxana be ready?

She says yes.

Let's go!

"It's time for women to stop being
lovingly annoyed."
Leymah Gbowee, Liberian activist, Speech for
the reception of his Nobel Peace Prize in 2011.

Kiev, November 14, 2009

Red tie, fluorescent green shirt, beige coat, Nestor Choufrich is a deputy from Yanukovych's party[17]. He arrives at the Parliament for a committee meeting when five furies throw themselves at him. His first reaction is to protect himself. Then he raises his eyes, looks at the young girls, their provocative necklines and their long legs perched on heels... Then he smiles wryly, before giving in to the avalanche of arms and voices that assail him.

---

17. Viktor Yanukovych, Prime Minister and then President of Ukraine from February 2010 to February 2014.

Around him, the policemen in charge of the surveillance of the accesses to the headquarters of the Ukrainian democracy are disoriented, paralyzed by the distant mistrust of the Slavs in front of the woman who rebels. And by the fear of being ridiculous. Especially since today the woman in question looks like she just came out of a night club for oligarchs in an after party. High heels, push-up bra, shiny thigh-high boots, garter belt and pink fur handcuffs. There is enough to destabilize a parliamentary teller numb with cold at 8 o'clock in the morning. From the shade of the grove of the Oligastka square, where they exchanged their parkas and their brodequins against affriolants finery, the girls appeared in a fraction of a second like a drunken students' hullabaloo. In front of stunned and laughing passers-by, they ran away shouting "*Ukrayina do not brothel*[18]! Interpellant there of the onlookers, blocking here the traffic of the cars.

This is the first time Femen has directly attacked a key center of political power in Ukraine. No one would have imagined that the girls, who have made a name for themselves with a few minor actions against corruption or animal trafficking at the Kiev zoo, would attack the political class so directly.

Everything was meticulously prepared. Anna and Sacha studied the terrain, hid in front of the Parliament for several days, planned the surprise attack, chose the day of the session open to the public, chose the main time for the arrival of the deputies and above all for the setting up of

---

18. "Ukraine is not a brothel!"

the cameras of the television channel that broadcasts the debates of the deputies in session.

The girls are about fifteen in all. They belong to the Femen movement, born in mid-2008. Some will only participate in this action. They came "to see", or even "to laugh". Others are here to last.

Three or four of them rush to the Ukrainian peacekeepers, tear off the dark blue caps of the policemen, shoot them so that the onlookers take them. It is an unstoppable tactic that was born that day. The girls will perfect it later. The Ukrainian police itself, through the voice of its national director, will praise its effectiveness two years later, at the time of the great Festival of Europe, future high point of the golden harpies: "The police can not afford to lose their cap, because it would be deducted from their pay, he said, so they must be careful.

A partridge of Ukraine without its galure is only half of itself. The unfortunate civil servants are agitated and cannot but...

On this November 14, 2009, the traffic is now totally blocked. Two girls are sitting on the hoods. A third one climbed on the roof of a blue Dacia, a driver with a cap gets out and yells.

Other girls, even more numerous, climb the gates, and there it is the stampede: a guard falls backwards, a Femen astride him, another tries in vain to catch one by her wig, which remains in her hand, a third has taken out a truncheon but hesitates reasonably, in front of so many amused passers-by, to use it. The driver with the cap has grabbed a leg.

This is one of the first major political outings of Femen.
Many Ukrainians discover them.

And a lot of police officers too.

What to do? Impossible to seize these furies in tight shorts without risking to be considered as a big pig groping young girls! And then the girls resist, fight, free themselves, and the shame is added to the shame for police officers unable to control girls. The gates are stepped over. The girls run under the columns brandishing signs, slogans and pink handcuffs. The patrol withdraws. The heavy doors of the Parliament entrance will be their fort Chabrol. No more ceding ground.

After half an hour of this hullabaloo, reinforcements finally arrive. A grouping is made around the deputy Nestor Choufrich in green shirt and red tie. The activists demand measures against the sex industry and prostitution in Kiev. The green shirt promises everything. Especially since the TV is filming. Nestor is a grassroots MP, he has never been on TV. But he will come back...

The police control the identities, including mine - I am the only photographer controlled, I say to myself that it is a story of face -, but do not stop the girls. After about twenty minutes, everyone got out of the wire mesh trucks that had been parked in the flowerbeds of the Parliament garden.

There are now a lot of MPs. Many of them came out when they saw the situation calming down, they don't want to lose an opportunity to be in the spotlight. Microphones are set up and they all say more or less the same thing: that they understand this sympathetic movement of pretty girls in anger and that they are, each one, different from their colleagues who, it is true, are big lazy corrupt people. A fool's game that convinces nobody.

But the good news is that the operation is the first media victory for Femen.

And Nestor.

Sacha and the others regrouped after a last series of photos in lascivious positions around vulgar deputies - they repented a few hours later when they discovered themselves, slimy with ridicule and incontinent with lechery, on the front pages of the capital's newspapers.

The goal is achieved.

Femen was born there, for me, and for some other Ukrainian and Russian photographers.

I met Anna two hours before, I find her after the assault. The first arrests will come soon enough, and also the police violence.

For today, we savor.

We head towards the greenish bar which serves as a meeting place for the girls. It is 11 o'clock in the morning, and the Protesgkai street is still freezing. The Kievians are walking fast, dressed in coarse overcoats and closed jackets. The heads are covered with warm hats and caps that cover the ears, the collars are hidden. It is still only November.

I hesitated to come. Notified at the last moment, I had to incur plane and hotel expenses... Wasting money, time and energy.

Now I don't regret anything. I have the distinct impression of being at the beginning of something.

A philosophy
at the bottom of the coffee

"The emancipation of the workers will be the work
of the workers themselves. The most oppressed
man can always oppress a being, who is his wife.
She is the proletarian of the proletarian herself."
Flora Tristan, *Peregrinations of an outcast*, 1837.

Revolutions are born in cafés.

Femen's is no exception to the rule.

In Khmelnytskyï, in the cafés of the Market Square, then in Kiev, first at the Ban'Ka, then at the Cupid, the Femen will foment their actions, feed their passion and found their claims.

Sacha and Oxana first feel the injustice on the skin and react passionately. Anna is the first to distance herself intellectually, out of character. But Oxana and Sasha are not slow to form a relationship.

Between 2000 and 2007, they read. They also think.

Femen was really born from the intellectual encounter of these three friends and the pooling of their revolt.

However, it is difficult to say at what moment the movements that will preside over the great causes take shape...

From a formal point of view, it is a girls' club that will prelude Femen: Nouvelle Éthique is born in February 2006, itself an emanation of the Center for Perspectives within which the friendships were forged.

The three friends chose the name New Ethics for their association, which was officially declared in the Khmelnytskyï town hall, "because it seemed to us," says Anna, "that this is what our generation needed, ethics, but at the same time the rules set by the communist society were breaking down[19].

New Ethics is not a feminist movement, "well," moderates Sacha, "it is, yes, but we didn't like the word, we were conditioned by our culture." In the Ukraine of the 2000s, feminist is a dirty word, an insult, a political and mental category that calls for subversion, even perversity. In the countryside, people still believe, as in the eighteenth century, that it is the disease of effeminate men... "In Khmelnytskyi, we can not even say that feminists, resumes Sasha, were frowned upon in our families, simply nobody knew any!" Internet, revolutions and the fall of the Wall have brought some news from the West... "But religion stifles everything." And also, the immeasurable disposition of their generation, they believe, not to be interested in essential things.

---

19. Unless otherwise noted, quotes are from interviews conducted by the author between November 2009 and September 2016.

As in Paris in 1971[20], in London in 1918[21] or in Bologna in 1236[22], in Khmelnytskyï, in Ukraine, in 2006, women who stand up for their rights are suspect: feminism is the left and debauchery! "Besides, Oxana points out, it will be the same in France, when Alain Soral will talk about us after the action in Notre-Dame, he will call us "Ukrainian whores"[23]. And in the cafés of Paris, Kiev or Brasilia, the jokes that revolve around Femen also primarily convey this image.

Feminist equals prostitute. The cliché is as old as Herod, and it is enough to make the three friends hesitate, even though they carry within them, since 2006, all the claims of feminism, but unconsciously refuse to qualify themselves as such. They are 22 (Anna), 19 (Oxana) and 18 (Sacha) years old, New Ethics is going to serve them to test the Ukrainian society on this fight which is not yet called. "We were only young girls, children even, but we went to schools, to orphanages, to give care and bring books. And also to bring the message that boys are simply not superior to girls. It's amazing how much doubt, even hostility, we encountered over that simple statement!" Verifying this blatant natural injustice strengthens them in their struggle.

---

20. "Manifesto of the 343 sluts" who declared to have had an abortion.

21. The suffragettes, often called prostitutes, obtain the right to vote for women over 30.

22. Bettisia Gozzadini, disguised as a man, obtained a chair at the university, her "virtue" was often questioned.

23. *ERTV*, November 2012.

A philosophy at the bottom of the coffee

The journalist from the Italian magazine *Grazia*, who interviewed Sasha in 2012, was taken aback by this tradition of founding groups, clubs, movements, naturally associating it with politics, the 1917 revolution, Bolshevism... Were Anna, Sasha and Oxana already revolutionaries? "No doubt," says Sasha, "but in any case, founding clubs is common here, it is a Slavic tradition, we meet." In the Eastern democracies, youth associations are the legacy of the Komsomol of Sasha's parents. Young people have been coming together since the October Revolution to act, to participate in nation building, as well as to exchange stamps. Clubs and associations are places of socialization. "What you need to know about the Ukrainian society of the 2000s and even before is that it is very boring," Sasha continues. So they founded clubs.

In Lola Lafon's beautiful book, *La petite communiste qui ne souriait jamais (The little communist who never smiled)*[24], the unforgettable Romanian gymnast, Nadia Comaneci, also speaks of the boredom that reigns in the East and of the gathering places that are so many opportunities for youth: "These are convivial places where friendships are born as much as fights, in Romania, for example, we lacked everything and so we lined up in front of the state stores with our tickets, and these queues became places where young people met, we prepared to go, the girls put on makeup."

---

24. Actes Sud, 2015.

The same goes for the children of Khmelnytskyï, who gather in the park to talk about emancipation: "We liked it, our friendship was strengthened there." Femen was born.

At the New Ethics Club, girls arrive from all over the region. They discuss politics, but very quickly the testimonies follow one another on the multiple manifestations of men's power over women in Ukraine. "We realized that girls were beaten, sometimes raped, that they were often subjected to heavy situations, and that even in families where this did not happen, like mine, machismo was everywhere, from the distribution of roles to access to bank accounts," says Sacha.

Excluded from the neighborhood hall because it was "too subversive," New Ethics would meet in the kitchen of Viktor's parents' small apartment, then in a park or on the street. "We wanted to act!" Sasha and Anna develop team thinking contests on themes that revolve around feminism: "It was a game with groups of girls from different high schools, the facilitator would provide a topic and each team would write an answer in a short time." These competitions still exist in Khmelnytskyï.

Today, Femen's commitment is theorized in a small manifesto book[25], which simply repeats the three main themes already defined at the time in Ukraine by Anna and Sacha: the fight against religion that oppresses women, whatever

---

25. The book was presented at the Espace des femmes Antoinette-Fouque on August 29, 2015 by Femen France.

the religion; the fight against the sexual exploitation of women; the fight for equality between women and men.

The Femen's passion and necessity are often the law, and they quickly add another commitment: the fight against all forms of dictatorship in the world. Not won...

At the root of the Femen philosophy is Anna's reference to intersectionality. This principle of struggle, theorized in the early 1990s by the American sociologist Kimberlé Crenshaw, approaches forms of domination through the links that connect them: intersectionality studies and fights the relations of domination induced jointly by sexism, racism or homophobia.

Intersectionality - at least in the sense defined by Anna, which is more about fighting on all fronts than actually studying the intersections of these struggles - was a trademark of Femen at birth. At the time, in Ukraine, it was said that they wanted to "interfere in everything".

Anna knows that the fights against dictatorships or religion are very long term, if they are not windmills. And she affirms that she can "obtain real progress in the fight against the sexual exploitation of women and in particular prostitution. That is concrete". She also thinks that denouncing the exploitation of women will provoke an awareness that will naturally lead to the fight for equal pay, the sharing of tasks in the household, etc. Sacha confirms it: "The three main axes were defined in 2010, when the movement grew and we realized that our revolts were multiple. But it was the fight against the sex industry that was our first struggle."

When I meet the "girls" (Anna, Viktor, Sacha and two young girls who will soon leave the movement) for the first time in the winter of 2009, we have a long discussion on this subject. I try to understand what these two-breasted Amazons want. Do they have an agenda? Do they have goals?

Anna first talks about her training, her studies and her awareness of the "societal" inferiority - in the sense that it is inscribed in the popular DNA - of women in relation to men, in Ukraine and in the Eastern countries that have just opened up to the so revered Western liberal world. But very quickly, the central subject emerges. It is the prostitution which motivates, initially and in the urgency, the revolt of the young girls.

For the writing of this book, I found a small notebook where I had noted at the time these words of Anna: "I am going to put the equation to you and you will understand immediately: on the one hand you have Ukrainian women who are young, pretty, poor, submissive and ignorant... and on the other hand older men, determined, immoral and rich. Who do you think is going to fuck whom?"

Yes, it is.

When it does not kill people, Slavic metaphysical nihilism gives faith in a better future.

But Ukrainian women are not really quick to revolt, which deeply irritates Sasha: "Sometimes I feel like saying to girls my age who are beaten by drunken husbands or crying under the yoke of old men who bought them: 'By not opposing this patriarchal situation, you are encouraging it!"

He who does not say a word consents.

Femen girls do not consent anymore.

From August Bebel to Angela Davis

"To argue that women have not been interested in the political movement until now proves absolutely nothing. From the fact that women have not, until now, been concerned with politics, it does not follow that they should not. How was it once the case for men?
August Bebel, *Woman and Socialism*, 1883.

"Toppled walls become bridges."
Angela Davis, *Black Feminisms*, 1970.

November 2009, Maidan Square

It is the Independence Square, the historical place of big gatherings in Kiev - as in 2004 for the Orange Revolution or during the winter of 2013-2014 for the second revolution. The Maïdan is the equivalent for Kievians of the Puerta del Sol for Madrilenians, of Tahrir Square for

Cairoites and of the Place de la République for Parisians. During the Soviet Union, the Russians renamed it Soviet Square, then Kalinin Square (first president of the Supreme Soviet), and finally, when the metro was built in 1976, October Revolution Square. Until the beginning of the 19th century, the Kievians called it Kozyne Boloto, the "Goat Marsh", and then, when the first wooden houses were built in this unhealthy area, it became Market Square-Khrechtchatyk, named after the main commercial artery that runs through Kiev from this central point. Finally, in 1991, in honor of the liberation from the Soviet yoke, the Maidan became the Maidan Nezalejnosti, the Independence Square.

Around the Column of Freedom, topped by a statue of Berehinya, a pagan goddess and protector in the Slavic cosmogony, political life is organized: the Parliament is just a few steps away, as is the presidential palace.

The Maidan is a strategic place that is constantly under surveillance. In 2001, the mayor of Kiev, Alexander Omeltchenko, had the square fenced off for work - Moldovan and Belarusian workers erected three new monuments to Kyi and Schek, the Cossack horsemen who founded Kiev, and to the city's patron saint, the Archangel Gabriel. For many weeks, the square was closed to the public. The first consequence was to nip in the bud, by preventing gatherings, the discontent that was rumbling in the streets, cafes and even in the media, against the president of the time, Kuchma. For Anna Hutsol, there is no doubt: "If the square had not been closed and guarded by the police in 2001, the Orange Revolution would have happened three years earlier[26].

But Femen was not ready in 2001, the girls were barely 14 years old. Destiny was waiting for Sacha and her friends.

In 2004, it was on the beautiful Maïdan theater that the whole world discovered the mats of Yulia Tymoshenko and the greasy face of Viktor Yushchenko[27], her political ally - although personal enemy -, probably poisoned with polonium by the Russian secret services.

The square will again be the nerve center of the February 2014 uprising, there will be fighting with a violence unknown in Ukraine since the Second World War. Hundreds of dead and thousands of wounded will mark the pavement of the Maidan with their blood. For weeks, the pro-European opponents of the Yanukovych government lived in the cold, organizing an improbable camp of canvas, wood, sand and tires. On the other side, the "Afghans", former Ukrainian soldiers who fought for Russia in Afghanistan, will defend the pro-Russian camp. FSB agents[28] will infiltrate the opposition groups. From the windows of the massive carcass of the Oukryina hotel, snipers will aim at innocent targets. The war.

A few months later, Viktor and Anna will tell me that this "second Ukrainian revolution" was only "fear and

---

26. Unless otherwise noted, quotes are from interviews conducted by the author between November 2009 and September 2016.

27. Viktor Yushchenko, Prime Minister then President of Ukraine from January 2005 to February 2010.

28. Russian Secret Service.

From August Bebel to Angela Davis

death" when the first one, the Orange Revolution of 2004, had been only "hope".

For the moment, we go along the Khrechtchatyk, the Kievian Champs-Élysées. The shop windows are amazing: Lanvin, Cartier, Bulgari, Dior... The biggest luxury brands organize a permanent parade of limousines, letting the wives of oligarchs, Saudi princes, local politicians appear stealthily... While we contemplate this merry-go-round worthy of Milan's *via* Montenapoleone, Anna evokes the importance of understanding the connection of struggles. She learned it from Marx and Bebel, but also from Angela Davis, the champion of minority feminism. She read her autobiography, and also *Women, Race and Class*[29], to put an intellectual concept on a notion she only had the intuition of: intersectionality. True, in Ukraine there are no African American minorities seeking civil rights, "but gays are persecuted, workers are exploited, women are dominated, it creates a conjunction of goals." This is why, in addition to the fight for equal rights for women and men and against the sex industry, Femen will include in its successive manifestos the fight against tyranny, whatever its nature and origin, and the fight against all forms of oppressive religion, "and they all are", concludes the young woman with red hair. If Femen willingly shares the anticapitalist struggle of the great "priestess of Black feminism", the limit of Angela Davis's influence lies in her relationship to religion.

---

29. Angela Davis, The Women's Press Ltd, 1981.

I point out to Anna that the black American muse is historically, and today more than ever, an active militant for the respect of religions, while the Femen are active militants for the disappearance of all religions, or at least for the disappearance of their influence in male/female relations. In front of us, a bimbo disguised as a Russian oilman's wife pulls out of a Ferrari and rushes into Chopard: "You're right, but I think Angela and I would agree to confiscate this slut's car and purse, and to distribute the dough to a school for orphans!" Anna says these words calmly, with the cool, greedy attitude of an anarchist in front of a burning prison.

What brings Anna and Angela together, and above all what seduces the Ukrainian in the American, is courage, combat and contact. And it is still paradoxical because Anna almost never[30] takes part in Femen actions, whereas Angela has been on the front line since the 1960s.

I have sometimes thought, without writing it in any report, that Anna was not, unlike Oxana or Sacha, ready to expose herself, to risk her physical integrity, in short that she was cowardly... I no longer think so. There are three strong reasons why she rarely appears in Femen actions. First, she shrouds her movement in a mystery that befits rebel organizations. When the time comes for controversy, journalists will gloss over her real role - and that of Viktor (see chapter

---

30. Of course, Anna tried. She participated in some actions. There are even collector photos of Anna topless. But she quickly understood the advantage of being in the background.

From August Bebel to Angela Davis

22). By constructing the most obscure hypotheses, they will only strengthen the legend of Femen. This is a tried and tested marketing method, and Anna is an expert in marketing. The second reason follows from the first: enigmatic in the eyes of the public, she naturally acquires an exclusive and original position within the movement. Not participating in the actions, she becomes legitimate to plan them, to organize them and, on a general level, to decide the political line. Its distance is an asset. If it is not in the action, it is in the reflection. Finally, from a practical point of view, Oxana and Sacha are not very inclined - especially Oxana - to the daily management of accounts, administrative procedures and relations with the press. It is Anna who takes care of this. The mass of information she gathers, the position she enjoys, offers her the role she aims for: that of an eminence grise. Anna never cites Lao-tseu in her personal references; yet she willingly applies one of his maxims: "Those who speak do not know, those who know do not speak." She is a model of political prudence.

And it is armed with this prudence that she will prevent any drift, any temptation to slip. If Femen slips into violence or illegality," I heard her reply curtly to an English journalist one day, "it will be lost in advance for our cause, and we want to win.

When we talk, a few months later, about European terrorism and the years of darkness in France, Italy and Germany, Anna will tell me about her fascination for the Red Brigades, but it is a romantic, virtual attraction, a human sympathy for those who once wanted a better world and went astray.

Political violence has never been on the Femen menu. Aggression is. The confusion made - sometimes in good faith, but most often in bad faith - by many of its opponents is due to the feeling of the "receiver", who feels or says he is attacked by this appearance of half-naked women who do not smile.

As long as they were in Ukraine, the European media did not question the political and intellectual formation of Femen, contenting themselves with reporting, amused and empathetic, the actions of a group of feminists of a new kind.

In Ukraine, however, the "traditional" feminists happily hated them from the start. When we shoot, with Cyril Denvers, a subject for Ali Baddou's program[31], we will meet some of these women, members of a Catholic feminist organization. They will tell us their total rejection of the Femen girls: "They are prostitutes who want to make a name for themselves. They are ignorant and just want to gain notoriety and money. They will also tell us that a woman's place is "at home with her husband and children". This puts their feminist revolutionary credibility into perspective.

---

31. *Le Grand Mag,* broadcast on Canal+ in summer 2011.

Meanwhile, in Kherson...

"It is a vain ambition to try to resemble everyone,
since everyone is composed of everyone and everyone resembles no one."
André Gide,
Le Prométhée mal enchaîné, Gallimard, 1925.

Inna grew up in Kherson, on the edge of the Ukrainian Crimea, more than 600 kilometers away from Anna, Sacha and Oxana. She has nothing in common with her future companions in struggle, who are already, each one, very different...

Mr. Shevchenko is a military man. One only has to attend a training session of the Femen soldiers led by Inna at the Lavoir moderne in Paris to be convinced. Mr. Shevchenko is a military man, and so is Inna. Or almost.

Moreover, the new leader of the movement does not hide it. Inna says in interviews that she has been a leader since her childhood and that she sees a paternal heritage in this way of being as demanding with herself as with the others.

We'll see.

The other central element of the story of Inna en marche is that she is, according to the popular "male-centric" imagery in force in France as well as in Ukraine or in the south of Cambodia since the darkness of time, a "tomboy". She climbs trees, runs - not the countryside because the family house is located in a dense suburban area - the construction sites, throws rocks, fights with boys, kisses no one, hates dresses and pink.

Inna Shevchenko is Tom Sawyer under Heidi's braids.

A few years later, a bit of make-up and a pair of high heels will instill a note of femininity in this portrait; but inside, Inna has remained the determined daughter of her father's major.[32]

Inna has a sister whom she lovingly ignores. Understand that they have nothing in common and that her older sister's life path - family, couch, work - is the opposite of the fearless blonde's dreams of greatness. Inna also loves her mother, but she says that her example, like that of her sister who is now married and has a child in Kherson, "represents the submissive Ukrainian woman, which is everything I did not want to be.

---

32. In various interviews and notably in her "confession" to Galia Ackerman for *Femen*, Inna says that her father is a "major", which refers to rank correspondences, varying according to the country, from warrant officer to general. To the question I asked her in 2011, Inna replied: "Captain equivalent". In her book, *Inna*, Caroline Fourest makes him a colonel.

At school, Inna is applied, because, she confides to Galia Ackerman, author of the first book[33] on the movement: "I quickly understood that there was a hierarchy at school: some children are more loved by the teachers who, as a result, help and stimulate them.

Inna wants to progress.

It is his inner drive, ambition.

In the amphigoric legend that the pretty Khersonian builds for herself, she never forgets to mention her responsibilities as a class leader and how she took her role to heart in leading the whole class to its own choices. At that time, in public schools in Ukraine, each class in turn is responsible for the maintenance and security of the school for a week. Inna's team kept order. Her stature is growing. She who only likes to hang out with the scruffy boys in the neighborhood behind the major's pavilion makes new, brighter friends. She is able to build on them and is elected president of the school's student government every year for three years in a row. The position is not only honorary, it contains real commitments in terms of maintaining order and implementing the political directives of the Ukrainian National Education.

A few years later, in February 2011, in a hidden room in Zaporoje before a blitzkrieg against "Greg the dickhead" (see Chapter 15), Inna will tell me the importance of her high school involvement in her overall political education:

---

33. *Femen*, Calmann-Lévy, 2013.

"Especially since it leads to the Orange Revolution in my last year[34]."

The "tomboy" grows up. He realizes, while watching his more feminine friends, that success with boys consists less in knowing how to guide them in the construction sites of the Soviet towers of the suburbs of Kherson to steal nails or plaster than in dazzling them with a pretty dress and a smile. He nourishes a form of bitterness that makes his appearance change. We can date from this period the oxymoronic birth of *"the high heels warrior"*.

In 2004, in Ukraine, who could be the idol of a 15 year old girl who was opening up to the world if not Yulia Tymoshenko? The hatred that Inna would later vow to her was equalled only by the love she had for her. Yulia, the high priestess of the struggle against the successive pro-Russian presidents Kuchma and Yanukovych, represents a model for Inna. The young girl especially likes her ease and her speech.

At the same time, in Khmelnytskyï, Anna, Sacha and Oxana are also seduced by the Ukrainian-Russian-Latvian muse. But they quickly come back, reproaching her for the fortune she made during the Russian perestroika in the gas industry. They also did not understand her center-right position and, as loyal Marxist beginners, were suspicious of any exaggerated incarnation of power or counter-power, preferring already "an idea to a person". At the time, Yulia

---

34. Unless otherwise noted, quotes are from interviews conducted by the author between November 2009 and September 2016.

Tymoshenko created an opposition party modestly named the BlouT, the Yulia Tymoshenko Bloc. It was this party that she put at the disposal of Viktor Yushchenko, her front ally - whom she hated, but whom she brought to the Orange Revolution - to overthrow Yanukovych, who had just been fraudulently re-elected.

Inna does not have the reservations of Khmelnytskyï's three friends. The personality of Yulia is precisely what seduces her. Perhaps she sees in her what the others do not? Perhaps she appreciates in the woman who married Alexander Tymoshenko at the age of 18 - the son of the most important political leader in Dnepropetrovsk, a man who one could bet would secure her future and that of seven generations of descendants - precisely what Anna, Sasha and Oxana hate: calculation, opportunism, Machiavellian prudence, which will make Tymoshenko a foolproof political animal.

Inna likes Yulia's appearance so much that one day she goes to school with her hair braided in the style of her idol, which will earn her a serious reprimand. Kherson has always been a small conservative town. His mother was also seduced by Tymoshenko, "but in secret she didn't even dare to tell my father". Major Shevchenko, on the other hand, hates the Gazprom *pasionary*. Despite the revolutionary fads of the young Inna, he accompanies her to Kiev, just after the revolution of 2004, to support her during her entrance exams: the tomboy, a construction site runner, wants to become a journalist.

His father's support is equivocal. He does not like journalists, Kiev or the revolution, but he loves his daughter.

And he wants the best for her. No doubt he also senses that this will happen far from Kherson, as he remembers that he was once driven by the same ambitious flame. But Inna's ranking in the university entrance exam does not allow for a free education[35]. The small Shevchenko family will make an effort to finance her studies in Kiev. The young girl seems motivated. Journalism appears, in the eyes of the father as well as the daughter, a good springboard to rise to interesting spheres. The major has great confidence in his daughter, and his daughter has great confidence in herself.

Inna will say that her first weeks at the University of Journalism were difficult. Mostly because she is directly confronted with the privileged caste in this country, the one that has access to everything, by right and without paying. While she, Inna, has to take seven exams in one week and get financial help from her parents to attend classes. She also knows that some students already have their diploma in their pocket even before starting their studies... The social elevator is still lagging behind in Ukraine. She will have a hard time adjusting to life in the capital, far from her family and friends. The boys obviously notice this pretty girl. But if, in Kherson, the former president of her high school students was the queen of the ball, here in Kiev, there are so many queens...

---

35. In Ukraine, only the first ranked students in the university entrance exam are entitled to free education, but these places are often unduly allocated to the children of apparatchiks and oligarchs.

She was obviously unaware of it, but during her last years of adolescence, in Kherson, Inna made the decision that would determine her destiny. After school, she skipped the long beer and cigarette sessions in the café with her friends for an evening course suggested by her father...

The major's daughter is learning English.

Ukrayina does not Damn'!

> "No one is more arrogant toward women, more
> aggressive or contemptuous, than a man worried
> about his manhood."
> Simone de Beauvoir,
> *Le Deuxième Sexe*, Gallimard, 1949.

Kiev, May 24, 2011

Cyril and I are walking along Kresnarhechr, the boulevard that connects the Maïdan to the posh residential areas
in the east of the city. I am back in Ukraine for a film[36]
about Femen. Cyril is a film director, he is notably the
author of magnificent episodes of " Des racines et des ailes
" in Moscow or in Croatia. He must bring to our subject
his technical mastery, I must bring my knowledge of the

---

36. *Trends Ukraine: topless feminists*. Broadcast on July 2, 2011, *Le Grand Mag*,
Canal+.

field and my relationship with the girls. We arrived the day before. Tomorrow, it is the big day of shooting with the planned intervention of the girls at the Festival of Europe. There is danger. They are known now, they are expected everywhere. The wolfhounds of power will be there to make sure that the cameras of the whole world film the majesty of the city center or the speech of the good president Yanukovych, and not a bunch of ranting and scruffy furies.

While walking, we observe the Ukraine where Anna, Sacha, Inna and Oxana revolt: it is the post-communist Ukraine which discovers the joys and the jungle of liberalism, the fortunes made in one day, a political class adoubted, co-opted, never renewed. Customs duties fall, borders open, Apple, Vuitton, Vivendi, Coca Cola or McDonald's foxes have a field day in this virgin henhouse. In a few months, the storefronts of Kiev, Odessa or Donetsk will be adorned with the jewels of Western good taste: H&M, Levi's, Desigual... whose civilizing mission is to replace, at one month's salary each, the high-waisted ribs and wide-necked shirts of the Ukrainian youth. Cargill is taking over the oilseeds, Monsanto is transforming Europe's breadbasket into a GMO paradise. Exxon and Chevron are buying gas pipelines to annoy Putin; Hunter Biden, son of US Vice President Joe Biden, is taking over Burisma, the country's largest private gas producer... In short, in the early 2010s, Ukraine is a supermarket without a security guard after an earthquake: Western looters are on the shelves and nothing escapes them. And especially not the most tempting of all goods: Ukrainian schoolgirls.

If Pasolini had been able to know the Ukraine of that time, no doubt he would have named it like the Berlusconi Italy that was born before his eyes on the overturned corpses of the working class and of the great Enrico Berlinguer, "the last of the disasters, the disaster of all disasters".

We return to the hotel.

"I am not really a prostitute, I need money and I like to have fun[37]." Olga is 26 years old. She was waiting for me, along with about twenty others who like money and fun, in the big hall where there are benches and sofas. She was waiting for me... or someone else, as long as that someone else or I was obviously from Western Europe.

I choose Olga, at random, and simply check that she speaks English. We go up to my room. I choose Olga at random, but I make sure she doesn't leave her bag with anyone in the lobby, that she doesn't make any conniving signs to this one or that one... Anna warned me well: "The girls' bosses are sometimes in the hotel, it can be problematic if they find out you're doing interviews." Indeed, the relationship I'm looking for with Olga is a bit unusual. It is simply a personal interview about why she "chose" prostitution, and first is it a choice? I offer the requested fee, $100 for two hours, but I say that I am a writer and that I want to find out about the condition of prostitutes in Kiev, because my heroine is supposed to have fled Ukraine to escape prostitution. I more or less cobbled together a

---

37. Unless otherwise noted, quotes are from interviews conducted by the author between November 2009 and September 2016.

Ukrayina does not Damn'!

scenario in two minutes, just before I approached Olga. The girl is immediately cooperative, that's okay, but she wants 150 dollars. Talking is more expensive.

Logical.

In one short hour, Olga traces, with naivety and in spite of herself, a bewildering picture of the situation of prostitutes in Kiev.

She was a student when she was approached on the street six months ago on her way to college by a man who left her a pamphlet and a phone number. The job was to waitress at a bar at night.

"I was not foolish, even then, I understood what it was all about, I could refuse, but I went, to see."

There are hundreds of touts in Kiev in the early 2010s. They are posted outside universities, but also schools, administrations, employment offices "and even marriage registration offices! These recruiters are the first interface between young girls and prostitution: they are young, friendly, never impolite or even insistent - there is so much supply. Their mission is to put the young girls in contact with the possibility of prostitution, to make it enter their daily life without them even noticing it and therefore defending themselves.

The girls see these boys regularly, are not afraid of them, and get used to their presence. The day they go to the night bar or the "restaurant", this known face has already familiarized them with the world of prostitution. They have already taken the first step in their minds, unconsciously, almost innocently. The second step is decisive and pushes many of them away. The direct contact with the client is sometimes traumatic, even if the girls' mission is only to "be pleasant".

For Olga, the first attempt was negative: "I ran away, I was dressed in an evening dress and heels in a dark bar, the men were old, they were drinking and laughing loudly, they scared me." But to leave, it is necessary to do violence: "The doors of the bar are guarded by guards who do not move away easily, even if they do not have the order to hold us. We lose the money of the evening."

Then Olga came back. "After that experience, I thought I had been stupid, I met a girl in college who had done it and was making money, I decided to go back."

To never leave.

"Obviously, here I can earn 300 euros a night, that's three times more than in a month for many girls employed in companies in Ukraine, and much more than a student."

In Ukraine, the average salary does not mean much, because the disparities are gigantic and "the caste" does not live, literally, in the same country as the rest of the population. There are no reliable studies, but the comparative orders of magnitude speak for themselves: a doctor in Kiev rarely earns more than 300 euros a month, a secretary 100, a bank employee 150... In Khmelnytskyï, Sacha's parents, a little better off than Oxana's or Anna's, earned 200 euros a month in 2008. In Kherson, Major Shevchenko, who has to finance Inna's studies, earns hardly more.

To find housing, we do miracles. Students live three or four to a room in dilapidated apartments in huge towers, some of which have not had an elevator for a long time. It is not uncommon to have to walk up twelve flights of stairs to get home. Rents remained low until the early 2010s. Real estate is one of the last economic sectors to be affected by the Western liberal octopus. But from 2011 onwards, the center, then the second crown, then the third crown become unaffordable for Kievians without support or fortune. Sacha will have a hard time finding an acceptable rent when she decides to leave the slum she shares on the outskirts of Kiev with a friend. The speculation linked to the installation of luxury businesses and the arrival of new oligarchs is in full swing for three years. It will take the dramatic events of 2014 and the war against Russia to stop this price explosion and, inevitably, to burst the real estate bubble.

In the early 2010s, life is not expensive for those who do not splurge. Basic goods can be found on the markets and if the basic prices are regularly increasing, one can eat decently in Kiev. The same cannot be said of the deplorable health care system. There is almost no social protection for Ukrainian citizens. The public hospital is free but dilapidated. Among the doctors, those who specialize in plastic surgery or dentistry are about to make real fortunes, the others are about to starve with the rest of the forgotten people of the new growth. Anna, Sacha or Oxana treat themselves on the Internet, often diagnose their illnesses themselves from specialized websites and buy their medicines on the black market when grandma's remedies are not enough.

This is the situation that throws the young and beautiful Ukrainian women into the pimps' pincers. And this jungle is even more ferocious.

Olga is lucky, she doesn't have a boss, well not really. "I have to give 20 percent to one person in the hotel so I can stay in the lobby." To which person? "A man that another girl pointed out to me." In Kiev's hotels, waiters, receptionists or chambermaids get part of the earnings from the prostitutes who hang out in the lobbies. This is also where the police regularly come to take their share of the money. That's why a prostitute is not free to work whenever she wants. She supports people around her, and these people want her to work, even if they are not really pimps... On the *other hand*, if she is too present, she will be told that it is time to go home and make room for someone else. People are lining up to become prostitutes in Kiev in 2011.

By the way, does Olga know the Femen girls? "Yes, of course," she smiles. She has already seen Femen's actions in the streets frequented by prostitutes, but Olga never works in the streets. However, she has a surprising opinion: "I think that Femen are useful because it is not possible that in this country all girls become prostitutes."

Olga is blond, thin, pretty. She is 22 years old. Some girls are 17, sometimes less, it is not rare. During their actions in the streets, Oxana and Sacha have already met girls of 12 years old. For Sacha, "the mechanism is always the same in this case, it's not to finance studies or to earn more money, it's just to earn a little money, it's survival prostitution, it's the most revolting". Femen's actions have sometimes brought to light extreme cases of girls being raped and even killed. Members of parliament have promised to help them (see chapter 6), but each time they run into the

Ukrayina does not Damn'!

same obstacle: the corrupt government, which welcomes the foreign currency linked to the development of prostitution, while officially taking offense at it so as not to shock its very religious electorate.

Olga is lucky, she works in a hotel. She owes it to a receptionist who let her "come here for services...". Olga refuses to work in discotheques.

The discotheques... Precisely, we must turn the next evening to the Shooters. It is one of the most famous discotheques of the Ukrainian capital.

I suggest Olga to accompany us.

She accepts.

It will be an additional $150.

In the hell of the Shooters

> "Don't insult those unfortunate women you meet
> in the evening on the street. Remember that most
> of them have been given up to prostitution by
> hunger and have dropped into the stream so as not
> to throw themselves into the river."
> Victor Hugo, *Post-scriptum de ma vie*,
> Calmann-Lévy, 1901.

Kiev, May 2011

At midnight, the doors open and the men rush up the stairs. Most of them are Western Europeans, Turks or Russians. But Russians are not popular. Russians are boorish. Not that the others are poets, "but at least they are not violent[38]", says Olga. On the other hand, Russians have at

---

38. Unless otherwise noted, quotes are from interviews conducted by the author between November 2009 and September 2016.

least as much money and libido to satisfy as the others, "so the girls go anyway.

Discotheques are the first place of meta-prostitutional contact in Ukraine, in other words, "they are not brothels but almost", simplifies Sacha.

Sacha accompanied us to the entrance, but his presence would put us in danger inside the nightclub. The physiognomists know his face and those of the main members of Femen. In 2009 they entered Shooters, interrupted the music and held up signs "*Ukraine is not a brothel*[39]". The reception was very harsh. The Shooters' heavyweights are worse than the Ukrainian police. Sasha came out of it with a swollen face and torn clothes: "Even though I wasn't wearing much," she smiles.

It is Olga, the young woman in the lobby of my hotel, who will be our guide inside the temple of Ukrainian class entertainment. At the entrance, we are scrutinized and searched, Olga parleyed and then told us that we have to pay a higher fee. Olga herself is the reason for this extra charge, because by entering at midnight together we did not comply with the rules. Here," Olga explains, "women have to enter around 10 pm. And at midnight we let the men in." During the two hours when men are not allowed through the airlocks, the women dance, deafen themselves and get drunk at the bar where drinks are free or almost. The result: when the men enter, many of them, "the youngest

---

39. The registration was in English, as the vast majority of Shooters' clients are foreigners.

and least experienced especially", are drunk and do not even realize what they are doing. The sharks of liberalism applied to Ukrainian sexuality have a field day in this uninhibited reserve.

Olga should have entered before us. And then, coming already accompanied by a woman, we take away a possibility to another one inside... We pay the supplement.

The rush of men drags us along and provokes screams in the dark clarity of an immense room. Swarms of young women are scattering in a ribambelle from which the colored flashes of the sheath dresses and the stilettos spout out.

Very quickly groups are formed, the benches and alcoves are filled. Women dance in front of tables. And on the tables. Around the bar, the crowd is pressed as in a popular stand one evening of PSG-OM. Men drink and let their hands wander over girls who pass by them. Smiles are exchanged between strangers. Champagne, or what takes the place of it, flows freely, 200 dollars a bottle. I ask Olga if all the girls are prostitutes. "No, of course not, and even none. But they are all there for economic reasons. Economic purpose? In a bizarre way and in my amazement, I wonder if this is a euphemism or an understatement.

Some alcoves are darker than others, more secluded: "You have to pay to get in." Some girls dance among themselves. I say to myself that they want to delay the moment to throw themselves in the arena... "The night is long, they give themselves time", slips me precisely. "The night is long, they give themselves time", says Olga, pointing to the procrastinators.

But, if they are not prostitutes, who are they, these girls who frequent the Shooters? "There may be occasional prostitutes, but soliciting is theoretically prohibited inside the club." Most of the girls are students, employees, unemployed women... all pretty or prim. "Obviously, if a girl has a too unattractive physique, she doesn't come here, she has no chance with the competition." In the Ukrainian chain of predation, as in others, physical appearance is a compelling argument. And the canons of local seduction are particularly talkative: dresses and bustiers pigeon-holes, glittering satins and acrylics coruscants, makeup boasts, peroxidized hair, pumps raised, bare legs, oversized nails... The looks are complicit and vague, the attitudes are polite.

In front of these attractive night beauties, an army of more or less senior executives, full of hormones, drooling and dollars in their pockets, takes possession of the place. Most of the male hominids are in groups, but some have come alone. "The ones that are alone, they're either locals or cops, and nobody goes to the cops. The people from here, they will be chosen at the end of the evening by those who can not afford to return empty-handed, "explains Olga.

From time to time, the flash of a flash pierces the darkness, the customers photograph themselves with girls on their knees, in their arms and even on their shoulders. It is not expressly forbidden to film or photograph in this kind of place as long as it is done by drunken men who are having fun with morgue. It is much more difficult for us. We knew that before we came. The club owners are wary, they know that European TVs like to film the night debauchery of

Kiev to feed reports on prostitution. In the room, imposing thugs in dark suits and ties, shaved and tattooed, equipped with earpieces and telescopic truncheons visible at the belt, walk the aisles and are in charge of observing the clientele. It is not uncommon to see one of them approach a customer and search him or her, or check a bag. They also prevent fights, which are frequent, and expel the belligerents.

I am equipped with a pen-camera stuck in the pocket of my jacket. I have to be careful not to wear out the battery and especially not to let my gaze wander towards my pocket. With a pressure on the cap, I activate the camera and I turn to the scene where two girls dance with a man who holds a bottle with one hand and lets the other one walk without care on the body of his preys. Olga points out an adequately lit alcove where men in their sixties are drinking champagne while being massaged by probably underage girls.

Everywhere, bodies seem to be looking for each other but the atmosphere is not festive, I feel tension, the tension that the bouncers who look at me transmit to me - Olga tells me that they probably don't suspect me of filming, but rather that they are intrigued because I don't have the greedy look of the usual clients - and especially the tension that I read, finally, on the faces of these girls... Behind these polyester dresses, these supermarket make-up and these disposable heels, the misery of the filthy apartments of the suburbs where these young women live, the pain of their daily life, the humiliation of selling themselves by necessity, clearly show through. Yet it is difficult to spot the slightest suspicious exchange of money. It will happen later, in the hotel.

Here, the bouncers are also in charge of spotting the girls who would sell their sexual services directly on the spot.

The next day, I met Alex, a young French agricultural trader who has been living in Kiev for a few years. He explained to me that the phenomenon has become so frequent that the "real" prostitution places suffer from it: why go to look for in a gloomy brothel what you can find in a discotheque where you will save a semblance of appearance?

Olga, our pretty guide, is herself very solicited, but we bought her services for the evening and her mission is to guide us in this dancing whorehouse... "I hate this way of doing things, I'm in hotels, the receptionists have lists with photos, they offer our services to the customers, it's clear and square, here it's a slaughterhouse. I hate this way of doing things, I'm in hotels, receptionists have lists of girls with photos, they offer our services to customers, it's clear and square, here it's slaughter!"

The hour advancing, Olga makes us notice the girls who are more direct, as if it were still possible! However, I see them now approaching the men one after the other, showing off with an outrageous felinity, not hesitating anymore to lure those who are already accompanied and that are defended, claws out, by other drunken rags clinging to their disgusting lifebuoys... "Time is short", explains Olga, "they cannot afford to go back alone. Time is short", Olga explains to me, they can't afford to go back alone.

We are going home. Dumbfounded.

The next day, I meet Sasha and Inna again: "It was President Yushchenko who caused the rush of foreigners here by opening the borders." Since 2005, it is no longer necessary to ask for a visa to enter Ukraine from Western Europe, but also from Turkey and some Arab countries. I think back to Anna who explained to me a short time ago the class inequality between Ukrainian youth and the men who hunt them down.

These girls have no chance.

The time of the first actions

"There are no limits to achieving our dreams.
That's what my mother taught me, who learned to
read and write at age 68."
Fadumo Dayib,
presidential candidate in Somalia,
in *Le Monde*, January 20, 2016.

There are no photos from that day, fortunately[40] !"
Sasha smiles, "We handed out candy and released balloons, it was childish, almost ridiculous." It is Earth Day, April 22, 2008. No journalists are present. It's a harmless action. Well, not so insignificant: "It is a founding action, because it is there that we confront people, the street world. Of course, there was already the cry of rage in front of the hospital of Khmelnytskyï, "but nobody saw us except the

---

40. Unless otherwise noted, quotes are from interviews conducted by the author between November 2009 and September 2016.

people of the hospital". For Earth Day, the girls are facing the public. They hear and receive direct feedback. They are subjects and objects of their action.

It was spring 2008 in Kiev, the time when the name Femen was chosen after a bitter discussion that lasted for hours in the night in a kitchen, on the fourth floor of Vylkov Street, in the middle of the whitish towers of a suburb where Anna rents a squalid two-room apartment. Anna and Viktor, as intuitive advertisers, love the percussion of the word and its sound. Its paronymy with the words *"female"* or *"feminism"* also plays in its favor, even if etymologically it has nothing to do with the feminine universe, it means "thigh" in Latin.

Sacha doesn't really like it.

Oxana says why not.

The Earth Day action is not political or even meaningful, "but," adds Sacha, "it freed us, all of us who were there.

Inna was not there. She even mocked the action later in different interviews[41].

From the moment Anna and Sasha arrived in Kiev until the summer of 2008, Femen was looking for its bearings. When I think back," says Sasha, "I realize how difficult it was to overcome our shyness.

Past or present, the performances of the members of Femen, seen from the audience, seem to be obvious on stage. Everything is set. The scenes follow one another. The

---

41. See in particular Inna Shevchenko at the Dave Rubin Report, March 2016 (minute 22).

performance and the message make us forget that there is a half-naked 20 year old girl in front of the world, and that the fundamental violence that she is showing is first and foremost self-imposed. Sacha will wonder, Inna will have a nervous breakdown when she understands that she will not escape the topless. For Oxana it will be easier: as an artist, she knows she has to give herself up to the world; so a little sooner, a little later, here or there, topless or not...

In the summer of 2008, the girls carried out a series of civic actions but without any real political investment: in the metro to stigmatize the lack of security after the suicide of two people, in the squares of working-class neighborhoods against the too frequent power cuts... The most important of these actions took place in July. It announces the politicization of the movement. For weeks, the Kievians have been regularly deprived of hot water because of works at the power station on which the whole city depends. On July 15, the girls invade the fountain of the Independence Square and throw themselves dressed in the water with cries of "let's wash here since we have no more water in our houses! They are unaware that at the same time, a few thousand kilometers away, a god of women has thrown other veiled girls into the delightful fountains of Tehran, provoking the reproachful outbursts of the clerics and the anger of the police. In Tehran, the mullahs will ban bathing after deliberation. In Kiev, the police hesitate to intervene.

The operation was a success and will be repeated about ten times during the summer. Journalists being present from the second bathing, it is difficult for the police to repress.

The time of the first actions

And then there is no death of man! Just young girls bathing. Anna will be nevertheless arrested and will spend one morning at the station.

Unlike the actions of the metro or Earth Day, this "swim", which takes a slightly more political tone, interests journalists. They ask about the movement and requests for interviews come in. "The questions immediately turned to the financing of Femen, its origin, political support..." Assuming manipulation is a classic that is useful to everyone. It gives grist to the mill to journalists and arguments to political parties who can throw accusations of manipulation by activists at each other. It also allows the movement to be discredited even before it takes off on the national scene, and then... " It is also, insists Oxana, a macho argument that poses as a matter of course that 20-year-old girls are not capable of having a political conscience."

This awareness will however assert itself.

Since the girls are in Kiev, they measure every day the power and the stakes of the sex industry. And also the dramatic loss of references that the western invasion provokes among the Ukrainian youth.

From the beginning, Femen has refused to please. It is not a party looking for votes; it is a virulent protest movement that is preparing to enter the field of feminist activism with force. This clearly identified political objective is one that the girls have carried with them for a long time. It resonates with their detestation of patriarchy, which was already the basis of their involvement in New Ethics. The repetition of the blows dealt by men is so strong that it could be, especially for Anna, likely to provoke a gendered radicalization, refocused on a sexual opposition and a detestation of the strong sex. This is not and will never be the case, even if the temptation existed, notably at the creation of Nouvelle Éthique, in 2006, which excluded male participants, with the exception of Viktor. "Because we were 18 years old, but we fought against ourselves to understand that feminism had to go through men too." For Oxana, "of course men must also carry the fight, but at first in Kiev, we could not find anyone to align with us, and then it is feminism anyway, so it was first to the girls to go to war." And when men are involved in the actions, it happens that they take their legs at the last moment... Sasha Shevchenko or Oxana Shachko is not who wants to be!

They lead a war whose first battles are called "sex safaris".

Since November 2008, safaris take place in the red light district, behind the Maïdan. Armed with signs demanding "the simple application of the law that forbids the purchase of sexual services in Ukraine", the girls invade hotels, block the buses of Turks who buy *all inclusive sex tours* (travel, hotel and a different girl every night), interrupt "services" in the brothels that are open to the public... These actions confront them violently with reality. As long as they bathe in the fountains and release balloons, the politicians find them sympathetic. When they take pictures of Turks in the middle of *sex tours* to send them to the Istanbul press, when they harangue prostitutes to incite them to revolt, when they grab TV stars or insult deputies and ministers whom they accuse of owning brothels... they collide with

The time of the first actions

the system head on. And the system is not a good girl. It rebukes. The first arrests take place. The police watch from time to time the old sauna of the Bank'a, the bar where the girls have elected headquarters.

At the same time as their revolt grows, their consciousness is refined. Anna, Sacha and Oxana think, observe, learn and reflect. "We were not *no-sex* or puritanical activists, we were afraid to install the idea that we were fighting against sexuality when we were fighting against prostitution and the sex industry. They thus choose a concrete political creed, which gives body and object to their revolt. It will be the abolitionism and the criminalization of prostitution. They decide this only after having studied, on the Net, the attitude of the big democracies in front of the industry of the sex and the prostitution, apprehended the concepts of right, the individualism, the respect of the person, the liberalism, etc.

While I listen to Anna disserting on "the right to dispose of one's body" - a right that I defend against her, one evening of debate at the Bank'a -, Sacha intervenes to justify with precision and will the abolition of prostitution: "One can understand everything in an ideal world, but the Ukraine is not an ideal world, it is a world corrupted by men and money."

Certainly.

Sacha insists: "We can say all the humanist things we want, but at the end of the day we have to impose the law, because if girls have the choice between prostitution and misery, they will always choose prostitution.

But then Femen has the wrong enemy, it is against misery that we must fight?

"Of course, that's what the corrupt politicians here say: "We're going to create the conditions so that women don't have to prostitute themselves anymore," but these guys own brothels!"

So there is no solution?

"If, we have to go after the effect before the cause, we have to go after the client so that girls have fewer opportunities for prostitution."

Making their virtue in spite of themselves, right?

"You can say it like that, but look at Moldova or Belarus, the girls are even poorer and as pretty as Ukrainian girls, but these countries don't have these problems because Westerners don't have access to them yet. If we start arresting and even convicting Turks or Italians for buying sexual services in Ukraine, they will come less, they will be afraid, and the volume of prostitution will decrease. Of course, we won't be richer, but we'll go to school instead of the brothel, and that's better!"

Sacha is 20 years old.

I admire it.

Inna has the Euro in mind!

> "When you don't know how to do anything,
> you have to have a lot of ambition."
> Georges Wolinski

Paris, February 2, 2016

Sacha lives in Montmartre. A small apartment that her husband Dimitri found thanks to Russian friends. "Otherwise, finding a place to live in Paris when you're a refugee is a real struggle, even if you don't believe in God[42] ! The studio overlooks a small side street of the Place du Tertre. That's where I found her, in a café.

"We didn't choose the location, but we obviously like Montmartre. In the summer, it looks like the Maïdan on a protest day, except that people are all happy to be there!"

---

42. Unless otherwise noted, quotes are from interviews conducted by the author between November 2009 and September 2016.

In 2015, for weeks, months, after her exclusion (see chapter 39) from Femen France, Sacha was unable to pronounce the word "Femen." "When it was said around me or on TV, I felt physical pain." She consulted doctors. "You know what a psychologist told me? Do sports!"

The day before, I reviewed a small subject for German TV from 2012: *"Guten Tag, my name is Sacha Shevchenko, I'm 24 years old and I'v been arrested by police more than hundred times*[43]*."* This is how Sasha introduces himself...

"Get active!"

This is Sacha's drama.

Beyond the political motivation, beyond even the courage and revolutionary commitment, there is the action, the stress, the moment, the decision, the race, the blows... All this is impossible to forget. "But I don't want to forget anymore! When we first met in Kiev, I probably told you that I would be a Femen for the rest of my life? Well, my life is not over!"

Sacha is clearly in need of Femen.

Like Michaux on mezcal or Cocteau on opium, she drank from boldness. And her world emptied in a few weeks when she understood that neither she nor Oxana were wanted. "I thought my life was over." In fact, it stopped, a little...

Sasha orders a latte and says, pressing each syllable, "I am Fe-men." The strength of her commitment far and above the shenanigans that will try to lose her. "Ask around, in

---

43. "Hello, my name is Sasha Shevchenko, I am 24 years old and I have been arrested by the police more than a hundred times."

2004, the image of the Ukrainian woman anywhere in the world was either a whore or Tymoshenko and her braids; today, the image of the Ukrainian woman is a Femen. It is thanks to Oxana and me. We have changed the world! So when people tell me that I have to do sports and that it will pass..."

Does Sacha feel guilty for having introduced Inna into Femen, does she regret having opened the sheepfold to the wolf? "No, as I told you, it was good for Femen, Inna is brave and she is not afraid to go to the contact, and at the same time she knows how to be careful, that is the right attitude to be in Femen."

The four young women of Femen were the fourth wave of global feminism. I often think it's a mess. And also that we live on hope. Still.

Maybe one day...

Inna joined Femen out of a thirst for recognition and power. Like many other activists. But unlike Sacha and Oxana, she pursues a personal rather than a collective goal. This does not prevent her from playing a strong role in the group, at least as long as her interests and those of the movement coincide.

It is a particular event that will definitively launch her political career within the movement: the Euro 2012 held in Ukraine and Poland in June. This is the first adventure of international stature that Femen has faced.

And it is Inna who will take care of it, as Sacha promised her.

"Inna told me from the beginning that she didn't want to participate in meetings with prostitutes or things like

Inna has the Euro in mind!

that. I understood right away that she was not interested in the substantive work of the team, that she was looking for something more media-friendly. Since it was useful for the cause and she was not shy about it, I entrusted her with the Euro 2012 project."

Managing the Euro 2012 project at Femen means imagining actions, coordinating their preparation and execution. And above all, it means establishing a network of contacts, journalists and program managers.

The young head of the Kherson class puts all her heart into it.

She's good at it.

Inna carefully notes each press contact, solicits others, in short, quickly builds up an extensive repertoire. Inna is organized. She immediately understood the scope of the event. After a few weeks, she has built up a file of journalists who will be notified by e-mail of the movement's every move and will receive all press releases. She thus sets up, on the occasion of the Euro, a systematic occupation of the field of the press relations which will be very useful to her thereafter.

Well before the start of the games, and despite the lack of enthusiasm for the competition in the country, Inna called the journalists directly, who were waiting impatiently and in secret to understand what Femen had imagined for the occasion.

In parallel with the preparation of the Euro, Femen is gaining momentum. The protests against the sex business are becoming more and more successful. Sasha attacks Oles

Bouzina, a famous writer who has just written a book in which women are presented as toys. At the Intercontinental Hotel, she ransacks the Miss Ukraine election program live. The sex safaris in the red light district meet a public more and more divided... "People knew us better, they were more aware of our work. People knew us better, they identified us as "girls against prostitution", and so there were those who supported us and those who hated us." And in the middle, the most numerous, the hypocrites who display a façade of support while refusing to move things forward...

"From this point of view Yushchenko, Yanukovych or Timoshenko... it doesn't change anything", concludes Sacha.

Orange or blue, the government lives off this sex business that observers and journalists estimate in 2012 to be worth more than 30 billion for Europe, including 3 billion, or 10%, for Ukraine alone[44]. For the government pundits who are linked to the mafia owners of the clubs, brothels and discotheques, the business is too juicy to give up an inch.

Inna rarely participates in these actions. According to Sasha, she is jealous, in retrospect, of her participation in the Miss Ukraine contest. However, "she had refused to do it, I could have given her my place, because I knew that she dreamed of it, but she did not want to"... Perhaps because she knew that all Ukraine would watch... and in particular Major Shevchenko in Kherson. Unlike Sacha, Inna did not impose her revolutionary feminist choice on her family, she negotiated it, revealing what she can reveal, hiding what

---

44. Report of the Scelles Anti-Prostitution Foundation, June 2012, 3rd edition.

Inna has the Euro in mind!

must be hidden. She spares the goat and the cabbage. Her entire period in Kiev is marked by this tug-of-war. She hesitates to appear then regrets it. She refuses the topless in particular, Anna confided to me, "not to offend her family. At the same time, Sacha imposes her commitment more frontally, to the point of being sequestered for a few days by her parents, in 2009, and then accepting to see them again only in open places so as not to risk kidnapping...

In Paris, the best period for sex workers has long been the week of the Agricultural Show, because the men are in the capital while the women are looking after the farm. In Kiev, it is the big soccer matches that motivate the important movements of prostitution... And for the Euro, hordes of Russians, Italians and Germans are expected in Kiev, Donetsk or Kharkov, who will come as singles...

On the basis of studies, projections, articles of informed journalists, the girls expect an exponential increase in the number of brothels in Ukraine for the opening of the Euro and say that it is there that it will be necessary to act. This multiplication of the places of pleasure - secretly encouraged by the power which hopes for a strong entrance of currencies - will occur well... but for nothing or not much: they will remain almost empty!

But it was not good news at all, it was even sadder than we thought," laments Inna. In fact, the brothels were useless because prostitution was everywhere, in the street, in the nightclubs, in the hotels..."

The police, too, look favorably on the growth of prostitution, as they extort girls or even collect a tax in kind called "*soubotniki*", named after the practice of Saturday volunteer work under the Soviet regime. This variant of *subotniki* provides a police station or a group of police officers with a certain number of girls for one day. The place of crime is often a sauna. The policemen abuse the girls by drinking[45].

At the Euro, Femen actions were a success. The most famous one was the one filmed by Joseph Paris in *Naked War*[46], which saw Oxana, Sacha and Eugenia - a Femen activist - appear in the middle of the Poland-Greece spectators, on the parking lot of the entrances. Bare-breasted, equipped with fire extinguishers symbolizing male ejaculation - an idea of Oxana's -, the girls sprayed the dead drunken males. On their chests: "*Fuck Euro 2012.*" To the many journalists warned by Inna, they declare in an impromptu press conference before the police stop them: "Politicians have spent fortunes to build stadiums, but have done nothing to solve the dramatic problem of prostitution."

Each new action is an opportunity for Inna to make contacts, but also to present herself as a spokesperson for Femen. Her talents as an organizer and leader of the group undoubtedly gave structure to the movement. The limit will be reached, as we will see, a few years later in France.

---

45. On the subject: "Diving with the prostitutes of Kiev," investigation by the Swedish newspaper *Dagens Nyheter, Courrier international,* July 4, 2012.
46. *Naked War,* Joseph Paris, La Clairière Production, 2013.

Femen takes off the top

> "Cover this breast that I cannot see.
> By such things souls are wounded,
> and it brings in guilty thoughts."
> Molière, *Tartuffe*, 1669.

Paris, March 21, 2016

"No, I didn't want[47]."

As we walk on the sunny square of the Abbesses, Inna comes back to the trademark of the Femen movement: toplessness.

She was against it and said so clearly.

Moreover, today, the leader of the movement no longer appears topless, even if she still does not wear a bra and claims the right to live topless, for men and women alike.

---

47. Unless otherwise noted, quotes are from interviews conducted by the author between November 2009 and September 2016.

Inna was against topless actions. She made this known as soon as the idea was put forward. Her opposition was violent and she announced that she was leaving the movement that she had just started to attend.

After thinking about it, she didn't.

Inna was against the use of toplessness for all the bad reasons that the Femen's contemptuaries oppose her today, in substance: "It's antifeminist, it's exhibitionism, it's divisive, etc." And then probably also a little because of Major Shevchenko, over there, in Kherson... What will he say if he sees his daughter topless in front of the whole Ukraine after having bled himself to send her to study in Kiev?

The adoption of toplessness as Femen's modus operandi is anything but a whim. It is a project carried by the artist Oxana, even before the arrival of Inna.

And it's a stroke of genius.

From 2008 to 2010, the actions of Femen surprised Ukrainians on the street. They sometimes join in en masse to one or another of the performances, notably the one of the "Ministry of Dirty Socks", in March 2010, where 70 girls take off their businessmen's masks at the same time and put on their housewives' costumes to signify the place devolved to women in this Yanukovych government.

Until then, Femen was content to be a protest movement "within the law", it did not create scandal. When they planned an action, the girls sometimes even asked for administrative authorizations - they soon gave up. They find it difficult to interest the press. The public that observes them unannounced is often more puzzled than shocked.

Feminism does not raise any consciousness in this country dominated by patriarchy.

We need to find something...

Some actions will serve as a test or prelude to toplessness: like this happening against the promotion of pornographic sites by Google, but the girls are from behind, we do not see their breasts. A few weeks later, it is about protesting against a waste of public money invested in the construction of a huge useless clock in the center of Kiev. For this action, the girls compose a dial, one is topless but she wears a band that bars her nipples. Neither the message, nor the performance, nor the importance of the subject are enough to mark the spirits.

Femen is stagnant. And stagnation, when you make a revolution, is death.

Anna and her friends are looking for a second wind, a "quality jump", says Oxana.

Already, on August 24, 2009, the anniversary of the independence of Ukraine, the case becomes clear. Oxana takes off her top. The young artist senses things, seeks a route, wants to strike the spirits. For the girls, the slogan of this demonstration is: "Stop selling Ukraine"; it refers to the whole sections of the economy which disappear in the groups of the West and also... to the soul of Ukraine that shameful politicians sacrifice on the altar of the trade. The flashes start to crackle around Oxana. The crowd giggles. The police do not dare to intervene. Paradoxical provocation that these fragile breasts which at the same time deliver her and protect her.

It is the first time that an activist takes off her clothes, but the episode, in spite of its success, remains anecdotal, like the one that will follow. Oxana, again, partially undresses for an action against the refusal of the Kiev city hall to install public toilets in the city center. The performance was not very strong, but the media got used to Femen and... Oxana's breasts. The year before, the young artist went on vacation to the beaches of the Black Sea and felt "the freedom to be naked". Nothing to do, obviously, with the political offering of her exhibition on the Maïdan that day, but Oxana knows that she is not afraid of nudity. The others, not yet.

The third topless action is planned for January 2010, against an art center belonging to an oligarch close to the power, which exposes naked Ukrainian women and paintings degrading for the image of the woman, according to Anna and her friends. It is Sacha who has to do it! But if Oxana is already convinced by this new mode of action, Sacha is still reluctant: "I was not afraid to strip, even if I wondered about the scope and the meaning of this undressing..." What preoccupies Sacha is of a physical nature. She laughs about it today, while we evoke this episode, sitting at the terrace of a Parisian café: "After Oxana, I was the second one to have to take off my top and I was very afraid to shame our movement with my small breasts! But in the action, I didn't feel any fear, I understood that it was the gesture that was important and not the chest size!"

The performance that will set in stone the institution of toplessness in Femen's action takes place a few weeks later, on February 7, 2010, on the occasion of the second round of the presidential election. The Ukrainian people must elect Yanukovych or Tymoshenko. "Today we can see that it was a choice between the plague and the cholera, but at the time, it was not easy, because Tymoshenko had many supporters and seemed to represent progressivism," remembers Sacha. Femen refuses to choose between the two candidates and intends to make it known.

The girls decide to wait for Yanukovych at the entrance of his polling station. Anna and Viktor have prepared the action. Sacha will be the central element. She will be "crucified", topless, on a human cross formed by boys. Symbolically, the action is strong, it mixes political protest and blasphemy in a "porno chic" aesthetic à la Bettina Rheims. It's a pity that there is no image of this crucifixion... since it never took place! The two boys who were supposed to represent the cross got scared and ran away...

Sacha Shevchenko is angry, she recruited the boys.

What to do?

Acting anyway?

Viktor has warned the media, they are waiting for a Femen action. And all the cameras are there to immortalize Yanukovych's vote. Everything happened at lightning speed. The security guards see the boys running away and seize two activists who are unfolding their placards prepared by Oxana. Sasha rushes the two guards, frees one activist and then the other. She gives the order to undress. In an instant, the girls find themselves bare-chested, brandishing signs with calls for no choice and slogans challenging the

Femen takes off the top

honesty of the candidates and the respect of the democratic game. The performance lasts only a few seconds. By the time the security guards regained their senses and the journalists immortalized the protest, the girls had already jumped out of the polling station's windows and disappeared into the snow, shirtless, at minus 20 degrees. But Sacha and his accomplices are not yet experienced in escapes and traps... On the road, they try to stop a car to escape from the security guards who are chasing them... A vehicle stops, it's an unmarked van... Head for the station.

A few years later, Sacha would tell me: "It was a good memory, the policemen were happy to see us in real life. As it was lunch time, they shared with us the meals prepared by their wives. We drank tea and made jokes. We still had to pay a small fine and then we went home quietly." This is Sasha's one and only "good memory" of an arrest, in a career that includes more than a hundred!

The date of February 7, 2010 is essential in the history of Femen. It marks the beginning of both topless collective actions and political actions. And Inna is not yet officially a member of the movement... Her first action will take place the following month, during the action of the "Ministry of Dirty Socks" against the Yanukovych government elected after the elections of February 7. Inna was already coming to meetings and parties organized with DJ Hell, our German supporter, and I regularly asked her to come," says Sasha. That didn't stop her from giving her opinion on toplessness."

No one followed him. Fortunately, no one did.

Operation "Greg, Dickhead!"

> "A strong man?
> Are you talking about muscularity?"
> Françoise Sagan, *Un château en Suède*,
> Julliard, 1960.

Auckland, New Zealand, April 2011

"Hi, Greg?

- Yes, are you from Kena Radio ?

- Yes Kena Radio speaking, but I'm sorry to announce that your trip to Ukraine has been cancelled[48]!"

I can imagine this dialogue and Greg's face when the radio station that won him an all-expenses paid trip to Ukraine a

---

48. "Hello, Greg? - Yes, are you from Kena Radio? - Yes, we are, but I'm sorry to say that your trip to Ukraine has been cancelled!"

few days earlier tells him that it's out of the question. And especially when they tell him why his trip is cancelled...

Zaporoje, April 22, 2011

For once, Oxana had to leave her brushes and scissors behind. No masks to cut out this time. Rather, it's a digital precision work to be done to perfectly match the bottom of the face of an Auckland, New Zealand, resident with the glans of an erect male sex. The caption on the photo states, in case anyone missed it, "*Greg is a* dickhead".

The reason for Femen's anger is a contest organized by a private radio station in New Zealand where the first prize is nothing less than... a Ukrainian woman! Yes, that's right, a media in this country has imagined to put in play over several weeks a "sex trip", a sexual stay in Ukraine for the winner. Everything is very serious. The radio has contacted a "marriage agency", as there are so many here, which offers foreigners to come and "choose their future wife during a pleasant tourist stay in Ukraine". In reality, it is purely and simply a "tourism/prostitution" stay, as elsewhere in Pattaya or Tijuana. Technically, the "consumer" is offered a series of interviews during which he must choose the object of his predation. A bit like in Isabelle Mergault's lovely film, *Je vous trouve très beau, but* without the talent of Michel Blanc and Eva Darlan.

And it's a guy named Greg who is scheduled to come and eat his prize next month.

But there's a catch. A listener who was outraged by the game remembered a story in the *New Zealand Herald about the* topless girls with flower crowns on their heads who oppose prostitution in Ukraine. A few clicks on the Internet and she managed to contact Anna to explain what was going on and to tell her that Greg would be arriving soon.

Immediately, the Femen organized themselves. Greg's stay is planned for the beginning of May and should start in Zaporoje, a working class area without any tourist attraction, two hundred kilometers from Kiev and four hundred from Odessa. Greg will not be satisfied with Zaporoje since the tour includes Kiev, Kharkov, etc. But it is here, in the center of Ukraine, that he will come to "collect his prize". Oxana, Inna, Nadjin - new recruit of the movement, she will spend only a few months there - and Sacha are ready to receive him.

A week before the "event" in Zaporoje, Femen is hard at work, and so am I. A first press conference is organized to warn the local population about this shameful scandal. A first press conference is organized to warn the local population about this shameful scandal: "It's good," says a journalist, "but even if the Ukrainians are indignant, there is money at stake, these agencies earn a lot this way and they will only give up if the trip is not safe."

We can count on Femen to make Greg's stay more secure!

We arrived the day before and slept in an unattractive apartment on the seventh floor without an elevator of a massive and delicate building, in which any exegete of the architectural philosophy of the Third International would have recognized without any possible mistake a jewel of the 5th Plan of social housing in the Lower Union initiated by comrade Khrushchev. Today it is an old rotten HLM. The apartment is provided by the family of an activist, who will participate tomorrow in the demonstration on the town hall square.

It is the beginning of spring 2011. These are the golden years of Femen in Ukraine. The public knows them. It often applauds them, approves of them. But this growing popularity is inversely proportional to the capacity of the public authorities to tolerate these women who prevent the patriarchy from living in circles. The arrests multiply. Inna, Sacha or Oxana frequently spend several hours at the police station. The bullying is humiliating: body searches, no toilets in the police cells, confiscations, slaps, etc. We are not yet at the point of the assaults, kidnappings, and life-threatening risks that will come in 2013, but the situation is getting very tense. For this reason - and also because it costs too much - it is impossible for us to go to the hotel where we would have to fill in attendance sheets. And then Sasha and Inna are so recognizable! During the train trip, they often wore a scarf and glasses.

At the press conference organized in the premises of a friendly association, the journalists are rather young and benevolent - contrary to what awaits us in Odessa the following week - but they seem much more interested in the movement itself than in the scandal of Greg's arrival. The questions all revolve around Sacha's or Inna's personality and could be summarized in one astonished: "What a funny idea to be a feminist when you are 20 years old and have pretty eyes." Questions also come up about the financing of Femen. We want to know who is behind it... Without even realizing it, the young Ukrainian journalists reproduce one of the oldest macho schemes according to which women are necessarily manipulated (or hysterical) when they take the floor in the public space.

Yes, in the end, why would three beautiful young women choose to look like fools, get beaten up and sleep in jail if they weren't secretly being manipulated and even paid for it?

It also testifies to the biased level of perception now rea-ched in Ukraine: a New Zealand radio listener has won a series of sexual relations with a Ukrainian woman whose consent is at best due to stupidity, at worst to hunger and desperation, and no one is really indignant. Except Femen.

The action takes place in front of the town hall of Zaporoje. We arrive at two cars. About fifty journalists and photographers are already there. In a flash, the three girls jump out of the car. Sacha takes off her leather spen-cer and Inna her tee-shirt. On their breasts appear *"Greg Dickhead"* and *"Ukrayina ne bordel"*. Nadjin joins them by adjusting his crown of flowers. While continuing to shout that Ukraine is not a brothel, Sacha distributes the ruffles made by Oxana. In an instant, hundreds of portraits of Greg "dickhead" spread across the square. Some of them are posted on poles, windows, TV cameras film Greg's face, well the bottom of his face since the top of his head is a turgid sex.

Operation "Greg, Dickhead!"

In front of the town hall, there are three policemen on duty. Very quickly, they understand that they will not be able to do anything alone, they have to call for reinforcements. I see one of them pull a cell phone from his vest. The three are armed. They take out truncheons and put the straps on their wrists. In the meantime, the girls have settled down facing the square, with their backs to the beautiful town hall with its renovated façade. Everything is planned. It is 3 pm, the sun is behind the photographers. The photos will be beautiful. Inna, Sacha and Nadjin join the stoop of the building. At the bottom of their naked torsos, they wear magnificent skirts with red flowers. It is the traditional costume of the region, which one puts on the days of festival. The three soldiers of Ukrainian feminism suddenly line up as one man under "Freedom, Agreement, Kindness", the motto of the country. Arms stretched high to touch the twisted festoon of a balcony, without hatred or fear or smile, dominating the tightly packed crowd, they defy Ukraine, New Zealand and all the fools who believe that women can be taken because they are poor.

The cranial charm of that moment will always stay with me. This is one of the reasons for this book.

But the bliss does not last long. From the three streets that lead to the large Soviet square, five cars pour out, sirens wailing. The three policemen on duty suddenly feel strong and grab Sacha, she struggles and bites one of them. Nadjin comes to the rescue and makes the official's cap fly.

At the edge of the sidewalk, the white Trabant which brought us opens its doors, the driver awaits us, engine humming. But a zealous policeman blocks the door with his truncheon and prevents me from getting on board. It is Inna who frees me by giving a shoulder blow to the blocking officer. The car starts in a hurry. In the back, Inna and Sacha are recovering. The fight was harder than usual. The two friends turn around to look at the wide, empty avenue behind us. A police car has started at the same time as us, but it seems to have given up the idea of a pursuit. We still make some detours before going back to our hideout. I help Nadjin a bit to climb the seven floors. Sacha and Inna have already exchanged their flower crowns for caps that cover their hair, so there is no need to arouse the suspicions of a neighbor who hates feminism so much that he would report the Femen's rear base in Zaporoje to the police.

We find with pleasure the sordid apartment. I load my files on the computer. I think back to an insignificant episode that happened in the dingy room, just before the press conference: the girls are getting ready, I take pictures. While I am interested in Nadjin who is painting Sacha's breasts, Inna calls me in the small adjoining room. She smiles and tells me - in a low voice but Nadjin doesn't speak English anyway: *"Nadjin, she's gonna leave Femen soon, don't take pictures*[49]. I understand that I can, on the other hand, take all the pictures I want of Inna, who is wearing make-up with affetence.

---

49. "Nadjin is going to leave Femen soon, don't take pictures of her!"Unless otherwise noted, quotes are from interviews conducted by the author between November 2009 and September 2016.

Operation "Greg, Dickhead!"

I tell myself that the major's daughter likes the light.

The girls are showering. An hour later, we are sitting in a small working-class restaurant on the outskirts of Nikopol, on the banks of the Dnieper river. Sasha orders beer. The girls are laughing. Some friends have joined us. Nadjin and Inna devour *oseledet,* marinated herrings, and *dirouni,* a kind of potato pancake with fresh cream. Inna and Sacha monopolize the attention of an audience that eats them with its eyes. I understand by their gestures that they are telling the story. Here and there I manage to catch "Greg", "*Politsiya*" and "*Zalupa*", which, I am told, means "cockhead". Inna wants to see my pictures. She asks to be allowed to use them right away to put them on the Femen website. I agreed, of course. Inna tells me that the action is a great success: "All the journalists came, there was TV. In Kiev, Anna has already issued a statement. The owner of the small restaurant joined the happy group and brought more beers.

And Greg? In the newspapers, the following days, the girls will read that the New Zealander had to cancel his stay because of the "terrorist threat" which weighs on his coming... The victory is total.

Today, Sacha is more measured: "Maybe they just postponed his trip and had him come quietly... but at the time, we had won and we were happy."

Femen always, Femen every day...

"All united and resolute, grown and enlightened by the sufferings that social crises bring in their wake, deeply convinced that the Commune, representing the international and revolutionary principles of the people, carries within it the seeds of the social revolution, the women of Paris will prove to France and to the world that they too will know, at the moment of the supreme danger, at the barricades, on the ramparts of Paris, if the reaction were to force the doors, to give, like their brothers, their blood and their life for the defense and the triumph of the Commune, that is to say of the people! Then victorious, able to unite and agree on their common interests, workers, all united by a last effort...
[This last sentence was left unfinished.]
Long live the Universal Republic!
Long live the Commune!"
Louise Michel, at her trial on December 18, 1871.

Paris, April 21, 2016

"From 2009 to 2012, Femen is everywhere[50]", asserts Sacha.

April in Paris is springtime and Sacha is nostalgic.

We met in a small park in the Marais, close to the Mansart gallery, which was to organize Oxana's first solo exhibition.

We are waiting for Oxana.

Sacha thinks back to the great years: "Looking back, I cringe just talking about how busy our business was."

Once the communication mechanisms that will serve its action have been integrated, Femen multiplies the fronts of attack. Hypermedia performances requiring heavy logistics, a network and meetings with journalists take place two to three times a month. It seems like an acceptable rhythm," says Sacha, "but sometimes it takes several days of scouting to prepare an action. You also have to make the costumes and imagine the staging. After the action, it always takes a little time to heal the bruises "or even get out of jail when we are arrested".

In November 2009, the girls stormed the Parliament on the 14th and invaded the set of TV presenter Chouster on the 29th. In early December, they "attacked" the Miss Ukraine election organized by a company linked to Donald Trump

---

50. Unless otherwise noted, quotes are from interviews conducted by the author between November 2009 and September 2016.

and his wife, and then tore up the paintings of Dimitri Bratskov, a macho painter. In January 2010, they held a four-day sit-in in front of the Parliament to demand a bill to criminalize prostitution. On February 7, they took over the polling station where Yanukovych was about to cast his ballot for the presidential election; on February 20, they were spanked in front of the Ministry of Education to denounce the harassment of female students. On 17 March, they took part in the "Ministry of Dirty Socks" action to protest against the absence of women in the government. In April, they demonstrated against Prime Minister Azarov for whom "women are not capable of working sixteen hours a day [like him] for the good of Ukraine". At the beginning of May, they "welcomed" the Russian President Medvedev. On June 16, they tried to prevent the soccer match Lvov/Galatasaray because of the macho behavior of the fans. In July, they interrupted an Orthodox Jewish pilgrimage. In August, on the 14th, they charged the presidential platform during the national holiday, then participated in a motorcycle parade on the 17th. On October 27, it was Prime Minister Putin's turn to be received by the activists with cries of "You won't fuck us like Alina[51]". On November 3, they organized a picket in front of the Iranian embassy to support Sakineh[52], etc.

From 2011 onwards, the movement becomes more international, Femen attacks Berlusconi (February 2011), supports

---

51. Allusion to the gymnast Alina Kabaeva, who became one of Putin's mistresses.
52. In October 2010, Sakineh, a young Iranian woman, was sentenced to stoning for the murder of her husband in Tehran.

the victims after the Fukushima accident (March 2011), asks Hillary Clinton visiting Kiev to take the opportunity to educate President Yanukovych (June 2011), demonstrates in support of Saudi women who demand the right to drive (June 2011), prepares for the Euro... Actions abroad are also multiplying, in Belarus against the dictator Lukashenko (December 2011), in France against Dominique Strauss-Kahn (October 2011), in Egypt against the imposition of Sharia (October 2011 and November 2012), in Turkey for Women's Day (March 8, 2012) and against the Islamist power of Erdogan...

One of the most dangerous of these actions takes place in Belarus on December 20, 2011. It involves Inna, Oxana and Alexandra. The three girls demonstrate in front of the Belarusian KGB headquarters against the dictatorship of the pro-Russian president, Lukashenko. They were kidnapped after their action and disappeared for twenty-four hours. They were found the next day at the Ukrainian border, which they reached half-naked and cold. In the meantime, they were tortured, doused with gasoline and threatened with lighters, their hair was cut and dyed, they were stripped naked, raped and abandoned in the snow. Traumatized, they first reached a village and then the border by their own means, before being taken in charge by the Ukrainian consulate in Belarus. For Inna and Alexandra, this is the worst experience as activists. For Oxana, there will also be the Russian jails, after the attack on Putin's polling station in March 2012. She will be locked up for two long weeks without any link with the outside world, without knowing if she would ever get out. The only words I will extract from Oxana about this Russian experience are, "It was cold and I was hungry."

In light of this experience, the protest in St. Peter's Square in Rome[53], on March 12, 2013, seems like a walk in the park. But it retains a special place, "in retrospect, almost tender," smiles Sacha, in the history of the two friends. "It's just... our worst action. Nothing worked, train late, credit card swallowed, we "lost" our last euros at the police station, it was cold, the cell was very dirty, we were released in the middle of the night in a deserted suburb without a penny, we were immediately approached by some very disturbing boys, finally we managed to stop a car that took us to the airport where we slept while waiting for our flight booked for the next day." A cursed action... "We told ourselves that even their god was against us and that we should not do any more action with two, just Oxana and me!", concludes Sacha laughing.

At that time, Femen was unstoppable. In total, from the end of 2009 to the end of 2012, the girls will imagine, prepare and carry out more than a hundred major actions, not counting the sex safaris (see chapter 14) and the almost daily actions of "Femen promotion" which were, it suited everyone, Sacha's domain. "It was a matter of going out into the street and talking to the girls we met. It's banal,

---

53. Taking advantage of the conclave meeting that will lead to the election of Pope Francis on March 18, Femen decided to light a red smoke bomb in the middle of St. Peter's Square, demanding the abolition of the papacy.

but it's the only way we had at the beginning to make the movement known." And that's how Sacha recruited the majority of Femen girls.

You also have to manage a growing organization on a daily basis. And that's Anna's domain. Her position in the background," explains Sacha, "gave her the time to manage everything. In 2009 and 2010, Anna devoted herself mainly to developing the Internet sales site, which began to bring in some money. The girls have objects made "almost on demand" in the suburbs of Kiev, "especially T-shirts, painted cups, posters" that the growing fame of the movement allows to sell.

For Oxana, the difficulty was elsewhere: it was a question of reconciling her feminist commitment, her life at the side of her mother and her little brother Lyosha, her numerous trips to Kiev for Femen, and her creative activity. As an artist, she feels a need for land, for roots, for a cocoon: her birthplace, Khmelnytskyï, is important to her. However, she chose to join her friends and move to Kiev in early 2010. Her responsibility as "artistic director" of the movement could no longer accommodate a distance that the frequency and reliability of trains in Ukraine make even more uncontrollable.

"The others were unloading the whole costume, makeup, disguise part on me... so I was lugging tons of material around on the train all week long."

In addition, in 2010, she obtained a grant from a foundation for artistic creation and went to Egypt for several weeks. Unfortunately, the numerous works created under the Sinai sun will burn a few months later, in Khmelnytskyï, in the accidental fire of her mother's house.

When she is in Kiev, Oxana stays with Sasha, who lives in a shared apartment with several other girls, or with Anna, who lives alone in a room closer to the center, but tiny.

Oxana sometimes sells an icon, never very expensive. When an order for a wedding arrives, it is a few *hryvnia*[54] more. Her travels prevent her from working, but she never returns from a stay in Khmelnytskyï without some food to share.

Anna and Viktor sometimes get some money from an assignment in an advertising agency or from a media collaboration.

Inna earned a little money at the press office of the city hall, before being fired "because of her involvement in Femen".

For Sacha, this is a period of intense activity. She devoted herself to Femen, but she had to survive and pay the rent for the two-room kitchen, which was not very expensive and was divided among seven roommates. She has taken on odd jobs: "I was a coordinator in a worker placement agency for a few months. But she quickly "suffocated" in office jobs to the point of being "happy" when she was fired, because Femen occupied her time and her thoughts. So, more often than not, the young girl earns three pennies by distributing flyers or neighborhood newspapers in the street...

---

54. Ukrainian currency since 1991: 1 euro = 29.176 *hryvnia* (pronounced *grivnia*) approximately.

Femen always, Femen every day...

Femen functions as an ideal communist organization, based entirely on meeting primary needs and sharing: "We put everything in common."

Concretely, any money earned by Sacha, Oxana or Anna goes into a kitty managed by the group and intended to ensure the survival of all.

"Inna will have a little trouble with this system," says Sacha, "but we were idealists!"

I try to imagine the journalism students, computer scientists, assistant directors and writers of Femen France 2016 sharing rent, clothes, meals and pocket money... and I measure the chasm that separates the revolutionary organization, born from the passion of three friends, from the Parisian media-airdutempsist movement that it has become...

The fact remains that the money to be divided does not weigh much. In Galia Ackerman's book, Oxana details the budgetary problems: "We had an average budget of [...] $200. Almost all of it went to pay our rent. With the rest, we bought paint, paper for signs and banners, artificial flowers for our wreaths. And we ate very little[55]..."

With the success of the 2010 actions, the activists arrive. Femen must organize itself. At its *birth, in* mid-2011, the movement is a mechanical oscillation of three circles orbiting around a core. The core is made up of the founders: Anna, Sacha and Oxana, plus Viktor and Inna. No initiative is decided outside the political bureau.

---

55. *Femen, op. cit.*

Around this anion, for a while unbreakable, gravitate about thirty very involved activists. Their names are Nadjin, Jana (now also in exile in France), Irina or Alexandra... They regularly participate in the actions. The leaders know each of them personally. They are very involved activists who can give their feelings on this or that project or even suggest different types of actions and places of intervention. These girls sometimes go to the bars where the "historical" ones meet and, from the end of 2011, to the place that will be the headquarters of the movement. They also share the risks linked to the actions. Nadjin Velja will participate in the whole campaign against "Greg Dickhead" (see chapter 15), Alexandra Nemchinova will risk her life in Belarus in 2011 alongside Inna and Oxana, Jana will be arrested several times...

The second circle is made up of several dozen - "maybe 300 people", says Sacha - "mobile" activists whom the girls can call upon for specific actions requiring a particular skill or a large number of activists. These girls adhere to the message carried by Femen, but they wonder about their own capacity to take action. In May 2011, while we were shooting *Les Féministes topless*[56] with Cyril Denvers, Sacha and Inna chose Valentina and Eva, two activists from the second circle, to jump onto the presidential podium where the cameras of a good part of Europe would be focused, because they themselves were afraid of being recognized by the security service on the run. The two novices will fulfill

---

56. *Le Grand Mag*, Canal+.

their role with courage, but will be arrested and sentenced to five days in prison. Traumatized, Valentina will not repeat the experience. As for Eva, she will not go beyond a second action. This second circle will be reduced to nothing in 2010 with the definitive adoption of toplessness for Femen actions.

The last circle is that of the sympathizers and social networks. It gathers thousands of girls "and also some boys", says Sacha, who follow with interest the adventures of Femen. These girls participate in the exchanges on Facebook or Twitter. They encourage, give their opinion, send requests for information... but they don't take the step to act. It is this labile movement, with its delicate figures - "but the success was enormous, thousands of people", according to Sacha - that will ensure the penetration of the Femen phenomenon into the homes of the provincial Ukraine, from Odessa to Kharkov, from Sevastopol to Donetsk.

At the center of the system, a typical day for Sacha starts early - "anyway my roommates, who were not necessarily Femen activists, got up at dawn". Every day, between a bus that doesn't arrive, the cold that blocks an avenue and her empty pockets that prevent her from hailing a collective cab that would take her for 50 euro cents, she takes two hours to reach the Cupidon, the bar that is the headquarters of the Femen conspiracy. She meets Oxana, who arrives from the squat-studio she found when she moved to Kiev in 2010, and Anna. They drink tea. The owner doesn't charge them for tea or coffee, only for Viktor's beers, who arrives a little later. If an action is planned during the day, the girls prepare themselves in the back room, where Cyril and I will be the first to film them. If there is no operation planned, they sit at the round table on the platform in front of the bar and... think about actions. "Our days were days of revolutionaries who want to change the established order." It was also necessary to maintain the material, signs, paint, costumes, stored in a cubbyhole, and sometimes help Oxana with manual work. When the wi-fi arrived at Cupidon, in 2010, the girls were permanently connected, they answered to Internet users who called them from Kharkov or Crimea, then from Paris, Rio or New York.

Every late afternoon, Sacha leaves for his recruitment tour in the student districts. Oxana comes back to work at the squat-workshop, she sometimes spends her nights making costumes. Anna does the accounts. Inna goes back to the small apartment that her parents pay for.

After the actions, the program is often different. We hang out in the back room of the Cupid, the owner brings glasses and plates. In winter, we eat borscht, a heavy vegetable soup. In summer, we drink a little mead or vodka while re-discovering Ukraine... and the world.

The concept of sextremism

> "Assuming that truth is a woman, would it not be plausible to say that all philosophers, insofar as they were dogmatists, did not agree to talk about women? The tragic seriousness, the awkward awkwardness that they have deployed until now to conquer the truth were very clumsy and unseemly means to win the heart of a woman. What is certain is that the woman in question has not allowed herself to be won; and every kind of dogmatist now takes on a sad and dejected attitude, if she still keeps any attitude at all."
> Friedrich Nietzsche, *Beyond Good and Evil*, Foreword, 1886.

Saran Prison, France, February 1st, 2016.

Five Femen France activists are in front of the prison in Saran. They are holding up signs demanding the release of Jacqueline Sauvage, in their eyes and in the eyes of many

French people, unjustly imprisoned for the murder of her violent husband. Jacqueline Sauvage is serving a ten-year prison sentence. The murderer whose fate moves the opinion and who benefits from networks of media support will be partially pardoned by François Hollande. For this action, the girls decided to dig a tunnel in front of the prison to "simulate a symbolic escape of Jacqueline". They are filmed by an activist, and some journalists are present. The girls dig the earth with spades for a few minutes before being interrupted without violence by the police, controlled and then released. It was a one-off action in support of a woman to whom Femen and the social networks grant many extenuating circumstances. An action without much luster, without much at stake either, but visually successful... One obviously understands the meaning of the demand, the liberation of Jacqueline Sauvage; one understands less the symbolism... In other words: what is the point of being bare-chested for this action? Elvire Duvelle-Charles[57], to whom I will ask the question a few weeks later, will be embarrassed, synthesizing her answer in a laconic: "That's how we do[58].

Not enough for Sacha: "Femen is a sextremist movement, it makes sense, it is not about performing topless actions for the sake of being naked, it is about saying something with our bodies." So what do the bodies of the Femen defending

---

57. Young French assistant director who will be one of the first to join Femen France in November 2012.

58. Unless otherwise noted, quotes are from interviews conducted by the author between November 2009 and September 2016.

Jacqueline Sauvage say in front of the Saran prison this February[1]? Nothing, except that it is cool.

For Oxana, it's simple: "Inna has never understood anything about sextremism, that's why she was against topless and did it reluctantly."

Sextremism was born, at the same time as Femen, in the well-done heads of Sacha and Oxana. Like a contemporary art performance, sextremism needs to be explained. It is at the crossroads of several concepts, but not always the ones we imagine and especially not nudity and extremism. "It is not about naked politics on the far left!", Sacha and Oxana will explain to me in Kiev, after a very hot action against Europe Day on May 21, 2011. "On the contrary, it is about mixing the concepts of sexuality and radical feminism to send the patriarchy back to its frustrations and abuse of dominant position." This doctrine is the fruit of months of reflection, nights of exchanges, shouting and kissing in the bars of Kiev and Khmelnytskyï, readings of Bebel, Marx and Angela Davis, comments of feminist actions of Black Power...

In the same political gesture, the sextremism potentializes and diverts sexuality and radicality.

Sexism transforms, under the frightened eyes of husbands and priests, objects of desire into active subjects. A formula that Sacha sums up perfectly with : "*Barbie can speak*[59]."

This transformation is peaceful, but it generates violence because it shakes under the feet of its adversary a ground

---

59. "Barbie can talk."

beaten by two thousand years of monotheism and atavism. The rule is no more. The order is turned upside down. God is dead. This is what the solemn bodies of the Femen say.

That's why the world is afraid of it.

The first concept of sextremism is radicality. Radicality, not extremism. In this, the etymology of the term is misleading. It is never violent, or at least it was never violent in the actions in which Sacha and Oxana participated. He is never doctrinaire or domineering either. On the other hand, it is demanding and well grounded in principles, equality, freedom, which are the basis of identified claims: refusal of religious or political diktats on the body and reason of the woman, fight against sexual exploitation, equality of rights.

The sextremism, by the blurring of the codes of beauty, martiality, femininity and protest, poses peacefully that the body of the woman is always the stake of the men. And that this must stop. It is the continuity and the renewal of old movements from which it has been nourished without the founders even having a precise historical knowledge of them. They are 20 years old and their education is incomplete. Each reading of one of them benefits the others by emulation, debate, and permanent exchange.

If the girls have studied the modes of action of the Black Panthers, they have evacuated all forms of violence. They also know about the struggle of German feminists and English suffragettes. Sacha and Anna know the history of the MLF, they know that some actions of the French movement used the nudity of women's bodies, and in particular that bras were burned in Paris in 1968. Oxana was interested in African ethnic groups that used the naked body of women as the ultimate posture of protest: in 1930, in Nigeria, against English taxes; in 1952, in Ivory Coast, against French settlers in the northern villages; or in 2013, in Burkina Faso, against Blaise Compaoré, women stripped to the waist to express their concern for freedom or justice.

The second concept of the Femen mode of action is sexuality. Sexuality, not nudity. It is not a question of a sexuality conceived as an artistic provocation; on the contrary, it is a sexuality constructed in the eyes of the public or of its opponents - especially religious ones - who want to see in the exposure of breasts a sexual trans-gression when it is elsewhere (see chapter 18). If there is a relationship to sexuality, it lies in the object of the contestations and not in the posture of the subject. Femen are not sexual, they denounce - often - dominant sexual positions - the actions against DSK (see chapter 21), in October 2011 at his Parisian home place des Vosges and in February 2015 at the court of Lille are very telling in this respect - or use sexuality within performances to denounce prostitution or the sex industry, notably by the dramatization of degrading postures.

This type of action will be abandoned when they arrive in France, at the injunction of Inna who intends to limit the use of the body to its potential of media capture.

Finally, the Femen's modus operandi is based on surging. This is a dimension that is rarely analyzed in the reports of their actions. They simply describe or show the image, without dwelling on the magical moment of the emergence.

All is quiet and suddenly the girls are there, tragic and implacable, sprung from the street like Rodin of a *non finito*, in a staggering literary gesture.

Beyond the religious and ontological symbolism of childbirth - which is ultimately the opposite of unexpected - the emergence has long been violent and masculine, reserved for the domains of ambush warfare, combat, and hunting.

The emergence of Femen inverts roles and blurs genders in that it refers to ejaculation. A virile symbolism that girls will often use[60], fire extinguishers in action representing the emission of semen.

The genesis of the emergence is chaotic. It is a convulsion, the tressautement of a social body in tension. In philosophy, it questions the relationship of the man to the contingency. In psychoanalysis, it founds the dialectic of chance and determinism. In religion - what irony! - it is a Marian apparition. In art, it is the automatic writing of the surrealists, the *paint dripping* of Pollock, the flash of light of Turrell and that of the razor of Fontana... In art, the emergence is an intuition which refers to that of the Femen, a "truth of the feeling", dear to the thinker of the art and the word, Husserlian and centenary, Henri Maldiney.

In the street, the emergence is frightening.

At the end of the nineteenth century, it was the suffragettes of Emmeline Pankhurst's Women's Social and

---

60. Notably in very dangerous circumstances in Kiev, June 8, 2012, during the opening match Ukraine / Spain of the European soccer championship, or in Paris during the intervention against the Catholic fundamentalists of Civitas, November 18, 2012.

Political Union (WSPU) who invited the emergence of feminist political demands. The method anticipates that of Femen: working-class women, middle-class women and mothers stroll, chat or go about their business in a crowded London street. When the whistle blows, they take over the public space, chaining themselves to lampposts, gathering to listen to a flash speech by Emmeline - while she is being sought by the police -, sometimes even pulling baby carriages and shopping bags full of large stones that they throw together into shop windows, shouting "*Vote for women*[61]".

The struggle of the suffragettes lasted eighty years.

The Femen's is just beginning.

---

61. "Voting rights for women!"

Too beautiful, the Femen!

"Like laughter, intelligence is the property of men, and much more rarely of women, but this is of lesser importance because women, if they are beautiful, have little need to be intelligent. If she is ugly, she has even less need to be intelligent.
Pierre Desproges, *Manuel de savoir-vivre à l'usage des rustres et des malpolis*, Seuil, "Point", 1998.

Joseph Paris, director of *Naked War,* likes to say that "beautiful and rebellious rather than ugly and ugly again", the most beautiful film made about Femen, along with Alain Margot's *I Am Femen* (see chapter 36).

This is one of the most common criticisms of Femen: they are too beautiful, real supermodels, as far from the woman in the street as Kate Moss is from a worker at Conti.

This is a bad trial.

One of the strongest memories I have of my reporting on Femen is an image of Sasha in the tiny kitchen of a cold, dingy apartment she shares with a friend. She stands and declaims, facing the camera: "I will never be happy as long as a woman is exploited in my country[62]. I have the impression that it is Saint-Just speaking. A cold sincerity, an astonishing conscience, almost disturbing... In the months that followed, especially during a month that we spent running around Ukraine, from Dnieper to Odessa or Donetsk for actions, interviews and press conferences, I will hear several times the young woman refusing tempting proposals from television producers, film producers, casting directors, fashion photographers... When the movement spreads and its fame goes beyond the borders of Ukraine, the proposals will multiply. After the publication of my first reports, I myself received calls from production companies asking me for Sacha's contact details in order to offer her a small role or a career as a model... Perhaps a little burned by her brief experience as a teenage "supermodel", but more surely supported by her deep and unwavering feminist commitment, Sacha refused everything.

She is making the revolution, not fashion shows!

Sacha was the best recruiter of the Femen. Inna is her biggest catch. The most dangerous too. But Jana, Nadjin, Carla... were all found by Sacha.

From the first Ukrainian years until today, recruitment has always been open for Femen. Even in France.

---

62. Unless otherwise noted, quotes are from interviews conducted by the author between November 2009 and September 2016.

For Elvire Duvelle-Charles, it happened very quickly: "I sent a message to Inna at midnight. At 12:10 a.m., she answered. The next day I was in the office at noon. At 2pm I was taking part in a photo shoot for the *Nouvel Obs*. This refusal of Femen to select its members has its limits: "We don't evaluate the quality of the commitments right away," concedes Inna, "that is done over time, as is the specialization of the girls, those who have skills in organization, press releases, computers..." Not selecting activists is a difficult reality to manage, but it evacuates from the outset the argument of girls chosen for their physical appearance.

In Ukraine, I myself met Femen of different ages and morphology. Most were young, but not all. For the shooting of the film *Les Féministes topless*[63], in May 2011, I interviewed an activist with her mother, both Femen. But the images were discarded in the editing process. This is the other issue of the "standardization" of Femen activists: the choice of photographers, directors and cinematographers.

In the selection of images that I made in November 2009, during the assault on the Parliament, for the American agency Polaris, I chose mainly images in which Sacha appears, because she is the most photogenic. The other photographers will do the same. And if they don't, the photo directors of the magazines take care of eliminating the less blond and less pretty ones. It is therefore unfair to put the responsibility of a hypothetical emergence of a Femen "profile" on its leaders. It is the media system itself that tends

---

63. "Le Grand Mag", Canal+.

to essentialize the image of the movement's activists. When Femen arrived in France (see chapter 24), the multiplicity of profiles and origins naturally made this essentialization much less clear.

For Sasha, things are even simpler: "We have always accepted everyone, but for the actions, we choose according to different criteria each time." In Minsk, in December 2011, for the protest against the dictatorship of Lukashenko, Alexandra Nemchinova is chosen for her stocky figure that can evoke that of the Belarusian dictator. For the interventions on the TV sets, it is Sacha, who expresses himself brilliantly; for the more visual actions, Sacha and Oxana, etc.

In France, recruitment took on a more media-friendly dimension. Inna made a habit of inviting the press to training sessions, interviews, and Femen conferences, in order to impose the idea of a structured, demanding, and solid movement - she succeeded so well that the movement was frequently accused of having become a sect[64]. Inna also reserves the right to decide, without explanation or appeal, on the choice of participants in actions (see chapter 37).

To reproach the Femen who arrived in France in 2012 and 2013 for their beauty is a tendentious criticism. Lydia Guirous, spokesperson for the UMP in 2013, declared that Femen are "Barbie dolls with impeccable plasticity, without brains above their breasts[65]"! And she adds that they have "a form of discrimination that discredits their action: are there

---

64. Notably by the UMP deputy of the Rhône, Georges Fenech (see chapter 23).
65. "Debate: should you show your breasts to be heard?", *Elle*, September 6, 2013.

any round, old or colored women at their happenings"? Her question is pernicious. In 2013, the founders of Femen are still in Ukraine, where there are few women of color. As for the assertion of their stupidity, it lamentably sacrifices to a gendered inversion of the classic macho cliché "a beautiful woman is a stupid woman." Above all, Lydia Guirous does not see the essential: an "agent of the patriarchy" finds himself in a situation all the more uncomfortable that he is struck full force by the message of a body-object become woman-subject (see chapter 17) and the subversion is much stronger still when the message is carried by women with desirable plasticity! In the male unconscious, a beautiful woman, according to the criteria of the place and the time, is not supposed to take the word, but to stick to her role of stooge where the man thinks besides that she is pleased. *On the other hand*, the famous "agent of patriarchy" will easily justify the claim of a less beautiful woman, always according to the criteria of the place and the time, by frustration or jealousy. The message of the talking doll is therefore potentially stronger if the doll is blonde and beautiful.

During the same interview, Lydia Guirous also attacks the mode of action: toplessness. The message of Femen would be counterproductive, "a nonsense, a regression" that "feeds the cult of the woman-object" because they would enter into the seduction that men are looking for... It is of a total intellectual indigence. As we have seen, the exact opposite effect is produced on the men - and women - who receive the message. The Femen, serious and surging, totally desexualize the visual relationship.

For the philosopher Geneviève Fraisse, the Femen nudity is a way of saying: "our body belongs to us", in the prolongation of the feminism of the body of the 1970s demanding the right to abortion and contraception. "It is a way of saying that we want to dominate nature and no longer depend on it, to put an end to media chatter by imposing a powerful image[66]."

But the Femen body also raises the question of sexuation. Their martial posture, their total absence of connivance with the surroundings or the context, their insolence remove all content of desire from desirable objects. "It is a paradoxical use of sexuality," explains Sacha, "we tell men that our breasts are ours."

Femen do not expose themselves entirely naked. Their breasts are a call for freedom and equality, they are intimidating weapons. They inspire distrust rather than lust. It is the public intellect that analyzes them, once the stupefaction of the action has passed, as a sexual provocation, but this analysis is done *a posteriori* and according to acquired and not innate criteria, in a process of social or religious atavism. In the heat of the action on the other hand, men do not perceive girls as objects offered. It is quite the opposite.

Throughout history and geography, many societies view the female breast differently. In some Swedish cities, toplessness is allowed in swimming pools. In France, one walked around with open bras and exposed breasts at the

---

66. Meeting/debate: "Feminism and nudity: a historical body to body?", Paris, Le Grand Palais, January 5, 2015.

court of Agnes Sorel, revealing one's ankles was much more licentious...

It is still social gender conventions that have eroticized the breasts as the willingness to seduce and the stabilization of the consensual relationship have grown. In 2016, many societies in sub-Saharan Africa or Oceania do not make the woman's breasts an erotic issue.

It is surprising to note that these societies are often - Pygmies, Vanuatu, etc. - less religious, at least never monotheistic and more egalitarian.

The breasts of Femen have this particularity: they speak. Since they are the support of the claim inscription. Carnal vectors of claims expressed by shocking and short slogans, taking into account the dominant advertising needs and... the naturally limited size of bellies and breasts. Immediate corollaries of the adoption of the topless mode of action, the slogans dress the bodies at the same time as they question the contradicts, the adversaries or simple observers. *"Barbie's boobs can speak[67]"*, Sacha often ironizes.

____

67. "Barbie's boobs can talk."

The original error

"Tears sometimes rise to the eyes like a spring,
they are mist on the lakes, a disturbance of the
inner day, a water that sorrow has salted."
Philippe Jaccottet,
À la lumière d'hiver, Gallimard, 1974.

Paris, January 25, 2016

"Ukraine food not very good."

It is Oxana who expresses a definitive comparative judgment on the respective culinary traditions of France and Ukraine. Sacha laughs, she is proud of her borscht that she learned from her mother and that she cooks with Dimitri once a week in the small studio in Montmartre. For the rest, the Femen diet has often been burgers and dry cakes.

We meet in a small Italian restaurant in Vanves. On the menu, *Pasta ai funghi*, pasta with mushrooms. Oxana and Sacha have been in France for almost two years now, they often understand French well, but their oral expression is still hesitant.

"When I went to the employment office," says Sacha, lowering her eyes, "I was ashamed of my life because I was told that it was not normal to have been in France for so long and to speak French so badly[68]. She who endured without blinking the Slavic jails, the bullying of police and priests all over the world, the low blows of false friends and the bludgeoning of fascists of all kinds suddenly bursts into tears: "This had not happened to me in public since school!" Then, in the muffled rumor of the reception room of the employment agency in the 18th arrondissement of Paris, a screaming Femen voice bursts out: "I'm losing my family, my country, I don't understand anything, I don't have money and I don't have friends, how can I learn your fucking French?"

Everyone understands that it is not easy.

The mandatory courses related to becoming a political refugee are... mandatory but brief. I also know, in the case of Sacha and Oxana, that it is the accumulation of problems that leads to crisis. However, when they arrived in France, the god of troubles decided to prove his existence... The pitfalls follow the obstacles, the traps follow one another, and the icy welcome they were given, even though they thought they would be welcomed with open arms, at least by the French activists, is at the center of their uneasiness... Still today.

---

68. Unless otherwise noted, quotes are from interviews conducted by the author between November 2009 and September 2016.

What was Femen's biggest mistake?

I expect Sacha to talk about political philosophy, projects, or simply logistics. Was it a mistake to attack all religions with the same force? To put them all in the same basket? Did Femen grow up too fast? Did opening up too quickly to other countries corrupt the movement?

Sacha asserts: "Femen's biggest mistake is to have let Inna come alone to Paris.

She has no doubt.

However, Sacha put all his heart into recruiting Inna: "I met Inna at a party, we talked a bit, I liked her energy. I immediately wanted to recruit her, but she wasn't really excited about the movement. I went through her roommate to see her again, it was almost harassment!"

In 2009, the movement is in its infancy in the capital, with no money and almost no media coverage; Inna understands that there are only blows to be taken... And her military education makes her suspicious of any organized form of social protest. Inna is the child of the Marquise de Merteuil and Eugène de Rastignac, she believes in the individuality of the fights. Each one for himself and nobody for all.

In 2010, after weeks of hesitation, dismissed appointments and unanswered messages, Inna finally agrees to join the Femen movement. Sacha quickly understood that she had a good recruit. Inna is not afraid of the eyes. She confronts the police with courage and aplomb, her hard eyes fixed on the horizon. She has the makings and the dog. She's not afraid of contact, unlike so many other new activists who join the movement to "test their limits" and leave with fear and bruises. Inna is not one of them. During the actions that followed, she showed the same courage as Sacha, Oxana and others; she took all her share of the blows received before her escape to France.

The event that provoked this change in Inna's attitude towards the movement took place at the beginning of 2010: Sasha managed to get past all the security systems and onto a television set where a famous talk show was being held, hosted by Savik Chouster, a former Russian journalist who has become the most popular presenter in Ukraine. The theme of the show is prostitution, and the production has invited a "reformist" MP who is well known to Femen. A few weeks earlier, Nestor Shufrich had participated in a public roundtable discussion with the movement, which he had discovered during the action against the Parliament (see Chapter 6). In front of an enthusiastic audience, Nestor promised to support a bill to criminalize prostitutes' clients, which the girls support... Then he vanished, unreachable. Sacha left him ten messages to find out what stage the debates in Parliament were at, why he wasn't answering and whether he intended to defend this important project for the fight against the sex industry. Nothing happened. Nestor Choufrich played the girl in the air.

"Obviously, for this roundtable, he wanted to put himself out there because there were reporters there, but he had no intention of advocating for the criminalization of clients."

The opportunity is too good! Sacha calls the producer at the entrance, twists her arm and tells her that she is Nestor

Choufrich's personal guest - by "guest", the producer probably understands what we understand in 2010, in Ukraine, when a beautiful blonde is the personal guest of a powerful, vulgar and ugly man. So she lets Sacha pass, who smiles at the big men guarding the set, and goes backstage through a back door. Here she is, three meters from the cameras, only hidden by a set decoration. Like a professional of the happening that she is not yet, she chooses the end of an intervention out of stage to be sure not to be controlled before being seen live. This is it, it's time. Sacha adjusts her wreath, unrolls her Femen sign and... suddenly feels an immense weight fall on her chest. She who has just left her small provincial town, rather than even escaping from it because her mother and grandmother tried to convince her that Kiev and feminism were not for her, she who made the choice of her commitment against her family, who will disapprove, to say the least, of her appearance on TV, she who has just committed two or three offences punishable by imprisonment, she who only knows about life what one knows when one is 20 years old... She is afraid!

"I felt like a moment of loneliness, in an instant I wondered what all this was for, I was sure I was going to make a fool of myself in the eyes of the whole country, I thought of my parents who would refuse to talk to me, I thought of my future that I was ruining..."

There, behind his cardboard curtain, Sacha lives his moment of truth, hesitates, trembles, sweats and then throws himself onto the set, shouting. As if seized by instinct, the cameramen focus their cameras on the one who shouts "Liar, liar" and on her unfolded sign that addresses the Ukrainians: "We are lying to you live!" The set is indignant, a woman tries to grab it, Nestor Choufrich tries to take a composure but has no time, Sacha shoots the sign on his head. She addresses the camera: "This man is a liar, he had promised us to weigh in to pass the law 5223 but he did nothing!" And she leaves the set in complete confusion.

In her small student room, Inna has seen it all. And understood everything: Femen is the right way.

An escape in question

> "There is no man - or woman - who speaks
> and spreads a lie with as much grace
> as he who believes it."
> Jonathan Swift, *The Art of Political Lying*, 1733.

Kiev, August 18, 2012?

"At 6:30 a.m., there is a knock on the door. [...] Six men with ugly faces want to enter. [Inna moves away and calls Sergei: "Some men want to break down my door. I will jump from the kitchen balcony, come and get me." The lawyer had expected this. He even came at dawn to his office, two steps away from Inna's house. [In a few minutes, his car is at the foot of her window. Inna only has to jump from the balcony. [...] All she takes with her is her phone, her iPad and a $100 bill...[69]"

---

69. Caroline Fourest, *Inna*, Grasset, 2014.

It is Caroline Fourest[70] who tells the story of Inna's escape. She places it the morning after the slaughter of the cross in Kiev, that is to say August 18, 2012.

The story continues: Inna jumped from the balcony, but she is still followed, Caroline Fourest does not explain why. We can think that a car was watching and chased Inna and her "lawyer". Or that the six men with their grim faces, giving up on breaking down the door, ran back to their vehicle.

The two fugitives will therefore change cars several times and get rid of Inna's phone, which they suspect to be traceable. Then enter a car wash, where Inna will escape between the rolls, thanks to another accomplice. This second accomplice is in charge of taking Inna to a "small village", previously indicated by the "lawyer" where she can catch the Kiev-Warsaw train.

This is the official story.

But the novel of this escape is... a novel.

And the questions are legion...

First, the coincidences.

Serguei, Inna's "lawyer", is at the office at 6:30 in the morning when Inna calls him, devastated. He takes only a few minutes to join her. And the pursuit begins.

---

70. Solicited several times by the author for an interview, Caroline Fourest finally declined by email: "Hello. I'm sorry, I'm busy with other subjects, not much in France, and I'm running out of time. I think I have said the essential in *Inna*, which is above all a political book on feminism. Good reading and good luck with your book. Sincerely, CF.

More surprisingly, how did he have, just that morning, accomplices[71] and several vehicles to exfiltrate the activist?

One could think that Serguei was already in the apartment and that he prepared his escape plan with Inna. Serguei - which Inna will hide for a long time - is the young woman's Ukrainian boyfriend. Why does Inna hide this relationship even from her Femen friends?

"It's Inna," says Sasha, "she lives in secrecy, and then it was her private life, we knew it, but it did not interfere with our friendship or our activities[72]."

Why does Caroline Fourest give Serguei the role of a lawyer involved in the Femen cases when he is - Sacha is formal - "not the lawyer of our movement"?

I don't know why she says that," adds Sasha, "but what is certain is that we had two lawyers in Ukraine. Not Sergei, who was only Inna's boyfriend."

To say that Inna is calling for help is to say that Inna is alone at home that night. To Sacha, who speaks with her several times during the night, Inna also says that she is alone, but sometimes betrays herself in the course of a sentence.

"I understood that Sergei was there, I asked the question frankly because it was important for her safety to know whether she was alone or not in this room, but she answered neither yes nor no, diverting the conversation to something else, it's Inna!"

---

71. In *Inna*, Caroline Fourest specifies that "despite two changes of car thanks to accomplices, they are still followed".

72. Unless otherwise noted, quotes are from interviews conducted by the author between November 2009 and September 2016.

The train to Warsaw leaves Kiev every morning at 7:54. It makes its first stop in Kazatin Tovarij at 10:47 am.

If Inna took the train in Kiev, she had one hour and twenty-four minutes, between 6:30 and 7:54, to call Serguei, wait for him, change cars thanks to accomplices warned on the spot, lose her pursuers in a car wash, buy her ticket... all at the worst hour, considering the morning traffic in the Ukrainian capital.

In the second scenario, Inna took the train to Kazatin, but it takes two and a half hours without traffic to get there, so she had to go through the same obstacle course to lose her pursuers in the center of Kiev in an hour and twenty-two, at best, before setting out for Kazatin.

In both cases, this is an unprecedented achievement.

For the story and for Caroline Fourest, it is the sawn cross that is at the origin of the urgency to "exfiltrate" Inna. This Orthodox cross cut down with a chainsaw, on August 17, 2012, by Inna, with the active help of Anna, Sacha and Oxana, to denounce the discrimination of women by the Church and to support the Pussy Riot arrested in Russia[73], triggered the opening of an investigation[74] criminal

---

73. On February 21, 2012, the Pussy Riot punk singing group was arrested by Russian police in Moscow for singing and uttering anti-Putin slogans in Moscow's Christ the Savior Cathedral. See in particular *Le Monde*, February 21, 2012, "Pussy Riot, arrest of two hooded women..."

74. According to the Interfax-Ukraine news agency, a criminal investigation was opened on August 18, 2012, under paragraph 2 of Article 296, against "activists of the Femen movement on August 17 guilty of sawing down an Orthodox cross located in front of the Center of Arts and Culture, Zhovtnevy Square."

for "hooliganism". Inna and her accomplices are all facing jail time. However, Inna is presented as the one facing the greatest risk.

In the book[75] by Galia Ackerman, the escape, still told by Inna, is different, and closer to reality. It does not happen the next day, but four days after Inna sawed the cross. This version is less spectacular, but still specifies that "in the emergency, Inna does not have time to warn her friends that she is escaping".

In the telephone exchanges she has with Sacha, and via Skype, until around 2 a.m., Inna does not mention the slightest intention of leaving at dawn. "We were all being watched and we thought that Inna was perhaps in more danger than the others because she had physically operated the sawing of the cross, but we are all on the film pulling the stays that make the cross fall or keeping watch, we were all threatened."

In *Confession d'une ex-Femen*[76], Éloïse Bouton doesn't bother with dates, but offers a third version that she says she got from Inna's mouth: "Inna arrives [...]. Emaciated and preoccupied, she hid the stigmata of her escape behind a thick layer of foundation. She tells me about the action, the drumming on the door of her Kiev apartment in the middle of the night, the panic, her escape through the window, the complicity of friends to get to the airport, Prague and then Paris."

---

75. *Femen, op. cit.*
76. Éd. du Moment, 2015.

An escape in question

Airport, Prague, Paris...

Inna.

When the young girl "on the run" arrives in Paris from Warsaw, she is welcomed by Safia Lebdi, Caroline Fourest and Loubna Méliane[77]. At Inna's side, Caroline Fourest tells us, "two Austrian-Iranian filmmakers who are preparing a feature film on several peaceful protest movements, such as Femen[78]". Inna will never explain how they were warned that she was escaping, nor where they joined the Ukrainian activist. At the very least, we will say that, even at the most critical point of her adventure, Inna knows how to take advantage of every situation and keeps her feet firmly planted on the media ground. At the most, we will say that everything was orchestrated and that her escape was well planned.

The exfiltration of Inna was seen as a matter of urgency and danger. These are not absent since, since the sawing of the cross, all the members of Femen are under pressure. But one can also think that Inna got up that morning more normally than she said, because she had decided that it was the right time to leave, that she took a train to Warsaw a little more normally than she said. We can also think that she informed, in Vienna, a certain Arash Riahi, an Iranian-Austrian director she had met three weeks earlier in Paris, who was working at that time for Austrian television. One can also think that Arash Riahi joined the young woman,

---

77. Feminist activist and parliamentary assistant to Malek Boutih since June 2012.
78. *Inna, op. cit.*

as planned, in Warsaw, that they stayed there for a few days before taking a flight to Paris where the great adventure began... And one can think all this considering the fact that they arrived together in Paris.

From approximation to slight omission, from omission to complacency, from secrecy to renunciation, the myth of the *pasionaria* who slipped into the clutches of the heavyweights of the secret services was built. The press has a taste for these stories, and it would be unwise to try to instill a hint of doubt in this perfect construction.

The main thing about Inna's escape is true: she is in danger and she deserves to be granted political refugee status in France. But the context, the circumstances, the instrumentalization of her friends and the manipulation of the facts are nothing more than a sum of half-truths.

For Sacha, this consecution is tragic, "it built the legend of Inna and contributed to our eviction, even from afar".

Today, Inna, who has long maintained the vagueness, no longer hides from it: she left on August 21 and not on August 18 at dawn as Caroline Fourest suggests. Today, it does not matter.

Between August 18 and 21, in Kiev, the atmosphere was tense, but was the danger as imminent as Inna and Caroline would say? The danger is there, but it does not prevent Inna from having lunch with Anna and Sacha on the 18th, then spending the next day with Sacha and Oxana printing *"boob's prints" for* the customers of the Femen shop... All this in a "rather relaxed" atmosphere, Sacha remembers.

On August 20, Sasha accompanied Inna to the central station to buy an open ticket "just in case". "And as if by chance, she left the next day at dawn, without telling anyone", Sacha says seriously. No one... Except Arash Riahi, whom she will probably meet in Warsaw and who will arrive with her in Paris on the 27th.

Galia Ackerman, a few years later, while I was preparing this book, asked me the right question: "Could Inna have organized everything from the beginning, the sawing of the cross, the emergency escape and arrival in Paris? To premeditate everything in order to be able to leave Ukraine and ask for political asylum in France?"

The answer, it is Sacha who gives it with sincerity: "No, Inna did not saw the cross to have a pretext to escape from Ukraine, to take refuge in France and to betray her friends." But she skillfully used the events for personal purposes.

One last detail: you need a visa to enter France and Inna didn't have time to ask for it because the procedures take a week. She had a 90-day visa," recalls Sacha. We asked for it on June 15 to come and found Femen France in Paris with Safia Lebdi. June 15? Ninety days? Inna's visa would expire in less than two weeks! It was time to leave.

Inna arrives in Paris

"The way to conduct a war well is not to follow, but to precede events. A general marches at the head of the troops, in the same way a good politician must march at the head of affairs, in order to be always the master of acting according to his will, without ever being obliged to drag himself along with the events."
Demosthenes, *The Philippics*, 4th century c. B.C.

Paris, August 27, 2012

"Femen is an international movement born in Ukraine", Inna Shevchenko used to say. This is clear and it allows to evacuate the genesis and the history of the movement. In essence, this means: "Femen was born in Ukraine, but that's in the past, and what matters now is that it's an international movement and that I lead it."

The turning point in this evolution, according to Inna, was her arrival as a political refugee in France and the re-foundation, by herself, of Femen under the name Femen France.

This is not true.

Inna did not create Femen France. Safia Lebdi, Anna Hutsol, Oxana Shachko, Sacha Shevchenko and Inna Shevchenko created Femen France. This birth did not happen after Inna found refuge in Paris, but even before she cut down the Kiev cross. And this changes the perspective on Femen's history profoundly. Inna has always based her legitimacy over the movement on the idea that she was the one who brought Femen to France, following her escape from Ukraine. She is even less legitimate as the head of Femen France because she has maintained the legend of the foundation of Femen France after having installed in the public opinion the idea that she had previously founded Femen Ukraine.

In real life, it happened like this: after her romanticized escape, Inna arrived in Paris accompanied by Arash Riahi[79], and his brother, Arman. The two brothers are Iranian and have lived in Austria since 1982. They are preparing a feature film and a subject for Austrian television. In Paris, Inna was welcomed by Safia Lebdi and Caroline Fourest,

---

79. The Riahi brothers are the authors of the film *Everyday Rebellion*, a documentary presenting in parallel the rebellions against finance in Wall Street, against dictatorship in Syria and against machismo in Ukraine... The link between the three rebellions is difficult to see. The film has not found a distributor in France at this time.

who wanted to film the images of the arrival of the blonde *pasionaria* and make a documentary[80] for French television.

Safia Lebdi has been in contact with the Femen for several months: "Since they came to do the action against DSK, in October 2011," she explains.

Safia is the inspiration, organizer and logistician of the birth of Femen in France. Today she is no longer involved in the movement, but has continued her political career - she was elected as a regional councilor for Europe Écologie-Les Verts (EELV) in 2010 - and her work with associations. She is also behind the wonderful project of the Amateur Film Factory in Aubervilliers, with Michel Gondry. When I asked her to meet me for the first time, she said that she "still supports the movement", adding, when I mentioned a possible "war of egos" within Femen: "There is no war of egos within Femen, there are only a few of us fighting, we are not going to start tearing each other apart[81]. In short, the door seems closed. There is no swinging between the soldiers of feminism.

Safia changed her mind when she learned of the drama experienced by Sacha and Oxana. A few months later, she agreed to meet with me: "I had already left when their big problems started, but I knew Inna and Caroline, I know what they are capable of, they wanted power at any cost[82].

---

80. *Nos seins, nos armes*, Nadia El Fani and Caroline Fourest, Nilaya productions, 2013.

81. Email exchange with author, February 2016.

82. Unless otherwise noted, quotes are from interviews conducted by the author between November 2009 and September 2016.

Safia discovers the girls in Paris, on the occasion of the movement's first trip to Western Europe. Alain Margot, the Swiss filmmaker (see chapter 36), organized and financed the trip for the film *I Am Femen*, which he is currently making. After a brief stay with Alain in Switzerland, Sacha, Inna and Oxana sought to set up an action in France. DSK offers them a golden opportunity! On October 31, 2011, disguised as sexy maids, they stormed the door of the former IMF president's building, Place des Vosges, with buckets of water and mops. During this first "political" visit to France, Safia Lebdi introduced herself to the girls. The founder, with Fadela Amara, of the movement Ni putes ni soumises, was quickly charmed. From this first contact, an exchange of emails followed by a collaboration that will lead, in July 2012, to the birth of Femen France.

After exchanging for many weeks, comforted in her belief that Femen was ready for a collaboration, Safia went to Kiev in early March 2012 to negotiate the creation of Femen France. In her own words, Safia made "a deal": "I dealt with Anna and Viktor essentially." Safia wants to import their mode of action in France, to serve, in particular, women from the Maghreb immigration: "I saw a great marriage, between Arab and Ukrainian feminists! A universalist and feminist alliance.

An explosive mix.

Detonating mixture.

In the background of Safia Lebdi's political project, there is also the debate on prostitution in France, which agitates feminist associations at the beginning of 2012. Safia intends to fight against the mafia networks of exploitation of prostitution, but she is not abolitionist, she refuses the criminalization of the client which leads, according to her, "the isolation and the greater precariousness of prostitutes". The fight is going to be close: "I am facing all the other feminist organizations as well as part of the Socialist Party, who want to punish the clients at the risk of weakening the girls, all in the name of morality." Above the parties, the minister waits to make a decision: "Najat Vallaud-Belkacem could be influenced one way or the other, with Femen and Arab women in the street, I was sure to win."

The negotiations in Kiev are tense. Femen is focused on abolition, but Anna and Oxana, in particular, understand the particularity of the French context, different from the "brothel" that Ukraine has become. They agree, according to Safia, to "evolve on this issue".

Second stumbling block: homosexuality. Safia wants to make this one of the Femen's struggles in France. Here too, a national debate is coming up and she wants the Arab women/Femen alliance to be on the right side. Today, it seems obvious that Femen defends marriage for all or gay rights. It was not so at the time. Sasha and Oxana immediately agree. Anna and Viktor wonder whether they should take up this new struggle. Inna is very reluctant. This is surprising, especially in view of the sentimental affair between Caroline Fourest and Inna, but also from a political point of view, given the future investment of Femen and Inna herself in the fight for marriage for all. That," smiles Safia, "is after the negotiation. We imposed

Inna arrives in Paris

the homosexual struggle on Inna, she was not in favor of it at all. Moreover, she adds, I do not believe for a moment in the love plot of Caroline Fourest's book, it is just that she wanted to find an angle of attack for her book, a first work[83] having already been written."

But Safia is a political woman. In 2012, she did not deviate from her goal: to import Femen to France. For many weeks, she took care of all the steps and expenses. Finally, the association Femen, in France, was born on July 14, 2012, the date of its declaration in the prefecture, under the object (spelling mistakes included): "To improve the relationship between women and men; to create training centers for feminism; to denounce all forms of injustice in an innovative and collective way." Its headquarters are located at 28, rue Ménilmontant in Paris, where Michel Gondry's film factory is also registered. This address corresponds to the home of Safia Lebdi. The birth of the association appears in the *Official Gazette* on July 28, 2012 (Id. RNA: W751215645, announcement number: 1031).

At that time, Inna did not participate in the birth of the project. She was content to observe Safia's efforts, organizing meetings at her home and paying for the Ukrainian women's trips out of her own pocket.

Sacha confirms: "Inna did not create Femen France, we did, together, in July, before her escape. Safia was essential to this birth. When Femen was born in France, the leaders were: Anna, Oxana, myself and then Safia in France. Inna

---

83. *Femen, op. cit.*

is only legitimate in fifth position. But by escaping from Ukraine, she upsets everything.

When Inna organizes her escape from Ukraine, she knows that an association, which she did not create and which she does not direct, exists in Paris. She arrives in the capital on August 27, 2012. Caroline Fourest learns of her arrival from Safia Lebdi and decides to go and wait for her at the foot of the bus that drops off the pretty Ukrainian woman at Porte Maillot.

They had already met, a month earlier, at the recording of the program that the journalist devoted to Femen, on France Inter.

Inna moves to the Lavoir moderne. It was Safia who found this place and organized the first "Femen party" on the occasion of the girls' arrival in July. A few hundred square meters of free space in the middle of Paris, what a bargain! The manager of the place is Hervé Breuil, a figure from the popular Goutte-d'Or neighborhood. Contacted by Safia, he enthusiastically agreed to host Femen, first because he is a sincere man and a convinced activist, and also because Femen's notoriety would reflect on the Lavoir Moderne and could well delay the closing of the place, which was strongly considered by the city hall.

As soon as Inna was installed on the second floor, we started to think about ways to act. An "inaugural march" in the neighborhood was decided for September 18, a sort of political "appetizer" under the eyes of dozens of photographers and filmers warned by Safia and Caroline. Inna will walk at the head of the procession, but Sacha and Oxana

Inna arrives in Paris

will also be there, specially coming from Ukraine for this founding action... And also to try to calm down the first tensions between Safia and Inna. But nothing happens, a clash takes place the same evening. Nothing transcendent happened during the march, but Inna wants to value the action. She writes and distributes, without informing Safia, a press release whose racist and sensationalist content reveals the gulf that separates Inna from French reality. The press release insists on the dangers faced by the girls during "a high-risk topless march" in a "Muslim neighborhood[84]". The inhabitants are presented as hostile. We are in the heart of Paris, in a popular neighborhood where several religions mix, certainly not in a *"no go zone"* of the type that will ridicule Nolan Peterson[85] when he will report their alleged existence in Paris, following the attacks of January 2015.

Safia explodes: "There is no way the movement will take this turn!" Caroline Fourest, in her book, explains how she tries to mediate between the two parties. "In reality, testify Joseph Paris and Alain Margot, who frequented the place a lot at that time for the needs of their respective films, Caroline clearly chose her camp from the beginning." It's Inna's.

On prostitution, Safia also loses the fight: "In a few days, after the Inna/Caroline rapprochement, the situation had changed, Inna declared herself an abolitionist. It was Caroline Fourest who was behind it, that's clear.

---

84. *Inna, op. cit.*

85. The *Fox* News reporter talks, during the January 15, 2015 newscast, about *"no go zones,"* areas deemed off-limits to whites in Paris, including the 10th and 18th arrondissements.

In the weeks to come, relations will deteriorate further until Safia throws in the towel in disgust. Inna, on the other hand, spills out into the media about the deep differences with Safia, and, not shying away from anything, the alleged coup attempt on the movement: "As long as we were in Ukraine, Safia could act as she pleased, she spoke to the media on behalf of our association, etc. But when we moved to Paris in the fall of 2012, we realized that we had different visions of what our activities were[86]." The "we" is no longer understood as "Femen," but rather as a "Caroline and I."

Exit Safia. Politically, because it is now necessary to remove her completely.

In order to do this, Safia's legal power over the association had to be removed. The Femen association was therefore dissolved, with Inna and Caroline in the wake of this dissolution creating a new association, Femen France, which was born, according to the *Journal officiel,* on December 11, 2012 (Id. RNA: W751217624, announcement no.: 1367), an association declared in the Paris prefecture with its headquarters at the Maison des associations[87], 206, quai de Valmy, in the 10th arrondissement, and no longer at the residence of Safia Lebdi. Its object is unchanged. The

---

86. *Femen, op. cit.*

87. In this regard, the movement has sometimes been accused of being supported by the Paris City Council, and the fact that Femen France has its headquarters in the Maison des associations in the 10th arrondissement has been cited as proof of this connivance. This institution of the arrondissement groups together more than 150 associations in fields as varied as checkers, angling and, therefore, the defense of women's rights...

information appears in the *Official Journal* on December 29, 2012. Safia Lebdi no longer has anything to do, officially, with Femen. She is no longer part of the movement, even though she was at the origin of the movement's establishment in France and largely facilitated Inna's installation. It is also worth noting the change of name from Femen to Femen France, which provides legal cover for the association, which is now run by Inna alone, against a possible legal action by Anna Hutsol, founder of the movement in Ukraine with Sacha and Oxana. The move is precise and quite Machiavellian. But Inna's legal advisors are probably still wondering... Femen France could well be understood as a branch of Femen Ukraine and would therefore give the Ukrainian association a say over the French association. The risk seemed to be definitively averted at the end of 2014, when Femen France became, by a simple modification registered in the *Official Journal* on October 21, Femen International (RNA Id.: W751217624, announcement number: 1637). A title clearly establishing the hierarchical superiority of the French movement over the Ukrainian association yet born six years earlier!

This legal game of chance led, on May 2, 2016, to the declaration in the *Journal Officiel* of a new association (RNA id.: W751233865, announcement no.: 794) whose headquarters would be located at 8, passage des Abbesses in Paris, and simply named... Femen. The circle is complete: Femen became successively Femen France, then Femen International, before becoming Femen again.

The hold-up is legal.

And Inna is the only soul of this "new" association...

On the condition of eliminating Anna, Oxana and Sacha.

Today, Safia Lebdi is appeased. She withdrew without making any waves, refusing to influence her network to withdraw the Lavoir moderne from the movement. She has only two regrets: "The first is that it was Inna who came to France, I wanted Oxana, she is a leader, but she spoke neither English nor French... ". And the second? "The second is that I called Caroline Fourest myself to involve her in Femen!

Viktor, manipulator?

"In politics, what is believed is more important
than what is true."
Charles-Maurice de Talleyrand-Périgord,
quoted by Jean Orieux,
Talleyrand ou le sphinx incompris,
Flammarion, 1992.

Damned soul. "Viktor is the Mohamed of the Femen,"
says Safia Lebdi in Caroline Fourest's book[88]. She is referring
to Mohamed Abdi, who, according to Safia, manipulated
Fadela Amara when she was the head of Ni putes ni soumises.
Safia knows Viktor from having "negotiated" with him
and Anna the logistics and timing of Femen's implantation
in France (see chapter 21). She has no interest in denigrating him, but she also lacks the necessary hindsight to
understand that Femen have always used Viktor more than

---

88. *Inna, op. cit.*

the other way around. Safia also wants to impose herself within the movement and, who knows, take the lead, as she later confided to Le *Monde*[89], even if she says today that this interpretation is "a speech made at first degree, in the heat of the moment, to a journalist who transcribed it as it was[90] ". In reality, she says, "I would obviously have accepted to share power, that is what we had negotiated.

A cruel twist of fate: like the fate of Safia Lebdi, Viktor Sviatski was sacrificed because it was useful to everyone.

I met Viktor in the winter of 2009 at the Sauna bar. He organized the assault on the Parliament with Anna and Sacha. He takes part in our long exchange after the attack, about Femen's objectives, the political philosophy that is emerging, the means of action, etc.

Viktor also comes from Khmelnytskyï. He is Anna's childhood friend. That's how he was introduced to Sasha and Oxana when they met the pretty redhead.

When we were in Khmelnytskyï," says Oxana, "Viktor was essential in our political formation. It was at his house that the first meetings took place around the founding themes of Femen, the fight against the sex industry and, above all, the place of women in the unequal and patriarchal Eastern European society. It was a kind of mutual emulation," Sacha continues, "we gave him confidence because we listened to him, we shared with him political readings and, in the end,

---

89. "Le féminisme à l'épreuve du sextrémisme," Stéphanie Marteau, *Le Monde*, March 8, 2013.
90. Unless otherwise noted, quotes are from interviews conducted by the author between November 2009 and September 2016.

fights. But he also gave us confidence in ourselves, constantly telling us that we could change this patriarchal society."

When Anna, then Sasha and Oxana emigrate to Kiev, Viktor follows them. Although he participated fully and every time in the preparation of the actions, like Anna, he rarely appeared in public. "He did not want to, this role in the background seemed to suit him, he was always happy to be with us," recalls Sasha. After 2010, when the girls moved from the Sauna to the Cupid, a new, more central and trendy bar, Viktor was in his element, he was the only boy in this place, frequented by the youth of Kiev, who could get close to the Femen. He is probably a little proud of this. He settles comfortably into a secret role, but never a leading one. The arrival of Inna will upset this balance.

When Inna joins the group, Viktor is naturally more important than her. She takes umbrage with him. She never agrees with his ideas, first discreetly and then openly. She launches initiatives without telling him, taking the habit of calling Sasha or Anna directly, forgetting the boy. Viktor is quick to rebel at this little game. But Inna plays it fine and tight, pleading innocence, forgetfulness or paranoia of the Marxist mentor. Little by little, Viktor's image deteriorates in the group. He himself, confused, moody and probably frustrated, inexorably participates in his estrangement each time he complains to the others about his increasingly neglected place within the movement.

Even before reaching Paris, Inna has already gained the upper hand over Viktor. But it is from the French capital that she will eliminate him politically.

Viktor, manipulator?

However, Viktor is neither an insurmountable obstacle on his way to power nor even, at the beginning, a declared opponent. His disgrace will be a trial run, a repetition. In the same way that she will attack Sacha and Oxana by manipulating the French women (see chapter 30), she makes the Australian director Kitty Green, who shares the life of the Femen for a few months in 2012, the instrument of her fight against Viktor. Kitty, who does not like Viktor and is looking for a scripted hit, will let herself be used all the more easily as it makes her film more attractive. As a result, Kitty Green's film, *Ukraine Is Not a Brothel*, presents Viktor as a Machiavellian eminence grise who instrumentalizes the girls for indiscernible, but certainly unprincipled purposes.

From then on, the curse is triggered.

Viktor is mostly in Ukraine. He does not speak English. He is shy, has no direct personal access to the media and is of no interest to anyone... Facing the Venice Film Festival (where Kitty Green's film was presented in 2013), and facing Caroline Fourest and Inna Shevchenko, he has no chance.

In the film, Viktor has the bad role that Kitty makes him play. And Inna takes it upon herself to add a layer to the film, in a press conference, about "the mistakes of the past that must not be made again" and "the agents of patriarchy who are everywhere, even inside Femen". By making Viktor look like a manipulator, she pursues two objectives: first, to get rid of Anna's childhood friend for good, and second, to throw a veil of discredit over the movement's past in order to project herself as the head of Femen's indispensable renovation and cleaning enterprise (see chapter 31).

During my various reports, I had the idea of a Viktor dragging some frustrations, but happy to be enthroned in the middle of an army of soldiers. His self-effacement, his lack of scale and sometimes of discernment make him an easy prey for Inna. His vanity also serves him well. Viktor falls into all the traps. To some journalists, he talks about his "harem". The information taken at face value will spread on social networks. Following the Venice Festival, his new fame throws him under the sunlights, he is rather pleased. "He did not understand, until the end, says Sacha, that he was really perceived as the *bad boy*." After being in the shadows for years, he is interested in him, Viktor is happy.

And Sasha and Oxana, what did they think of the turn of events and of Viktor's pillorying? "We didn't participate, we were a bit overwhelmed and then we started to argue with him, we let it happen."

In France, the story of Viktor mentor "manipulator" is very popular. For Galia Ackerman, it is a clear sign of the machismo of our society: "We believed what we wanted to believe, that is to say that young Ukrainian women were not capable of leading a revolt, a man was needed behind! Macho among machos... It was Kitty Green who developed this credible scenario because it corresponds perfectly to an unconscious of our society. In general psychology, this is called "moving from cognitive dissonance to positive consonance through a cultural bias". In the history of religions, this is called "harmonistic concordist exegesis". In common parlance, it is called "one hell of a whore".

Viktor, manipulator?

During an appearance on Laurent Ruquier's show *On n'est pas couché*, on February 8, 2014, about the book she wrote about and with Inna, Caroline Fourest was questioned by Aymeric Caron in these terms: "I regret in your book that you did not do a thorough investigation especially on this Viktor who seems to be the éminence grise, the brain of Femen and who manipulates them, what about him?" Caroline Fourest's answer is embarrassed and tries to evacuate the subject a little: "Femen is a girls' movement, there have been personal struggles, Viktor is something else..."

In short, she says almost nothing about it.

She knows that the role she makes her play in the book is inaccurate and serves Inna's interests. But she is not the only one: *L'Obs*, *Le Figaro*, France 2, *Le Monde*... all the major media fall for it. However, the prize goes to *Libération* for an article entitled: "Viktor Sviatski, a manipulator in the shadow of the Femen[91]. Inna first presents herself as a victim: "We didn't know how to resist him. Then she settles her accounts: "He made us understand how much men can be bastards. Before closing the enterprise with a definitive statement: "Since I have been in Paris, I have been able to build the real Femen.

Sacha and Oxana are already condemned, but they do not know it yet.

In an interview[92] to *Spiegel*, Viktor will sink himself by declaring that he had control of the film's script in agree-

---

91. Quentin Girard, *Libération*, September 4, 2013.
92. "Femen's male mastermind: "I am no tyrant," *Spiegelonline International*, September 26, 2013.

ment with Kitty: "Kitty and I wanted to make the film more interesting by making me a bully from whom the girls break free at the end!"

The image of Viktor being able to manipulate anyone, especially Inna, Sacha or Oxana, has always amused me...

Even after his beatings in Kiev and Odessa, there will remain the eternal suspicion that attaches itself to a boy who is involved in changing the condition of women... and some of the questions that his family and his few Ukrainian friends kept asking him: Where is your interest? Why do you support them? Can't you see that they want to destroy you and all men? Are you with us or against us? How can a man be on the side of women?

Today, Viktor lives between Ukraine and Switzerland where he has obtained refugee status. He is still Anna's friend.

Eloise makes a passage

"The undisputed protagonist of the show is the man... so, because we have been crying for two thousand years, today, we women will laugh and even laugh at ourselves."
Franca Rame, *Women's stories*, Dramaturgy, 2002.

She is the most famous French Femen activist. And one of the very first. But Éloïse Bouton[93] missed her adventure with Femen, wrote a book and changed her ways.

Eloise embodies the hiatus of Femen's arrival in France. She is a feminist, her commitment is sincere, but her priorities and motivations are variable. She wants to serve Femen and also to use Femen.

Éloïse was 28 years old when she joined Femen. She graduated from the French Institute of Press at the Sorbonne-Nouvelle Assas. She collaborates with various magazines and

---

93. Eloise Bouton did not respond to the author's requests for an interview.

conducts investigations on the theme of feminism, which she offers to *L'Express*, Le *Parisien*, etc. Like many young feminists, she knows Femen. So, when the Femen from Ukraine set up the movement in France, with the help of Safia Lebdi, Eloise became enamored with the famous blonde from Kherson. From a positive point of view, we can say that Eloise and Femen have a convergent interest: militant feminism. If we are more prosaic, we understand, after reading her book, that Eloise sees in the Ukrainian movement emerging in France a fantastic opportunity. Unlike the Ukrainian women, Eloise does not intend to completely abandon her job to embark on the adventure, she intends to carry out her freelance activity and her militant commitment at the same time.

Éloïse Bouton has recounted her *Confession of an ex-Femen*[94] in a book in which she reveals, over two hundred pages, how she tried to keep herself in grace with Inna, with a view to being hired full time by the movement and becoming the first official employee of Femen France. She plays cat and mouse with Safia Lebdi, creator of the movement in France, and then with Caroline Fourest... each of the three courting, in their own way, the queen Inna.

Following Eloise, many activists will rush into the path. Sarah, Elvire, Marguerite, Pauline, etc., who are still today the base of the French team around Inna.

This is the "affair" that will lead the young girl on the path to exclusion. Eloise receives a phone call one morning

---

94. Editions of the moment, 2015.

in May 2014 and immediately understands, from the tone of Sarah, her colleague in combat, that something has happened... " Sorry to bother you," she tells her, "some extreme right-wing sites have published articles and naked pictures of you. They say that you are an *escort*[95]. Eloise almost faints, then recovers. She explains to Sarah what she will repeat to all her friends a little later at the Lavoir. A few months ago, in search of an interesting journalistic investigation, she registered on the Internet in a call-girl network in order to infiltrate it. "I create a profile half real and half fictional, I invent a character, practices, rates. I add photos of me taken a year earlier by a journalist and photographer friend[96]. Obviously, these photos are still lying around on the Web! Her friends are taking it in different ways. Inna is worried about the movement. French women don't care or even believe her, at least at first. Caroline Fourest, to whom Eloise will ask for help from the lawyer who advises her and takes care of Inna, sympathizes wholeheartedly but: "You know, my lawyer is very, very expensive[97]."

Not everyone is Inna; Caroline has selective solidarity.

Oxana remembers: "Eloise thought she could count on Caroline who also has a lot of problems in court, but nobody can count on Caroline Fourest if she does not have a personal interest in the case." And here, there are clearly only blows to take for the famous polemicist. On social networks, Éloïse

---

95. *Ibid.*
96. *Ibid.*
97. *Ibid.*

was dragged through the mud: "Femen, neither whore nor submissive[98] ?", asked ironically the sworn enemy of Femen, Alain Soral. In the end, according to Eloise[99], it was her ex-boyfriend who sold this information to extreme right-wing sites in order to take revenge for having been abandoned. A kind of "revenge porn" particularly violent considering the notoriety of the victim. Eloise filed a complaint and was partially successful. But at the Lavoir moderne, the Femen headquarters, the damage is done. Her friends moved away from her. Without saying anything, or almost without saying anything, Inna made her fall from grace. Caroline Fourest followed suit. Eloise, who had long cherished the hope of being the first employee of Femen France, was disappointed. This anecdote, however, symbolically poses the difficult equation of the existence of the movement in France and the reality of French militancy, which has neither the same history, nor the same motivation, nor the same leather as the Ukrainian girls, including Inna.

Eloise's other major achievement was to be the first Femen activist to be prosecuted and sentenced for sexual exhibition to a one-month suspended prison sentence (plus a 2,000 euro fine and 1,500 euro court costs). Her conflict with Femen took an irreparable turn when she asked Inna to pay the fine and the legal fees. Inna takes refuge, as usual, behind the poverty of the movement... except that

---

98. "Les Femen: ni putes ni soumises?", *Égalité et Réconciliation*, 26 November 2012.

99. *Confession of an Ex-Female*, Éditions du moment, 2015.

she herself lives on the movement's money and that the costs of the actions are covered by Femen (see chapter 26). This refusal is more than inelegant, it puts Éloïse Bouton in a delicate position - she lives soberly - and creates mistrust in the group... If Femen does not support its activists when they are condemned, we may think twice before committing ourselves... In 2016, the appeal of the decision concerning Éloïse Bouton will overturn the previous judgement and give reason to Éloïse. Inna will talk about a Femen victory in this matter, says Eloise in her book[100]. Inna is always there where there is a little notoriety to be had.

More generally, the problem of sexual exhibition refers, for Femen, to an inequality that they were already denouncing in Ukraine: boys can show their torsos, but girls cannot. This prohibition, which they largely attribute to the weight of religion, is one of the struggles they wage - even if Inna was fiercely opposed to the topless happenings of Femen (see chapter 14). In this perspective, Éloïse Bouton still leads debates and meetings on this theme. In particular, she published on her personal website, in February 2016, an interview with the artist Deborah de Robertis, author in May 2014, of the "exhibitionist" happening at the Musée d'Orsay in front of Courbet's painting *The Origin of the World* and then, in January 2016, in front of Manet's painting *Olympia.* The activist and the artist agree in particular on the essential political dimension of this claim and on the need to "desexualize" this fight.

------

100. *Confession of an ex-Femen, op. cit.*

Eloise makes a passage

In her book, Eloise settles accounts with her ex-friends and her ex-boyfriend. She also brings elements on the functioning of Inna with her militants. The "trainings" - races, boxing sessions, etc. - She deeply dislikes the "trainings" - races, boxing sessions, etc. In Ukraine, there was never any such training, despite the very difficult conditions of combat. Inna introduced them upon her arrival in France to give their content to magazines in search of Femen images. This imagery helped to establish Femen in the sectarian symbolism, to such an extent that a deputy - Georges Fenech of the UMP - wrote to the Interministerial Mission for the Fight against Sects (Miviludes) to denounce the functioning, the actions and the recruitment of Femen, which, according to him, are reminiscent of the satanic sects[101].

About Eloise's book, Inna will say: "I am not interested, and I will not comment on this book. Gossip has nothing to do with feminism and our common struggle. What interests us is the feminist community, and this trial for sexual exhibition. We are not "*freelance* feminists", as Eloise defines herself today, after having left many movements. We are full time feminists, and that's why we will be by her side, until the end, in this fight against gender injustice[102].

Classy for someone who had refused any support to Eloise during the first trial, which was admittedly much less publicized.

<hr>

101. "Un député saisit la Miviludes contre les Femen," *Le Figaro*, February 10, 2014.
102. "Éloïse Bouton, there is a life after the Femen," Camille Emmanuelle, *Les Inrocks*, February 7, 2015.

Femen France takes action

"Let the women keep silent in the assemblies,
for it is not permitted for them to speak there;
but let them be submissive, as the law also says.
If they wish to learn anything, let them ask their
husbands at home; for it is improper for a woman
to speak in church.
First Epistle of Saint Paul to the Corinthians
14, 34-35.

Paris, February 15, 2016

"Obviously, we saw it most often from there, but we were happy[103]."

From Kiev, Oxana and Sacha witnessed the movement's take-off. The French are there: "We knew that the French

---

103. Unless otherwise noted, quotes are from interviews conducted by the author between November 2009 and September 2016.

would appreciate the action of Femen because France is a free and independent country with regard to religion.

At the Lavoir moderne, generously provided by the manager of the old theater (see chapter 21), they are getting organized. Inna took possession of the studio above the training room. In *Inna*, Caroline Fourest writes: "The former student thinks back for a moment to the beautiful apartment she was able to rent when she was not this wanted and stateless "hooligan"..." Inna has always lived in dingy rentals, and no change was in the immediate offing.

Once Safia Lebdi was removed from the movement, Inna had a free hand. The first meetings take place. The recruitment campaign begins.

There too," Sacha recalls, "we saw that it was working very well, but we wondered about the motivations of all these girls ready to commit themselves.

In Paris, Inna doesn't ask herself any questions, she welcomes en masse, more and more often accompanied by Caroline Fourest. In the chaos of the Lavoir, Caroline occupies a lot of space and asserts her place with Inna.

At the end of 2012, Inna set up the training sessions that many activists dislike so much, but which are very popular with photographers. In Ukraine, they find it stupid, but they accept the idea that it is about installing Femen in the landscape as a radical protest movement. Alain Margot, for his part, is trying to shoot the end of his film *I Am Femen*[104], but it is not easy: "I was surprised, like the others,

---

104. *I Am Femen*, Alain Margot, Caravel Productions, 2014.

at Inna's hasty departure, but above all, her attitude towards me changed when she arrived in Paris, she became distant, she ostensibly ignored me, whereas she had always been welcoming to me."

According to Alain Margot, Inna understood that she would not be the central character of the film, and she resented having chosen Oxana as the heroine and made her pay for it. Similarly, for the Swiss director, Caroline Fourest is immediately hostile to him: "As soon as she saw me, she asked Inna in English in front of me what I was doing there, although we both speak French. Her goal was to get me away." The journalist wants to turn, too. Perhaps she fears that Alain will overshadow her? Yet, "our films were produced in different countries, we didn't tell the same story and I was two years ahead... It was stupid, but that's how she is."

At the Lavoir moderne, Inna is gradually finding her feet. She spends a lot of time surfing the web and talking with Anna or Sacha on Skype... At least at the beginning.

The neighborhood surprises her. The Goutte-d'Or is nothing like what she knew in Ukraine. She did come to Paris a few years ago on a school trip, but she had seen the tourist Paris, the Eiffel Tower, the Louvre... She came back later for actions and for the launching of Femen France (see chapter 21), but she had never set foot in the 18th arrondissement. With her direct language, she is sometimes astonished in public by the diversity of Paris, which is often unknown outside our borders.

At first, the actions are always decided in agreement with Kiev. Femen France has already proven itself, in London,

Femen France takes action

August 2, 2012. In the middle of the Olympic Games, Eloise and Safia hijacked the official slogan of the Games *"Inspire a generation"* which became *"Kill a generation"* in order to stigmatize the presence of veiled sportswomen. Inna and Sacha came from Kiev, travels paid on the own funds of Safia Lebdi, but they have no visa for England. It is thus Safia and Eloise, accompanied by two other activists, Loubna and Charlotte, who must take up the challenge. Fernando, Safia's companion, is also there, he speaks English and he will take care of the purchase of material on site: signs, paint, etc. This performance is the first one in which Éloïse Bouton takes part and she describes in detail in her book[105] the excitement, the adrenaline... In the end, this action, entirely financed by Safia Lebdi's personal funds[106], will be a success. Safia and Eloise were arrested and then released. There will be no prosecution. But already, in the train that brings the activists back to Paris, the first doubts assail Eloise, who regrets, while taking the precaution of excluding herself from the circle, the rivalries and the game of courtesans that is installed between the participants: "They tell their custody, they shout, they do not listen to each other. Each one has lived worse than the other, has had more pain, has shouted more, has had the worst cops[107]..." According to Safia, Inna had instructed Eloise to keep an eye on her. "She spent her time on the

---

105. *Confession of an ex-Femen, op. cit.*

106. "Train tickets, accommodation and expenses on site...", in *Confession d'une ex-Femen, op. cit.*

107. *Confession of an ex-Femen, op. cit.*

phone to inform Inna." Oxana would then compliment her on the importance and timing of the action, Inna would be "very upset."

On October 27, 2012, another Femen protest scored points in the opinion and in the press[108], the one against Ikea and its Saudi catalog without female models. With slogans such as "*Marianne is angry*[109]" and "*Women are here*[110]", Inna, Marguerite and Elvire took over the Ikea store in Gonesse Paris Nord II. They jumped on the furniture and brandished chairs under the stunned eyes of customers and salesmen who... took their picture.

But the action that will crystallize the sympathy of a large part of the opinion in favor of Femen is still in gestation...

On November 18, 2012 a large demonstration of opponents of the "marriage for all" law is scheduled. The Femen do not want to miss it. For Caroline Fourest, the opportunity is too good: this action will be the central sequence of her film[111] for France 2. Marriage for all" is also a fight that is close to her heart. For many French activists, Pauline, Marguerite, Sarah, etc., this is a first, a baptism of fire. And what a baptism! The girls burst into the Denfert-Rochereau district, dressed as sexy nuns and armed with fire extinguishers that symbolize "ejaculating males". Here and there, they sprayed anti-marriage for all demonstrators and

---

108. Notably "Femen invade an Ikea store," *Elle*, October 27, 2012.
109. "Marianne is angry."
110. "The women are there."
111. *Our breasts, our weapons, op. cit.*

Femen France takes action

marched shouting "*In gay we trust*", parodying the motto of fundamentalists all over the world "*In God we trust*". The public often reacts with violence to religious protests, much more than to political ones. This one is no exception. Barely have they time to walk a few dozen meters when they are assaulted, thrown to the ground and beaten by a horde of fascist thugs. It is the Catholic fundamentalist association Civitas that provides the ranks of these avengers of God. This association is known for its numerous appeals against shows where the image of God would be, according to it, debased. In 2012, it is one of the most active and extreme against marriage for all. When its activists see the Femen dressed as sexy nuns, they lose all common sense and engage in violence.

These men, dressed in black and often masked, are armed with truncheons, tear gas canisters or sticks. Several girls are wounded. Eloise and Julia are taken to task. Inna, never the least active in the heat of the action, leaves a tooth there. Oxana, who came from Kiev especially for this action, is rushed to the ground between two cars. She receives several kicks to the head. Caroline Fourest will say she was also beaten. A scene filmed by *Le Parisien*, still visible today on social networks, shows a person beaten against a car. It could be Caroline Fourest. The journalist has filed a complaint. The case is ongoing.

After the demonstration, the president of Civitas, Alain Escada, justified the violence against the young girls by their "aggressive attitude", their "provocation" and the throwing of smoke from their fire extinguishers which were aimed, according to him, at "a child in his stroller[112]". An untenable defense obviously. The girls will file a complaint. Civitas too, notably for violence, that's the last straw. If this aspect of the procedure is still not judged today, the Femen have nevertheless won their case, at the correctional court of Paris, on February 15, 2016, on the accusation brought against them by Civitas of "disturbance of public order" and "insults because of their belonging to the Catholic religion".

The main consequence of this action, once the blues are massed, is to install Femen in the French landscape as a legitimate movement of feminist or intersectional struggle. The sympathy of a large part of the public is won over. The frivolous and gullible perverts that their critics often denounce have earned their stripes as courageous and sincere activists. Femen France's popularity ratings have been rising steadily... until February 2013.

The second major action of Femen in France will bring this rating down to its lowest level.

Inna has made it a fixed idea, almost a fantasy: Notre-Dame must be attacked. It is the symbol of Catholicism. The Femen in Notre-Dame... that would have worldwide repercussions! But not everyone agrees. Around her, her court does not dare to rebel, even if several girls think that other actions are a priority, notably on gay rights or equal pay. After all, Catholicism does not really endanger French society, nor does it challenge the secular balance... At least

---

112. "The Civitas Institute will file a complaint against the Femen," *La Nouvelle République*, November 20, 2012.

Femen France takes action

not yet. Caroline Fourest, for her part, is resolutely against an action at Notre-Dame and will make it known. But Inna doesn't care. The action will take place.

Inna was suspicious of Caroline, she did not inform her of all the meetings or decisions taken. Joseph Paris remembers: "Inna believes, at that time, rightly or wrongly, that Caroline Fourest is playing a double game and that she could warn the government or the police of actions in preparation[113]. The reason for this distrust? Fourest's network, which she never ceases to mention in order to shine with her protégée. And Inna has a front row seat to see that Manuel Valls calls Caroline when she is in trouble in a demonstration and that the President of the Republic, François Hollande, sends her a text message to support her and to check on her[114].

Inna fears that the journalist will only receive support from the higher-ups in exchange for services rendered, "for example, keeping an eye on the Femen on behalf of the Minister of the Interior," says Joseph Paris. There is no question of the police preventing her commando from entering the cathedral. Caroline will therefore be carefully kept away.

It was Benedict XVI's renunciation of the papacy that provided them with the pretext. In the middle of the morning of February 15, 2013, eight Femen activists, including Julia, Elvire, Eloise, and Inna, entered the cathedral and made their way towards the enormous central bells. Armed

---

113. Email exchange with the author, April 2016.
114. *Inna, op. cit.*

with sticks carefully covered with felt - which will make the accusation of degradation formulated by the church fall apart - the stripped harpies suddenly assault the sacred bells in a hullabaloo to wake up a priest after a banquet. The tourists are astonished, several try to immortalize the scene. We laugh. But the divine reaction is not long in coming. In an instant, the night falls on the house of Esmeralda like the plague on the cities of the plain. The guardians of the temple have understood that these demons feed on light. The darkness will prevent their gesture... Las. The recent technological evolution of Mr. Gaedicke's and Mr. Mietke's flash powder is forgotten: the electronic flash, which now equips most cell phones and cameras. The gunfire is back in full swing. The clerks' trick backfires. Lightnings bathe the scene of a malignant halo. The cursed ones beat and bray to all rupture. It is necessary to seize them with rough hands and to leave them with kicks so that the insult finally ceases.

The damage is done.

Caroline Fourest will be furious, as Joseph Paris attests: "I was at the Lavoir when the girls returned, Caroline was there, she yelled at them and blamed Inna for having left her out of this decision making." Caroline Fourest herself would return to her opposition to this action, notably on February 8, 2014, on the set of Laurent Ruquier: "I had many reservations about this action, I expressed them to Inna."

In Kiev, Anna, Viktor, Oxana and Sacha applaud.

For Joseph Paris, these two actions, which receive a diametrically opposed reception in public opinion, speak to us first of all of a dull and sleepy irascibility: "The Femen are a revelation of this invisible violence which surrounds our society and which is ready to spring up as soon as we break a line or a rule.

For Inna, there is no doubt: "Whatever their religion, they all hit equally hard!"

Caroline and Inna
make history

"Cursed be all kings. They have no faith and are not faithful to their commitments. Woe to him whom God has struck with the scourge of their society; for kings have neither companions nor friends; they never love anyone: if they have regard for a man, it is only because they hope to obtain something from him [...]. If they have obtained from him what they desired, they have no friendship, no tenderness, no brotherly feeling for him. Book of Kalila and Dimna, *The Fables of Bidpai*, chapter IX.

Paris, March 15, 2016

"Come, I've spotted a terrace in the sun, we'll be quiet[115]."

---

115. Unless otherwise noted, quotes are from interviews conducted by the author between November 2009 and September 2016.

Inna leads me to a paved street next to the Sacré-Coeur. We find a table against the low wall, facing south. "The police have asked me, when I sit in a public place, to always have as few people as possible behind me." Inna is officially protected, and very legitimately so. Since the 2015 attacks, she has been among the potential targets of Islamist terrorists. "I take precautions, I also have instructions from the cabinet of Cazeneuve and an emergency number to call if necessary." For the rest, no secret agents on the horizon, we settle down.

We've crossed paths here and there, at press conferences or outside a courtroom, but this is the first time since 2012 that I'll spend more than an hour with Inna. The "world leader" that I find has changed. Salmon-colored mid-season raincoat, silk shirt, dizzying heels, Longchamp bag... She has become more middle class. Rather, she now has the means to assume the Inna *fashion victim* that she has long silenced in her because of an empty wallet or an inadequate political line. Installed in life and free of any critical look in her entourage, Inna does not hide anymore. She has grown cheeks too. She orders a salad. "When was the last time we spoke?" she asks with a smile. I remember it well, it was at the Trocadero, the first action in France, with Safia. Inna also remembers that I had given her, at her request, upon her arrival in France, several contacts of journalists who might be interested in Femen's actions. She thanks me.

Inna is suspicious.

Last week, I saw Elvire Duvelle-Charles, we talked about the future of the movement in France, new perspectives, militant action, etc. I realize that Inna knows everything about our conversation. I realize that Inna knows everything about our conversation. In detail.

We evoke memories, Odessa, the trains of Ukraine, the Cupid...

I catch a little nostalgia in his eyes.

I am wrong.

She is concentrated, voluntary, cold. It is Inna.

I look at her.

I know who she is and where she comes from.

I know what she did that is not being said.

She knows that I know.

Before our meeting, Inna asked me about my last reports, she asked me to tell her about Syria, about the Kurdish-Daesh front; she said that "everything starts from there"; that political religion is "absolute evil"; and also that she is so happy to see me again and that it is wonderful to run the world. I know she is anxious for the interview to end and hopes that we will stick to generalities.

The lunch goes on in a false rhythm. Each of Inna's answers ends up being a red herring. She dodges, deflects, smiles a lot and says as little as possible...

I talk about the year 2012-2013, his arrival in France.

She smiles again: "Those were the heroic times, many things have changed since then..." She doesn't say which ones.

She asks me if I have thought about the cover of the book I am preparing on Femen. I said no, not yet. She says that Femen is a "forward-looking" movement and that "a recent photo" is needed. She also says that she was recently in Italy

Caroline and Inna make history

for an interview about another book[116] that is coming out in that country: "A good book, I think, but I haven't read it." I say I know about it. The book covers the high points of the movement. Inna is on the cover.

I prefer to go back a few years.

In theory, throughout 2013, the actions are still decided in Kiev in a small council: Oxana, Sacha, Anna and Inna via Skype. Oxana, moreover, makes many return trips between the French and Ukrainian capitals. She serves as a transmission belt. A few months later, Oxana will read in Caroline Fourest's book that she was "the eye of Kiev[117] ", in charge of spying on Inna's actions and reporting them to the Ukrainian Politburo. This contemptuous slander of the French journalist did more damage to Oxana's head than all the blows of the cops of Europe: "I think back to that time and I measure to what extent those two lied to me, plotted, while I believed that they were our friends; I sacrificed my youth to this movement and that's how I was paid in return by those two wicked women.

In her love for Inna, Caroline Fourest does not lose sight of the benefits she intends to draw from Femen. She wishes to politically influence this modern and media-oriented movement, whose militant ideas she shares. But as always, without belonging to it. A little inside, a little outside. Inside when there is praise to be received, outside when there are

---

116. *Inna e le streghe senza dio. (Inna and the witches without god).* Massimo Ceresa, Tra le righe ed. 2015.
117. *Inna, op. cit.*

blows to be taken. Inside when it joins in the success of the actions or outside when it disassociates itself, along with the Socialist Party, from the action at Notre-Dame. With skill, she knows how to make herself indispensable to Inna and the movement.

I am talking about Caroline Fourest to Inna.

Inna sighs and shakes her head: "Caroline helped Femen, but she's not the only one, she's saying a lot of crap now." The romance, if it ever began, is well and truly broken.

At the end of 2012, Caroline Fourest was Inna's "press attaché" in France. At the end of 2013, Sacha and Oxana - and many others with them, from Joseph Paris to Alain Margot or Galia Ackerman - accuse her of having been the instrument of their eviction. Caroline, for her part, says she fell in love with Inna and that she bitterly regrets it[118].

Caroline first met Inna at France Inter in July 2012 for her program *Ils changent le monde*. This stay of Inna, a few weeks before her "escape", is essential in the story of the young Ukrainian activist. There she discovered the opulence of the media and the gentleness of Paris, a friendly press and smiling people; she also met Arash Riahi, the Iranian-Austrian filmmaker who would join her in Warsaw.

Inna met Caroline Fourest and saw that her charm was working. It amused us," says Sacha, "to see this journalist subjugated by Inna. Anna, Sacha, Oxana and Inna are there. Caroline interviews Anna but only has eyes for Inna. The others laugh about it. It will be time to cry about it.

---

118. Notably on the set of *On n'est pas couché*, France 2, February 8, 2014.

Naturally, Caroline, introduced to the place by Safia Lebdi, is there to welcome Inna at the end of summer 2012. After the few scenes shot at the arrival of Inna's bus (see Chapter 21), they meet at the Lavoir moderne. Since the announcement of Inna's arrival in France, many journalists have wanted to meet her. Inna does not close any doors, but she is wary; Caroline will guide her.

Inna does not deny it: "Of course she helped me, but she also wanted to use Femen, like everyone else!

The polemicist is very present in the French audiovisual and intellectual landscape. A former columnist for *Charlie Hebdo*, which she left in 2009 over a disagreement with "the Siné clan," she has an open mic on France Inter or France Culture. It is on this antenna that the most significant interview will take place, on September 20, 2013, in France, of the young Ukrainian activist by the brilliant journalist. Caroline also has access to many television platforms. She regularly participates in debates on her favorite themes: gay rights, secularism, women's rights, fundamentalism and the extreme right... On these subjects, the two women are perfectly in tune. Their opponents naturally brought them together, and it is easy to understand what attracted the former student of a private Catholic school to the young and attractive revolutionary figure with a legend in the making. After the release of Caroline Fourest's book, *Inna*[119], several details will separate them. But in 2012 and 2013, the sun shines on the relationship of the two young women.

---

119. *Inna, op. cit.*

Since the time of her first freelances at *L'Événement du jeudi* and the creation of *Prochoix*, a magazine defending the rights of women and homosexuals, which she founded with her companion Fiammetta Venner, Caroline Fourest has traced a relentless path. With a degree in history, sociology and political communication, she masters the codes of political and media infiltration to perfection. She has connections on both the right and the left, but her rather liberal convictions on economics and open-mindedness on societal issues bring her closer to the Valls current of the Socialist Party.

A tireless worker, Caroline Fourest has successively published in-depth and courageous books of investigation on religious fundamentalism. She is notably the first to directly attack the sulphurous Tariq Ramadan[120] in search of respectability on the French intellectual scene. She is also thinking about a sociological platform for living together[121]. The rise of the National Front worries her and she publishes an investigation on Marine Le Pen[122]. A few months later, on the set of Laurent Ruquier[123], she awkwardly tried to defend her very nice *Éloge du blasphème*[124] against a vindictive Aymeric Caron, who locked her in a controversy about a lawsuit against Rabia Bentot, a young Muslim victim of

---

120. *Brother Tariq, speech, strategy and method*, Grasset, 2004.
121. *La Tentation obscurantiste*, Grasset, 2005; *Le Choc des préjugés*, Calmann-Lévy, 2007.
122. *Marine Le Pen*, with Fiammetta Venner, Grasset, 2011.
123. *On n'est pas couché*, France 2, May 2, 2015.
124. Grasset, 2015.

Caroline and Inna make history

an assault whose circumstances Fourest disputed. Anxious to refocus the debate on secularism, the theme of her book, the author tries a pirouette: "I won my case, let's move on." This is a lie that Caron will establish a few hours later in an op-ed published on Mediapart[125] from which it emerges, with supporting evidence, that no appeal date has yet been set for the trial[126]. A faux pas that discredits his otherwise thorough work. But this is not the first time that the polemicist has dealt with the truth...

If her books have established her as a brilliant and respected activist, Fourest is also a seasoned debater. She handles language and concepts with agility, and her analytical mind chisels out an argumentative speech. She also handles the camera for Arte, France 2 or Canal+. These are the talents that she puts at the service of Inna from summer 2012.

But, as their ambiguous relationship unfolds, as Caroline shows us through her film[127] and her book[128], we can mea-

---

125. "Caroline Fourest : le mensonge de trop", Aymeric Caron, Mediapart, May 2015.

126. On August 31, 2016, the Paris Court of Appeals will establish that the plaintiffs were indeed out of time and their action time-barred. Caroline Fourest will therefore win her case for a technical reason related to the procedure and not to the substance of the case. She wrote on her blog that she had "demonstrated the lies of the propagandists" (in this case Ruquier and Caron). Aymeric Caron will react on his Facebook account on September 1, 2016 by confirming that Caroline Fourest had indeed lied on the night of the show, stating in particular: "I won my case and what you just said is totally inaccurate. No I was never convicted of defamation, I won my case," even though she had been convicted in the first instance.

127. *Our breasts, our weapons, op. cit.*

128. *Inna, op. cit.*

sure the gap that is opening up: Inna the Slav does not give herself away, but she understands all the advantages she can get from the French intellectual. She confides in us with discernment and parsimony... Giving us to see what the eyes and the heart of the journalist are waiting for.

Caroline is captivated.

Inna plays.

Where does the money come from?

"THE COMMISSIONER. - Let me do it, I know my
job, thank God. It's not today that I'm involved in
discovering thefts, and I'd like to have as many bags
of a thousand francs as I've had people hanged.
HARPAGON. - All the magistrates are interested
in taking this affair in hand; and, if they don't
make me find my money, I will ask for justice
from the law.
THE COMMISSIONER: All the necessary proceedings
must be carried out. You say that there was
in this tape?
HARPAGON. - Ten thousand écus well counted.
THE COMMISSIONER. - Ten thousand ecus!
HARPAGON. - Ten thousand ecus.
COMMISSIONER. - The theft is considerable.
HARPAGON. - There is no punishment great enough
for the enormity of this crime; and, if it remains
unpunished, the most sacred things are
no longer safe."
Molière, *The Miser*, act V, scene 11668.

Parliament Square in Kiev, May 12, 2011

We are shooting a twelve-minute story on Femen for Canal+. I was contacted by a production company that saw one of my reports in *VSD*. The idea is to make a short film about the movement, which is still little known in Europe. While Sacha was posing in front of the Ukrainian parliament, a man came down the stairs and approached us. He tries to prevent us from working by gesticulating. He is a conservative deputy. Instead of complying, we hand him a microphone and ask him questions: What does he think of the Femen movement? Has he ever dealt with young feminist activists? His answers are provocative, even if his speech is toned down compared to what is regularly published in the Russian and Ukrainian press. The man is not very familiar with the recent history of Femen, but he knows that "they are whores in the pay of foreign politicians, paid to destabilize Ukraine.

That's it.

Who pays? Where does the money come from? Does he have any proof of what he is saying? Why are these "whores" demonstrating against prostitution? Allia, our Russian fixer for this topic, translates, but she seems overwhelmed by the ranting flow. What comes out is a vague but rather well-oiled gibberish, like a polished speech based on conspiracy and the enemy within. One certainty, however: "Femen are supported by foreign powers." Good. Which ones? "Foreign powers. But what else? I try Russia in a slightly provocative way. "No of course, Russia is our friend." Then the United States? Hesitations, then the man drops: "Enemies of Ukraine, in the West, and also left-wing parties here." We will not know more but the method is classic. Conspiracy, secrecy, mystery...

The financing of Femen is the favorite topic of their opponents. For the supporters of the conservative Yanukovych, Prime Minister overthrown by the Orange Revolution in 2004 and then President from 2010 to 2014, it is Yulia Tymoshenko, the revolutionary muse with the world-famous braids, who is using the Femen to undermine the foundations of Ukrainian democracy. For the Church, it is the former communists and the Russians who finance the movement underhandedly. For the progressives, and in particular the supporters of Yulia Tymoshenko, it is the conservatives who are manipulating the Femen to provoke a civil war in the country. For almost everyone, there is, in any case, some hidden power behind Anna, Sacha, Oxana and their group.

This says a lot about the mentality in Ukraine in the 2010s. How can one imagine that young women organize themselves, of their own accord, within a movement that pursues political goals and proclaims humanist demands? It is simply impossible; women in Ukraine are not like that, they are docile, content to look for a husband and then keep his house when they have found one. Ukrainian women do not get involved in politics, except of course that harpy Tymoshenko, who everyone predicts will end badly...

Who can think that Femen are independent?

And yet, it is enough to watch the movement live to understand... that there is nothing to understand. Nobody knows where the funding comes from because there is no funding. In fact, there are almost no expenses. Each action decided jointly by the three founders is primarily evaluated according to its cost. If there are too many expenses, we give up. "It happened several times that we wanted to go to Russia, for example, when it was possible, and we gave up because we didn't have the money[129] ", says Anna.

Very quickly, the artistic originality of the girls, especially Oxana, will impose a Femen "universe", signs of recognition that the movement can monetize. At the time of the Café Bank'a, the former hammam, there was still almost nothing, a few t-shirts, but from the time of the Cupid, at the beginning of 2010, the friendly bar owner made available to the movement a showcase where they presented some objects for sale, imagined by Oxana and made in "just-in-time" and for two cents by craftsmen: mugs, headbands, t-shirts, and also posters, small paintings, etc. From the start, Anna, who has worked in communication and marketing, also understands that the game will be won online. She created the Femen shop on line. The beginnings are difficult, but the movement is launched.

In the years 2009-2011, the income from these small sales, at the bar or online, finances some expenses: "An operation

---

129. Unless otherwise noted, quotes are from interviews conducted by the author between November 2009 and September 2016.

rarely costs more than 6,000 hryvnia[130], explains Sacha in 2010, if it costs more we give it up, and the expenses are, most of the time, train tickets to go to the city where the operation is planned. For the rest, we eat sandwiches and sleep at the homes of supporters."

Supporters are the other source of funding that will develop. Femen has been present on social networks since the beginning, first through their Myspace page, then on Facebook and Twitter. They build relationships with young women across the country. As the movement's notoriety grew, a few donations arrived, a few dozen, a few hundred euros, which Sasha and Oxana, in full confidence, left to Anna, who gradually took over the administrative aspect of the movement.

A few donors are also coming forward. The first of them is a German *deejay*, DJ Hell, who supports the girls during a tour in Ukraine. He will be the main sponsor of the years 2009 and 2010. His donations rarely exceed 500 euros twice a year.

Another important name supports Femen in 2009. Jed Sunden was born in New York and took advantage of the opening of the Eastern bloc countries in the 1990s to invest in Ukraine. He made his fortune in the media. He is a young, modern, feminist press owner: "He was the first of all to give us money", remembers Sacha. Sunden will give almost 90 000 *hryvnia*[131] in 2009. Then he will stop, because

---

130. About 200 euros.
131. Nearly 3,000 euros.

Where does the money come from?

of ideological disagreement: "Sunden did not accept that we talk about religion, he wanted to limit us to the fight against prostitution. It is him who will pay the expenses of creation of the domain name and the first site femen.org. The name of Sunden will also be used, a few years later, to justify, on sites and in the circles of the extreme right as well as the extreme left, racist theses based on "anti-Christian conspiracy fomented by girls in the pay of the Zionists[132]".

In Galia Ackerman's book[133], Anna Hutsol dwells on the importance of these early donors, "The years 2009 to 2011 were tough. We had a budget of $200 a month, no more. That amount paid for our rent."

Among the sponsors of Femen, we should also mention Artemi Lebedev, who runs the most famous and expensive design studio in Kiev, and who, together with Oxana and the others, will create the Femen logo: two yellow and blue circles, separated by a vertical line, so as to evoke the Ukrainian flag and reproduce the Cyrillic letter ф (F).

Generally speaking, the daily life of the girls on the spot (see chapter 16) says enough that they have not benefited from any fortune from anywhere, even if, year in and year out, they manage to get by.

Things are going to get worse when Inna moves to France.

In *Inna*, Caroline Fourest insists on her impecuniosity when she arrives in Paris, in August 2012. This destitution

---

132. See "Why Femen Breasts are Zionist" on the CCLJ (Jewish Secular Community Center) website, www.cclj.be.

133. *Femen, op. cit.*

is relative and, in any case, it is incomparable with the dramatic state of debauchery of Oxana and Sacha who will arrive the following year. Caroline Fourest evacuates the question of Inna's income, to whom the group would reimburse, according to her, "just enough to eat and carry out the actions (a few shorts, posters and paint). [...] Far from being a salary that can be disposed of[134]".

In reality, Sacha and Oxana confirm that the movement provides Inna with 1,000 to 1,500 euros every month, not counting the costs of the actions, which are always reimbursed in addition. "We sent this amount to Inna by Western Union, because transfers were impossible from Ukraine, too expensive." But how could a movement that lived on $200 a month in previous years afford such an expense? "2011 and 2012 were good years, we sold a lot of Femen products, small donations were added, we were not rich but it was during those months that we had the most money, and we sent it to France." This money, collected each month to allow Inna to live in Paris, corresponds, according to Sacha, "to more than 80% of Femen's monthly budget."

In Ukraine, we tighten our belts and we take blows. In Paris, Inna is preparing her coup at the expense of the movement. To these 1,000 euros at least, one must add free accommodation, reimbursement of her telephone and travel expenses, and of course frequent and generous support from her new friend Caroline Fourest.

---

134. *Inna, op. cit.*

With Femen France, financing is becoming more opaque. The money arrives more and more quickly. Donations from supporters are paid into the account opened and managed, at the beginning, by Safia Lebdi, who, as we have seen, has also paid a lot of money out of her own pocket for Femen's travels and the financing of actions.

In November 2012, when Safia and Fernando left the movement, Caroline Fourest noted in her book that Inna, "from one day to the next", took out "in cash what was left of the 8,000 euros paid by Calmann-Lévy for the writing of a book on Femen[135]". Galia Ackerman confirms that the payment was indeed 14,000 euros: 6,000 euros for her and 8,000 for the girls. "The girls. That is, the four of them! Oxana, Sacha and Anna, on the other hand, affirm that they never received anything from this retainer. They did not even have access to the Femen France account. Oxana explains: "What was planned was that the profit would be shared between the four of us. I even said that if everyone did it, I could give up my share for the movement...". In fact, this is what happened: Oxana, Sacha and Anna gave up their share... While the least important member of the organization, the one who joined last, pocketed the whole sum...

Sacha, annoyed, confirms that there was no tacit agreement between the four girls for Inna to use this money to live and finance actions in Paris: "No and no, again, Inna received a salary and the actions were reimbursed."

---

135. *Inna, op. cit.*

When they arrive in France, beaten and hunted by the Russian secret services, Sacha and Oxana ask Inna for financial help. She refuses them.

Éloïse Bouton, when her book was published in 2015, gave some figures on the functioning of Femen France. For the year 2013, she notes, in response to an official question in the National Assembly from Valérie Boyer, a UMP deputy, on the financing of Femen: "At the end of the first general assembly, on January 24, 2014, Femen France's account is in credit of 3,259.65 euros, a sum resulting from 20,965.76 euros of expenses and 24,225.41 euros of income in 2013. Over the same year, donations from private benefactors represent 10,669 euros[136]."

In all likelihood, especially in view of the perfect synchronization of the sums and details, Eloise will provide these figures to Solène Cordier, a journalist at Le *Monde*, the only journalist to have investigated the financing of the movement during this period. Eloise is not named in the article in Le *Monde*[137], which refers to an activist under a pseudonym. But, at the headquarters, Inna seriously suspects her of being at the origin of the leak. This incident will worsen their already tense relations. Solène Cordier brings however information which is not published elsewhere. It appears in particular in the article that the movement counts more than hundred members who contribute each one to the

---

136. *Confession of an ex-Femen, op. cit.*

137. "Comment sont financées les Femen," Solène Cordier, *Le Monde*, February 21, 2014. The figures, as well as many of the terms in the article, are, in detail, the same as those cited by Éloïse Bouton in *Confessions of an ex-Femen*.

Where does the money come from?

amount of 10 euros per year. The investigating journalist also notes that 19% of the 2013 operating budget comes from insurance reimbursement following the fire at the premises (see chapter 30) - and 5% from merchandise on their website. This item has increased enormously over the course of 2013, 2014, and 2015, but the Femen association refused to tell me the current funding structure.

It seems that the association does not receive any subsidies from the Île-de-France council or the Paris city hall. However, it can be estimated that the provision of a Parisian theater and the tolerance of housing in a squat in Clichy constitute an "operating credit" of a value that the journalist of Le *Monde* estimates, according to the "masked treasurer", at around 15,000 euros per year. This is a minimum, considering the occupied surface of nearly three hundred square meters.

As we have seen, derivative products are one of the first sources of financing imagined by the founders. Oxana, the artist of the team, has never touched a cent on these products which are however, in great majority, her creations.

Joseph, at the heart of Femen

"The photographer Art Shay gives us to see with this photo of her naked in her Chicago bathroom another Simone de Beauvoir, no longer a philosopher or feminist but sensual and sexual...
- It is only sexual if we adopt your patriarchal sexist vision of a woman as a sexual object, whereas for me, it is the subject that says the sexual [...].
- But she was complicit, she just said *"naughty boy"*!
- I don't know anything about Simone's reaction, we only have the version of the photographer who took a forbidden and inappropriate photo. You see sexuality, I see a clean Simone de Beauvoir.
Les Chemins de la connaissance,
dialogue between Florian Delorme
and Christine Delphy,
France Culture, October 15, 2015.

Paris, Les Halles, February 12, 2016

He is the one who first understood the power of the issues and ideas behind Femen's actions.

"They were barely 20 years old[138]", recalls the young director Joseph Paris as he sits beside me on the floor of Le Père Tranquille.

From our first exchange, we share an essential analysis: Femen is an instinctive movement.

They were only 20 years old, but they had brilliant intuitions.

They were only 20 years old, but they changed the face of the Ukrainian woman.

They were only 20 years old but, in their own way and for a generation that would not have received the message so well in other terms and in other places, they advanced the cause of equality, feminism, humanity.

From the birth of the movement, and even in the embryo of New Ethics, the girls had decisive intuitions. Like a blind painter guided by a flash of insight, they composed a picture of the exploitation of women and imagined answers. They understand instinctively the strength of the emergence, the strength of the non-smile, of the immobility, of the topless, of the message painted on their breasts... They

---

138. Unless otherwise noted, quotes are from interviews conducted by the author between November 2009 and September 2016.

apply, without mastering all the stakes, a reversal of the genders which will destabilize deeply the Ukrainian patriarchal society, triggering reactions of an unheard-of violence, which exceeds each time the symbolic or even blasphemous violence that they impose by their presence or the messages written on their bodies.

The strength of *Naked War*, Joseph Paris' film, is to match concepts with Femen's actions, to put an intellectual discourse on an anger. "I wanted to help theorize the instinctive."

Sasha and Oxana did not take off their shirts one day on a dare to "make a buzz." It was a profound act that involved their bodies (see chapter 14). But were they aware of the disruption of the codes they were going to impose? They had the intention to destabilize the patriarchy by showing him the object of its desire flocked with a revolutionary liberating message, but were they conscious of the deflagration that this antagonistic confrontation was going to produce? Did they expect such a success and such violence in return? No, clearly not.

Joseph Paris first shows that this violence is expressed with unexpected force, "because it is already in our society in a latent state[139]". The Femen are only the revelation of it. Secondly, they reveal what is happening and what is hidden on a daily basis: "They bring to light this world of control that speaks to us of freedom of expression, but that watches

---

139. Documentary Film Month, Lille 2 University, November 7, 2014.

over us from behind its screens, ready to emerge when we touch specific places.

The writer and critic Annie Le Brun intervenes several times in *Naked War*. The specialist of Alfred Jarry and André Breton - she participated in the surrealist movement until his official death in 1969 - has been working for years on the categories of the nude. But the Femen nude does not belong to any known category.

On this subject, beautifully filmed in low angle, Sacha explains: "We are sent back to our nudity by assimilating us to the prostitutes who are part of the industry that we denounce, but the men deny the fact that it is not the same nudity, they are in bad faith by confusing the two nudities." Annie Le Brun agrees and sheds light on the matter in the light of a distanced sociological reflection: "The nude is very well tolerated in our society, provided that it remains categorized[140]."

It thus establishes a certain number of categories of the nude corresponding to the values and necessities recognized in our societies - Western at least. The sports nude, the advertising nude, the medical nude, the media nude... are very well digested and never stigmatized by the republican morality, except when confronted, here and there, with religious dogmas where hypocrisy vies with absurdity (the display of nipples in Anglo-Saxon societies, for example). These categories of nude induce, for Annie Le Brun, a fragmentation of the body - "We have a body for fashion,

---

140. *Naked War, op. cit.*

another for work, another for the house..." - which takes away any perspective on the being, notably female.

Through a reading grid more "Bebelian" (*La Femme et le Socialisme*, the work that inspired the Femen) than Marxist, we understand that this parcelling out of the body is indispensable to the market economy for two reasons: first, because by successively and separately addressing each part of this dismembered body we can sell it almost anything, and above all useless things; then, because by separating this body it authorizes the most disembodied exploitation. A body considered by apartments is no more than the addition of its components; reducible to its functions, corveable to death. The process of saving individuation[141] exposed by Cynthia Fleury[142] is a philosophical answer to this dehumanizing fragmentation.

The naked breasts of Femen are another. Frontal and carnal.

Annie Le Brun continues, "Femen recompose this body and automatically make it more difficult to trade." The Femen body, no longer destined for a specific use, but affirmed in its essentiality and returned to its humanity, "prevents any capitalist trade[143]". In this sense, the nude

---

141. Construction by an individual of his own destiny from his experience which makes him irreplaceable. The individuals thus conscious are able to imagine a common destiny not by addition of interests, but by political claim. Liberalism and fascism deny this appropriation by the woman or the man of his own narrative.

142. Cynthia Fleury, *The Irreplaceables*, Gallimard, 2015.

143. *Naked War, op. cit.*

according to Femen does not fit into any existing category. Neither naturalist nor hippie. Neither sexual nor seductive.

This awakened awareness of the female body as an issue has been deeply rooted in Sacha and Oxana since 2008, even if the words to say it have sometimes been missing. Instinct preceded reasoning. Like a genius mathematician perceives his result without yet mastering the process.

Coming from both men and a part of feminism, especially materialism, the argument of the "woman object", a cliché to which Femen's act of stripping is supposed to refer, is also instinctively contradicted from the very beginning of Femen: "People tell me that I behave like a woman object by offering myself to the sight of men, but it's quite the opposite, because my attitude is that of a subject who acts", Sacha explains. To expose a body object, but to act in subject: it is this paradoxical territory which frightens the men. This "body-subject" which asserts itself in its entirety comes up against two thousand years of patriarchal domination.

Nabilla's submissive breasts are tolerable, Sacha's brandished ones go to court.

I remember an anecdote from our first meeting in 2009: while we were taking some photos on the Maïdan - Sasha's first public posed photos - and the 18-year-old woman was giving herself away with great availability, she suddenly stopped and stared at me with the smile of a mannequin: "*Barbie can speak, Barbie can speak, Barbie can speak*[144]...", she repeated, nodding her head from right to left like a doll

------

144. "Barbie can talk."

out of *Blade Runner*. This image is one of the strongest that Femen has given me to see.

Without possessing all the dialectical keys of reasoning, Sacha synthesized in three words the essence of a thousand-year-old struggle.

The paradoxical body of Femen is both imposing and fragile. Immobile and evanescent. Its message is powerful, but it is based on the gratuity of a naked body, offered and apparently defenseless. Sacha and Oxana understand very early that this fragility is their best friend, their best weapon...

Law enforcement is only justified because there is adversity - the thief is the policeman. The strength of the offender justifies the intervention of the force of law. If his adversary is powerful and dangerous, then the force of law is justified in opposing its own power, in proportioning it to master his adversary's body, but it cannot master a frail body. Left, ashamed, clumsy, hesitant, it only reinforces the message of the body, and if there is only physical courage, as Michel Foucault says, then Femen's display is all the more striking because the social disproportion of forces is great.

Naked War is Joseph Paris' first film, made with a tourist camera and two lenses, it is a challenge to aesthetics and technique. With his small camera constantly at the heart of his subject, he establishes a warm and thoughtful complicity with Sacha and the others. More with Sacha.

Joseph has known the movement from the inside. And although he has lost interest in it since Inna made it a "personal toy", he has followed it since 2011 after the

Joseph, at the heart of Femen

action against Dominique Strauss-Kahn (see chapter 21). He witnessed the exclusion of Sacha and Oxana at close quarters. He saw Inna and Caroline Fourest "instrumentalize the group of French women" against the two friends from a hypocritical position of neutrality. He was also a victim of what he calls "the little shenanigans of Caroline Fourest". "She viewed my presence in a bad light because I was shooting a film, but I was there before her." For the same reasons, Alain Margot, director of *I Am Femen*, has the same criticism. Quarrel of chrono-cinephages aiming at the same bone? Joseph smiles: "It went much further, I was in her way, like an embarrassing witness." And so also in Inna's way?" Yes, but Inna was trying to ease the conflicts with me, she wanted to spare everyone, at least at the beginning, while Caroline Fourest was trying to keep me away; yet our two films could cohabit." Jealousy? "She also wanted to hide her real role around Femen and Inna. Her real role? "Caroline has a journalistic network but also a political one, her project for Femen was to make it a media-friendly movement. So a movement that would stick to the government's policy? "It's a hypothesis, it's plausible, and that's what Femen has become.

At the time Joseph was attending the movement, in 2013, the most controversial action was the intervention at Notre Dame (see Chapter 23). He remembers well Caroline Fourest's position on this operation: when Inna talked about it, most of the girls approved. Only Caroline said that it would be negative for the image of Femen. So it is the image of Femen in the public opinion that worries her? "Yes, and perhaps also not to displease the government..."

This would explain why Inna did not keep Caroline informed of the implementation of her project. "Fourest was mad with rage when she discovered that the action had been decided behind her back, she even told Inna that it could be bad for her future in France."

In Ukraine,
the situation is deteriorating

"If there were only one cannon left on earth,
nothing but a cannon and a last day of war,
we would be revolutionary
If there was only one prison left on earth,
Only one whore, only one misery,
We would be revolutionary."
Robert Ganzo, excerpt from "Si même",
Tracts, in *Paroles de révolte*, Albin Michel, 1996.

Kiev, July 27, 2013

"Where are we going? Why? Who are you?" Sasha is afraid. She and Oxana are surrounded by two men in the back of a car with dark windows. In the front, two men as well, one of whom is wearing the uniform of the Ukrainian police, she had time to recognize him before they put a bag over his head.

When she came out of her building with Oxana and Dimitri, men appeared on both sides of the street. Several dozen of them, in civilian clothes, but armed with truncheons. They threw Sacha to the ground and beat her. Dimitri, a Russian journalist who has been following Femen for a few days, tried to help her, but he left two teeth. Who are they? She understood immediately, they were the men of the FSB, the dreaded Russian secret service. Oxana found herself lying on the sidewalk, men kneeling on her back, grabbing her and lifting her into the car. On the other side of the street, another car loads Dimitri. He will be released in the evening.

Ukraine has almost no secret services[145], and not forty men capable of intervening at the same time on an operation that requires a minimum of logistics. Even if, in the end, it is only a matter of kidnapping two or three defenseless girls. "Police Ukraine, it's drunks with broken arms, not afraid[146]", Oxana summarizes me one day in the peremptory and concise style that characterizes her, "but FSB, Putin, dangerous".

---

145. The Ukrainian secret police SBU (Sloubja Bezepky Oukrayiny) took over from the Ukrainian branch of the KGB when Ukraine became independent on 24 August 1991. The Russia-Ukraine handover agreement and then the Slavic Union treaty (December 8, 1999) authorized the Russian secret services to act on Ukrainian or Belarusian territory. See "Comment les russes ont infiltré les services secrets ukrainiens," *Slate*, March 12, 2015.

146. Unless otherwise noted, quotes are from interviews conducted by the author between November 2009 and September 2016.

The pressure is especially huge since the action at the Hannover Fair on April 8, 2013, when Oxana and Sacha jumped on Vladimir Putin visiting with Angela Merkel. When they reached the Volkswagen stand, they broke through the security guards and jumped onto the stage shouting *"Fuck dictator!* They were quickly stopped by a muscular security service and violently evacuated. The Russian president tried to save face by ironizing on the nudity of the girls, but his prestige is reached. He will not forget...

In Kiev, for the past few weeks, the tension has risen a notch. Every day, when she leaves her studio, Oxana immediately notices the men with very short hair, closed faces and dark clothes. They come in pairs.

At the foot of his tiny apartment, in the lost street of a rotten suburb, Sacha has noticed for several days the presence of a black car, always the same, and comings and goings, even at night. Especially at night.

On July 25, Viktor was attacked and taken to the hospital with several broken teeth, a cracked jaw and a lot of blood loss: "A professional job", said the police officer who recorded his complaint. On the 26th, it was Anna's turn to be attacked in a café, her face was disfigured, her dog was kidnapped and found dead a few blocks from the attack...

The night of the 26th to the 27th, Sacha slept at her place with Oxana. Dimitri joined them at noon. They had lunch and talked. They did not notice anything suspicious outside. The group left the apartment reassured...

As the car drives to an unknown destination, Sacha understands in a flash. Tonight, in Kiev, the "Sabbath of Gangers"

In Ukraine, the situation is deteriorating

is planned, in the presence of Patriarch Kirill, whom they attacked in 2011, and of... Vladimir Putin. All these attacks that follow one another, Viktor, Anna, the dead dog, they kidnapped... it's that bastard Putin who warns them: "Do not come to piss me off as in Hanover!" The irony is that they obviously had not planned any action. Femen is on her knees. Knocked out lying down under the repeated assaults of the barbarians.

Beyond the extra pressure of the last few days, the two girls have been followed for almost a year, as if locked up in an invisible panopticon, at the central watchtower occupied by a trained and penetrating eye. "Most of the time, these bastards just want to impress us with their presence", explains Sacha. Understand: "We see you and you are in danger." If it also aims to inform a possible action in preparation or to prevent any outburst, the primary objective of this message is to establish in the girls this guilt-inducing fear so coldly described, at the twilight of Leninism, by Evgeny Zamiatine in *We Others*[147], brilliant counter-utopian work that will inspire Aldous Huxley and George Orwell. This climate of paranoid suspicion is the hallmark of controlled societies. "You have to be Soviet to get used to it, but it's very hard," says Sasha.

The car stops. Sacha has difficulty walking. But she is satisfied to have understood the reason for this repeated violence. And she even feels a little proud... Yes, she feels proud that, in his office in the Kremlin, that bastard Putin

---

147. Gallimard, 1979.

has asked his henchmen to prevent any action by the Femen against him. Putin was afraid of her, Sasha Shevchenko! She is proud, but mostly afraid. At this moment, she thinks she is going to die. At 25, because she wanted boys and girls to be equal in her country. And elsewhere.

Since 2011, men have been present at almost every Femen action. At the Festival of Europe[148] in Kiev or during the protest on the Odessa staircase[149], I notice these secret agent faces, as impressive as they are ridiculous in their unsurpassable typicality. Several times, Sacha or Inna would point out these men to me at the time of an action, but I believe that my childhood readings would have been more than enough for this edification: Tintin or Rantanplan. These shaven and dark-rimmed goons always appear a few minutes after the intervention has begun. If the girls are arrested, as at the Fête de l'Europe, they film from a medium distance, with cheap cameras, motionless, without looking for an angle, without any allocentrism, with no other purpose than to document an archival scene that nobody will see.

In July 2013, for a few months Femen Ukraine has been dormant. Actions are rarer. The girls are constantly summoned to the police station, to court. The trials are piling up. The lawyers are afraid. Anna is a little less present. The spleen has set in. Recruitment is very difficult: "In France, there is a queue to register; in Ukraine, the girls understand that there are only blows to take." In Ukrainian

---

148. See Chapter 10.
149. See Chapter 1.

In Ukraine, the situation is deteriorating

opinion, the idea of feminism has a hard time settling in: "Ukrainians still think that we do something in exchange for something, they don't conceive of disinterested political commitment." Femen no longer has the charm of novelty, and suspicions about its financing persist. Israel, George Soros, the Americans and even Italian criminal organizations are mentioned. "The girls don't even have money to buy medicine when Sacha falls ill.

But there is hope. In France, the movement is taking root, Inna is doing a good job. We can count on her... These are some of the thoughts that assail Sacha as the car, driven by a Ukrainian policeman, takes them to a secret location: "To the right of the driver, there was a Russian, Oxana and I were behind, flanked by two other Russians." Sacha thinks about Inna, her friend, and the future of Femen in France. The secret agents do not speak or speak well with each other. They took off their bags so that they could breathe, but they held their heads down against the front seats so that they could not recognize the streets. The car stops, they are given the bags. They are unloaded without care: door of building, staircase, descent, Sacha thinks of a cellar, she hopes that she will not be raped before dying. One presses on her head, undoubtedly to pass a door. One throws it to ground, still. She almost faints, recovers, she is in the overheated room of a deserted court. She is however frigid. She is struck again. She will spend a night and a day here. A night and a day of anguish.

She thinks about France and Inna, again.

In Paris, Inna may be coming out of one of those romantic dinners that Caroline Fourest likes to offer her[150] ?

Femen France is doing well. This is thanks to Inna and Caroline who are working hard to impose the movement on the media scene. And also thanks to Sacha, Oxana and Anna: "That year, we gave everything for France", remembers Sacha. Starting with the money of the movement, entirely devoted to the organization of actions in France and to the heavy burden of the "salary" paid to Inna (see chapter 26).

On the evening of the second day, without explanation or consideration, Sacha and Oxana are thrown out into the street. Free? They don't know anymore. They returned to Sacha's house. His friend Eugenia, a not very active Femen sympathizer, is still there, on the verge of a nervous breakdown. She was at the window yesterday and saw Sacha being beaten up. She called the police. When the officer on duty heard Sasha Shevchenko's name, he hung up.

Sacha collapses for a few hours. Oxana is nervous. Desperation seizes them. They need a change of scenery. What time is the train to Odessa?

Sun and dachas. Odessa the sweet will restore hearts and nourish souls. Sasha has been here many times. She loves the climate, the time to live, the mixture of Marseille and the Black Sea. She dislikes the police and the conservative pro-Russian politicians who have been running the *oblast*[151] and the city since the *oblasts* and cities existed. She remembers

---

150. *Inna, op. cit.*
151. Administrative region.

In Ukraine, the situation is deteriorating

having her ribs caressed here. And elsewhere. Sasha's ribs have a hard life.

They stay with a friend. They eat out of the friend's pocket money. And Anna has some savings. Viktor joined them as soon as he got out of the hospital in Kiev. The five of them bathe and go for a walk. Tears dry, hearts grow fonder. Life begins again. At noon, they often have a picnic on the white sand of Arcadia, the big beach. In the evening, they take a bus to their room, near the baroque theater where Pushkin and Gogol play.

In Ukraine, there are small lights in front of the stoops of the houses. This is an architectural tradition from the time before urban lighting. The small light, often a long candle, indicated the house to the one who came home at night. Gas came and electricity, but the tradition has endured. And the small room of the friend, on the stoop of a single-storey house, is equipped with this approach light. But on the evening of August 18, it is broken. Viktor can see it from a distance. He has a bad feeling. Has someone entered their room? A burglar? He hurries up, Anna follows him. Sasha is in the background. Oxana returned yesterday to her mother's for a few days. Before he reaches the door, which he now sees open, Viktor is dried by the first knock. The man has emerged from a perpendicular alley. He has a baton, a black jacket and sunglasses, but it's evening. Viktor will only remember a man and a rain of blows. He will lose almost an eye and completely lose his memory for several days.

When she sees the scene, Sacha understands in an instant that the war has started again. She doesn't have time to rush, some men grab her and throw her to the ground. She takes the position of the egg. She is used to it.

Two hours later, the friends are in the room. They pour water on their wounds. Viktor was taken to the hospital. Neighbors have called the emergency room. Sasha is crying. She goes to call Inna.

Femen is me, me, me!

> "It is better to treat an enemy whom you hate openly than a friend from whom you hide your true feelings."
> Mirabeau, Letter to Sophie Ruffei, 1777.

Odessa, August 18, 2013

"Inna, we're going to leave, here they'll kill us."

Sacha speaks via Skype to his friend in Paris. She tells us about the aggression of which the group has just been a victim once again. She is still crying. Then she stops and looks at her friend on the cracked screen of the old computer.

Inna is frozen. But it's not the drama of the attack that grips the Parisian leader, Viktor who returns to the hospital, Sacha's blood, Anna's bruises. What freezes every square inch of her skin and every part of her being is that they will come.

In Paris.

She will no longer be alone.

The others, those to whom Femen owes everything, those who have always been Femen. Those who have suffered the most.

They will come to Paris and the world will watch them. They and not her.

"*Don't come, I don't want you, Femen is me, me, me*[152]!" Her eyes flow with rage. Her mouth is bad.

I saw a woman I had never seen before," says Sasha, "she was foaming at the mouth and I understood that she hated me[153].

Inna has been in France for a year. A century.

Actions took place. Girls came, a lot. Safia, Eloise and others left. Disappointed. Caroline is both mentor and object. Inna plays with her and benefits from her teachings. The journalist made a film[154] about Femen - she went to film in Ukraine where Sacha and Anna ran many risks to help her. She is writing a book. Inna and Caroline are behind dozens of programs, articles, interviews... in which they have presented the face of Femen that Inna wanted to give her: her own. There was no question of these "*bitches*" taking advantage of *her* movement! Of *her* friends. From *her* city.

In Ukraine, the girls cut off communication. They were shocked and distraught: "We talked to each other for a

---

152. "Do not come, I do not want you, Femen is me, me, me!"

153. Unless otherwise noted, quotes are from interviews conducted by the author between November 2009 and September 2016.

154. *Our breasts, our weapons, op. cit.*

while, but in any case we had no idea where to go, the Femen movement was already established in France, thanks to us, so the question of going elsewhere did not even arise." Femen already exists in Germany, but the movement is in its infancy, and all the effort and investment in recent months has been focused on France. It is the safest and most obvious refuge.

They set out for Kiev and hoped that things would calm down. They are still determined to leave, but feel unable to travel. We will see in a few days. And then, it is not a detail: they do not have a penny.

When they returned to the Ukrainian capital, events took a sudden turn. The following week, police officers arrived at the premises at 21 Mikhailovskaya Street. They had received an anonymous phone call indicating that weapons were hidden in the Femen house. They forced the girls to leave during the search. They refused vehemently: "They laughed, but they were hesitant," Sasha recalls, "I saw that they were embarrassed, as if they didn't know where to start. Sacha continues: "They block us against the wall and then they make us leave by pushing us towards the door, like in a demonstration. One of them has a big bag in his hand, it's so obvious that it's a trap! I refuse to go out, they grab me and put me outside. Five minutes later, I escape and I come back: they make surprised faces while looking under the lamp and they say "Look what's there". They even finish taking stuff out of the bag in front of me. They look like kids, they are playing very badly, I am ashamed for them and for my country, and I am angry, but I see

Femen is me, me, me!

them extracting from under the lamp a grenade, a gun and portraits of Putin."

Police station, interrogations, violence. Sacha and Anna refuse to speak or sign anything.

Oxana found refuge in the French embassy.

The next day, a Ukrainian policeman comes to get Sacha and Anna in their cell: "He tells us that we are now accused of terrorism and that we will go to prison for twenty years." Sacha sees her life falling apart. But the civil servant adds that he has not yet received the official order and therefore: "He has the right to free us for the moment..." Sacha understands that the young policeman is helping them. He adds by opening the door for them: "Ukraine, it is finished for you, girls, you must leave quickly. Without this fair young man, they would probably be behind bars.

There is not a minute to lose.

They come back to the local.

Some clothes, a bag, the passports hidden in a corner of the room, direction the French embassy where they find Oxana. "The FSB and the Ukrainian police suspected that we would go there because the movement was present in France, they regularly called the embassy to tell them that we were going to do an anti-French action inside the embassy, they had called the day before, but the French didn't believe them, they sheltered us," explains Oxana. And she adds, "As soon as the three of us were inside, we were relieved, we understood that we were treated well, people knew us, they knew that the police were after us, but that we were not terrorists."

Two days later, on August 30, 2013, they landed in Paris. Skype, cell phone, SMS... Inna does not answer anymore.

At the airport, there is no one to welcome them. But Anna has informed some editorial offices by e-mail, there are two or three journalists at the Lavoir moderne. So, when they get out of the cab, Inna comes out of the building, all smiles, and embraces her friends. Sacha and Oxana are stunned. Anna plays the game of effusions. Inna is the only one who speaks English correctly and now even a little French, so she addresses the journalists and explains that the "Ukrainians" are visiting France. We will learn later," says Oxana, "that Inna let it be understood that we were just passing through, not that we had come to take refuge. The journalists leave after a few photos.

Inside, several French women welcome them, there is Marguerite, Pauline, Elvire... "But we understand right away that the atmosphere is bad. But we immediately understand that the atmosphere is bad, I even hear a *why you come*[155]*?*", says Oxana. They go up to the room that Hervé, the manager of the Lavoir, had put at their disposal each time they came before. And they fall asleep. They spent the first few days like zombies. Oxana suffers a lot, but she is cared for by Alain Margot, who came from Switzerland to help her. Without Alain, his beautiful film, his beautiful madness and his faithful friendship, Oxana might not have survived the doglit that will follow.

---

155. "Why did you come?"

Femen is me, me, me!

On September 20, they were awakened by the sounds of conversation and music, and applause. They do not dare to go downstairs. Downstairs, a party is taking place, for the first anniversary of Inna's arrival in France[156]. There are about a hundred people there, regular journalists, close politicians, friends, Nadia El Fani, co-director of *Our Breasts, Our Weapons,* is there, Angie has come from Mexico City at her own expense to present Femen Mexico, even Safia Lebdi, who has nevertheless left the movement for a year, has come with Fernando. Caroline Fourest is there, of course.

This is the perfect opportunity to announce to the world the repression of Femen in Ukraine: the torture, the kidnapping, the imprisonment, the flight of the three friends who, like Inna, are going to ask for political asylum in France... But Inna is careful not to make the slightest allusion to the founders of Femen who have taken refuge on the upper floor. Around her, Pauline, Marguerite, Éloïse, Sarah... don't dither either. Everyone obeys Queen Inna.

The star of Femen is her, and nobody else.

For a while now, Oxana had been having doubts. She came to France much more often than Sacha. She had rubbed shoulders with Caroline Fourest. She saw Inna impose herself... for the better of the group, she thought at first. She said to herself that a leader was needed. And then, she did not consider for a moment competing with her for the leadership of Femen France. But with hindsight, today she

---

156. The film of the evening can be seen on YouTube under the title, "Femen debate for the 1st anniversary of Femen France, September 20, 2013."

confides: "I think I had understood for a long time that Inna would betray us, probably as soon as she started managing Femen France, but I refused to tell the others because it was admitting an unbearable reality."

A week after their arrival, Anna goes to find her sister who lives in Zurich and Viktor who has friends there. Both of them will ask for political asylum in Switzerland.

For Sacha and Oxana, it is a new hell that begins.

In the hell of Femen France

> And long hearses,
> without drums or music,
> Scroll slowly in my soul; Hope,
> Defeated, weep, and atrocious, despotic Anguish,
> On my inclined skull plants its black flag.
> Charles Baudelaire,
> *Les Fleurs du mal*, "Spleen", 1861.

Paris, March 15, 2016

We meet in a small bar in the Marais. Sacha has just finished her French class. She is making progress, but she lacks friends to talk to. We decide to start the interview in French and then resume in English when she is in difficulty.

Oxana is in a bad period. *"Artistic crisis"*, she warns. Sacha smiles. Oxana is no longer sure of exhibiting in June. I suggest that she meet a friend who runs a gallery: *"Why not, but* for the moment, *artistic crisis!*

Oxana is sulky, but her anger is stronger than her sulkiness. We go back three years.

After the first few days, after their chaotic arrival from Ukraine, they take their marks. Paris is not unknown to them. Oxana came regularly and sometimes for long stays. Sacha came for several actions, notably against Dominique Strauss-Kahn in 2011, against the burqa in 2012 and for the interviews of the book of Galia Ackerman. They know most of the girls who have joined Femen France. Sacha liked Safia, but she left.

And now? The organization in Ukraine is dead. Anna continues to run the Femen online store, but the activity is dormant. She will soon restart it, unfortunately for her own benefit[157].

A few weeks later, the Venice Film Festival arrives to change everyone's mind. The film of Kitty Green, *Ukraine Is Not a Brothel,* is selected. The Australian spent several months with the girls. She was staying at Sacha's house.

---

157. The Femen website is still the object of a war between Inna and Anna Hutsol. According to Inna, Anna has "completely abandoned feminist activism". However, she continues to cash in on Femen's online store, which is accessible through the sales sections of femenshop.com and femen.org. On the Femen France Facebook page, messages warn that the femenshop site is a fraud. Customers also testify that they do not receive the ordered goods. At the same time, Femen France created a new shopping site supportfemen.com to market its products and enhance its merchandising. According to Inna, "negotiations" are underway with Anna to find an agreement. It is impossible to have a precise idea of the sums generated by these sales. The only certainty, in the middle of this legal and commercial muddle, is that Oxana and Sacha will never get anything, even though their image is used and Oxana is at the origin of many creations.

It is this film that will install the idea that a manipulative male is instrumentalizing Femen and persecuting Inna (see chapter 22). The girls only learned about it the day before, in Venice: "It's a bad film," says Oxana, "it went to the festival just because Femen were fashionable, but nobody is himself in this film[158]. Today, Sasha regrets not having denounced the deception of the film more strongly: "I told a few journalists, but I did not put myself in danger to deny the falsehood of the film." Even Inna is now spitting in the soup served to her by Kitty. At our lunch on March 21, 2016, she will have this strange confession: "Obviously, Viktor was not manipulating anyone, but this is Kitty's film! She did it for scripted stories."

Beyond the direct testimonies of Sacha and Oxana, all the close observers of that time, from Safia Lebdi to Alain Margot, or Joseph Paris, agree: together, Inna and Caroline Fourest monopolized the media and did not hesitate to twist reality to serve the interests of the young refugee.

Low blows are raining down.

"Inna, the new Marianne", headlines the press[159] in this summer 2013. It is the consecration. After Brigitte Bardot, Catherine Deneuve and Laetitia Casta, Inna Shevchenko is Marianne!

On July 14, 2013, François Hollande himself presented the stamp that will now be used in all post offices in France

---

158. Unless otherwise noted, quotes are from interviews conducted by the author between November 2009 and September 2016.

159. Among others, "The face of the new Marianne...," *L'Express*, July 15, 2013.

and overseas. The controversy begins when one of the two designers of the stamp (David Kawena and Olivier Ciappa) announces that he was inspired by the leader of Femen Inna Shevchenko for the creation of the vignette.

This is not true.

It is Olivier Ciappa who makes this announcement, David Kawena, for his part, is not aware of anything. And if Inna is - perhaps - one of the elements that inspired the new Marianne, she is far from being the only one: "Olivier Ciappa called me to ask if he could say publicly that he had been inspired by the attitude of the Femen girls for his drawing, and in particular the head carriage," Sacha recalls, "but he never mentioned Inna. Why then did he do so a few hours later, naming the leader of Femen France? "Because Caroline called him," says Sacha.

In the wake of this conversation, Olivier Ciappa tweets, "For all those who ask the model of Marianne, it is a mixture of several women but especially Inna Shevchenko, founder of Femen[160]." Two lies in one hundred and thirty-nine characters. Even three since Ciappa implies that he is the father of the design while he has an Israeli designer, Shaul Dadon, who officiates under the pseudonym of David Kawena and claims "exclusive authorship of the stamp Marianne[161]", adding that he is "the only person responsible for the design of the stamp Marianne and the only creator and artist of

---

160. https://twitter.com/olivierciappa/status/356457915416190977

161. Notably, "Stamp Marianne: David Kawena claims to be the sole author and files a complaint against Olivier Ciappa," www.yagg.com, February 25, 2014.

the stamp. Through his lawyer, he will disassociate himself from his partner: "Mr. Kawena wishes to remove any doubt and clarify that the Marianne stamp was not, in any way, inspired by or related to Ms. Inna Shevchenko[162]. He states that he had never heard that name before.

For Caroline and Inna, it doesn't matter about the controversy. Even today, millions of French people believe in good faith that Inna Shevchenko is Marianne.

On March 28, 2014, a madman armed with knives and cleavers burst into the Lavoir moderne. Here is Caroline Fourest's account of it on her blog: "Last night, a man came to the Lavoir moderne to assault Inna and the Femen. When he couldn't find them, he attacked the spectators. After the attack on *Charlie Hebdo*[163], the Lavoir moderne which burned down and now this assassination attempt... Will those who put on the same level the symbolic violence of blasphemers and the - real - violence of fanatics (be they Islamists or nationalists) wake up[164]?"

There was a theater show that night, and the man had taken a room in a shabby hotel across from the Lavoir moderne. But if Inna was not there, it is wrong to say that the Femen were not there, because Oxana was at the show, she even opportunely interposed herself between the spectators and the man. She pushed the benches to prevent the attacker from passing, narrowly avoided a bloody stabbing

---

162. "Femen stamp: the cartoonists are divided," *Le Figaro*, February 27, 2014.
163. She refers here to the fire of the premises of *Charlie Hebdo* in 2011.
164. "Attempted Murder at the Modern Washhouse...," www.carolinefourest.wordpress.com, March 29, 2014.

and protected the evacuation of a part of the audience. "I was as scared as everyone else, I just tried to help someone in the panic," Oxana would later recount.

If Caroline Fourest ignores it, it is unfortunate for someone who claims to be reporting on it publicly. If she does not ignore it, one may wonder why she does not mention the presence of Oxana and center the attack on Inna? Especially since, according to witnesses and Oxana herself, at no time did the gunman mention Inna Shevchenko's name, he only spoke about "Femen sluts" and declared that he was acting "for the Front".

Once the man is arrested, Oxana spends part of the night at the police station to make a statement. Then she goes to sleep a few streets away, at Apolline's, the daughter of Hervé Breuil, the manager of the Lavoir moderne. In the morning, she returned to the Lavoir. In front of the entrance, she finds Inna and Caroline who are agitated, microphones that are tense, cameras that crackle.

Nobody is interested in Oxana. She goes forward. Marguerite and Pauline tell her to go back into the theater. Oxana gets angry. She tries to call a journalist. Femen France interferes again. She wants to know what Inna and Caroline are saying. But it is Caroline who is speaking, Oxana does not understand anything, except that she is not wanted. She goes back into the theater.

The next day, Caroline published her report on her blog and the press took up the same story: the attack took the form of a presumed attack against Inna Shevchenko. In *L'Express* we read: "Two injured, one of them seriously, but it is Inna Shevchenko who was targeted[165]" and in *Le Parisien*: "The day before his madness, the man would have passed by several times demanding to see Inna Shevchenko[166]"...

In the chapeau of her paper, Caroline Fourest also refers to the fire at the Lavoir, suggesting at least that it may have been a criminal act. This is the impression that will remain in public opinion after Inna's statements: "Since the fire started right next to the open window, it is perhaps a sign that this fire was planned, that it was an attack planned by someone[167]. "Femen have many enemies who have been trying to stop us for a long time[168] ".

Pauline Hillier, the only Femen activist on site, told AFP that she was sound asleep and that "suddenly the fire, the sound of breaking glass and the crackling sound[169] " forced them to rush outside. The "glass noises" will also be reported by Inna, who, although absent at the time of the disaster, confirms that a window was open that night[170]... Glass noises, open window... Everything is clear! An enemy

---

165. *L'Express.fr*, March 29, 2014.

166. *Le Parisien.fr*, March 30, 2014.

167. Inna Shevchenko, LCI, July 21, 2013.

168. Inna Shevchenko, marieclaire.fr, July 26, 2013.

169. See in particular *L'Humanité*, "Les locaux des Femen incendiés," July 21, 2013.

170. In *Inna*, Caroline Fourest says that the young woman "slept for a few days at the home of an activist who had gone on vacation. According to Galia Ackerman and Joseph Paris, Inna was staying at the Cité des Arts in the Marais. When I asked her directly, she confirmed that she had lived for a while in the artists' residence that "Caroline [had] obtained for her".

of Femen has thrown an incendiary object in order to reach the organization!

The reality is quite different, according to Oxana: "When Pauline returned to the Lavoir with her boyfriend, she was stoned and so was he, they got into bed with lots of candles lit around them and they were smoking. Two hours later, they were evacuated, completely soaked, after Hervé had called the fire department. "Anyway," Oxana adds, "all the access doors were locked from the inside."

Perhaps it is an electrical fire?

It's better for the insurance.

Or an attack?

It's better for the image.

The press blesses Inna

> "My brother, who has a hard right ear and a hard left ear, is asked if any of his classmates are smart. No," said my brother, "he talks too low."
>
> Louis Scutenaire,
> *Mes inscriptions, 1943-1944*, Allia.

Paris, February 22, 2016

"The French media had Inna, that was enough for them[171]." Sacha sighs.

When they understand, quite late, that their exclusion is decided and implemented by Inna and her acolytes of Femen France, Sacha and Oxana try to defend themselves. It is their character. They are immediately confronted with the inertia and simplism of a part of the press.

---

171. Unless otherwise noted, quotes are from interviews conducted by the author between November 2009 and September 2016.

On April 14, 2015, I speak on the phone with my colleague at *Libération*, Quentin Girard, who has been following Femen since the movement resided in France. He is knowledgeable and informed. He has already met the founders Anna, Sacha and Oxana. He has even been to Ukraine at least once. In the course of our exchange, I mention various papers in *Libé* or other newspapers where Inna is too often presented as "the inspirer and sole leader of Femen". However, she only joined the movement two years after its foundation and is therefore neither the founder nor even the soul of the movement. Quentin's response: "I know, but she is the one who is known and the others don't speak French or English. This seemingly innocuous simplifying laziness is one more element that leads to the impasse in which the two founders of Femen found themselves when faced with the rise of Inna. Not only did they have to face the "internal maneuvers" of Femen France, but, in a cynical paroxysm, the free press of a free country turned away from them, choosing the beautiful and understandable lie over the less beautiful and more complex truth.

Quentin Girard's mastery of the language of Molière or Shakespeare is not just a pretext for the sincerity argument. He is simply putting into practice a major axiom of journalism 3.0, based on precariousness, urgency and extreme simplification: better a lie in a language spoken by a journalist than a truth that requires a translation.

In Kiev, when I met Anna or Sacha for my reports, they spoke almost only in Ukrainian or Russian. Viktor too. I had to hire interpreters, fixers, and spend money for that.

Sasha and Oxana now speak excellent English and French, but that was not the case then. All it took was a little time, kindness and respect to listen to them. And a willingness to tell the truth, of course.

The French press, which has very largely outsourced - and by way of the law of the sensationalized and "simplified" market - its "Reporting" services, has no time, no means, no desire. In 2013 and 2014, nobody hears Sacha and Oxana. They tried to contact several journalists, including Quentin Girard. All the doors were closed: "The answer was often: 'It's much too complicated to explain who you are when the French public already knows Inna well' ", remembers Sacha.

On September 20, 2013, during a "Femen Party" intended to raise funds, Sacha and Oxana approach some of the journalists present, but they notice that Marguerite or Pauline pass behind them... Are they spreading the rumor that they are going to be excluded from the movement? Sacha and Oxana strongly suspect it. In the same way, "they doubted, without hiding too much, the persecutions of which we had been victims in Ukraine". As Sacha and Oxana express themselves with difficulty and discretion, the journalists do not seek to know more. Nobody wants to hear their cry. False messages are passed on to the public through these journalists, who are complicit by dint of their complacency.

On February 15, 2013, on France Culture, Caroline Fourest introduced Inna: "So Inna you are one of the co-founders of the Femen movement." A few minutes later, Inna answers a question about the sex industry in Ukraine: "It's modern slavery, and so we started to say no to that in

The press blesses Inna

2008 by going, we women, to the streets, to say, 'We are not prostitutes, don't treat us like one.'" This time, Inna joins the first "pink brigades" and "sex safaris" of Femen, which roamed the streets of Kiev in 2008 and 2009 to alert opinion. Inna has never been part of it.

It is a detail. But detail lie after detail lie, journalist convenience after journalist convenience, Inna imposes the idea that she created Femen. The others, meanwhile, are persecuted in Ukraine.

July 15, 2013, in *20 Minutes*: "Inna, founder of Femen, posts anti-Islam tweet..."

October 21, 2013, at the microphone of Jun Peters, on Radio Brussels: "Inna Shevchenko, founder of Femen, escaped from Ukraine..."

February 15, 2015, in *Le Monde*, following the Copenhagen attack: "The feminist activist, founding member of Femen, Inna Shevchenko..."

The list of simplifications and amalgams is endless, and each time it happens, Oxana's and Sacha's heads are pushed a little further into an ocean of oblivion.

Even when they know the truth, the journalists do not mention the important role of Anna, Sacha and Oxana. Inna is "convenient", the others are far away or difficult to access, or blocked by Inna...

The doxa is established. History is rewritten. The legend is born. Simple, pretty, square and ready to be consumed: a pretty blonde with naked breasts founds a feminist movement and then takes refuge in France, home of human rights, to escape from a stupid police. Why look any further? Especially since she is Caroline Fourest's friend, and feminist movements are reaching out to her. What would nuance, investigation and complexity have to do with this idyll?

Journalists have editors to whom they must sell a story in a few minutes. And editors like easy-to-understand stories because they think the public is not receptive to complex stories; and they are often right.

Besides, no one ever really lies in this case. An interview with Inna given to *Paris Match* on September 18, 2013[172] singularly illustrates the laziness of the press, its refusal to name and see. Its choice of simplicity and sensationalism. The interview, conducted by Marie Desnos, is only one of hundreds of articles that completed the novel, but it is worth studying closely, so much antiphrasing and omission, the unspoken and the avoidance are put in the service of a collective compromise.

Let's go beyond the usual amalgam of the title which associates "woman" and Femen: "Femen, in the beginning was the woman"; whereas Femen, as we have seen, means "thigh" and embodies much better the concept of "sextremism". The chapeau of the interview already contains an error and an absurdity: "During our meeting at the Lavoir moderne, Inna Shevchenko, one of the founders of Femen, who became the leader of the movement by reinventing it in Paris, told us, etc."

---

172. "Inna Shevchenko: Femen. Au commencement était la femme," Marie Desnos, *Paris Match*, September 18, 2013.

The press blesses Inna

First question: "When did you discover Femen and when did you decide to join the movement?"

Inna's answer: "At the end of 2008, beginning of 2009, it happened by chance and quite naturally. I had never heard of Femen before, because the movement was still in the process of being created and was probably not yet called Femen. At the beginning it was a gathering of activists. [But we didn't even call ourselves feminists yet. It was not an organized group.

Inna's answer adds up the lies and suggests that Femen did not exist before her.

The second question is about toplessness: "And it's also a bit of a coincidence that your breasts became your main weapon, seeing that it was a good way to get media attention?"

Inna's answer is confused and opens doors, "the breasts are symbolic", "the breasts of women and men are perceived in different ways"... She avoids the fact that she was totally opposed to the process. Above all, she ignores the fact that it was Oxana and Sacha who invented and imposed the toplessness of Femen, giving birth to sextremism.

Third question: "[...] Why did you choose France?"

Inna's answer: "[...] There have been internal clashes (within Femen), which are mentioned in the film *Ukraine Is Not a Brothel*. So much so that I wanted to leave the movement two years ago. In the film, we see me discussing this with a Femen, who asks me: "Where are you going to go? And I answer, "To Kherson or Paris, to found the real Femen." I dreamed of rebuilding the movement in light of the mistakes we have made and acknowledge - without really knowing how to do it. I was afraid Viktor would come back. A man doesn't just abandon something where he has power."

Can Marie Desnos, who follows Femen, ignore that Inna is rewriting history?

When she gives this interview to *Match*, Inna is at the Lavoir moderne, in the girls' training room. Upstairs, in their room, Sasha and Oxana are sleeping. They have just arrived from Kiev after being kidnapped and raped by the Ukrainian police and the Russian secret services. Inna is careful not to wake them up. She does not forget to mention the persecution of her friends, whose courage and glory reflect on her, the spokesperson and self-proclaimed leader of the movement.

The French media have Inna, that's enough for them.

Every day feeds the pain...

> "Abusing the trust of his friend,
> it is the worst and most abject betrayal."
> Jean-Jacques Rousseau, *The Confessions*, 1765.

Between the day they arrived in Paris in August 2013 and the end of their story with Femen a year later, Sacha and Oxana's daily life is an ordeal.

"There were FSB agents, they didn't let us go when we arrived in France[173] ", attacks Oxana. It was when Femen started to attack the Russian president that the "very" big trouble began (see chapter 28). Sacha and Oxana spot, from time to time, around the Lavoir, this conspicuous presence that now makes Oxana laugh because: "Russian agent Goutte-d'Or, you spot right away!" Sacha also remembers, "It lasted until spring 2014, they never bothered us or

---

173. Unless otherwise noted, quotes are from interviews conducted by the author between November 2009 and September 2016.

approached us, but they were there. I saw the last of them at Place du Tertre when I was already in the studio, it was in April." It seems that the FSB went away as soon as they were sure that Oxana and Sasha's French exile was real, that the "terrorists" were not up to some dirty trick at Vladimir Putin's expense. The Femen problem, moved to the country of human rights, would no longer interest them... It would even be rather good news, provided that they were sure, so they were watching. Besides," Sacha continues, "the Russians have so many agents all over the world that they have to be kept busy, so they prefer to monitor in pure loss rather than run a risk."

But Sasha and Oxana have so many other things to worry about than the master of the Kremlin!

When they arrived in Paris in August 2013, the two friends were given free accommodation at the Lavoir, as were Inna and other French women, notably Pauline and Marguerite. Even though Safia Lebdi, who found this magnificent place, left Femen, (see chapter 21), the founder of Ni putes ni soumises refused to put the Femen movement in trouble, which would have been hard pressed to find almost three hundred square meters of free space in the heart of Paris. Moreover, after the burning of the Lavoir, it was also through Safia's friends that the Femen found the squat in Clichy. Elegance and political conviction go hand in hand at Safia Lebdi.

At the Lavoir, we are far from the micro society of sharing that Sacha and Oxana had set up in Kiev. Here, everyone pays for their sandwiches, make-up and cigarettes.

Sacha and Oxana can't afford to smoke, or sometimes to eat. As early as September 2013, they asked Inna to allocate them something from the membership fees of Femen, or from some donation that comes from time to time. After all, when they were in Ukraine, they bled to support Inna in Paris (see chapter 26), so it would only be fair! Inna categorically refuses: "She told us that the association did not have the means to give us money, especially since she was not going to receive anything from Ukraine now!" A comble. Money comes in, but no one knows how much, and Inna, still today, maintains total secrecy around it. She is the only one, as president, who has access to the bank account. Inna's relationship with money is "just like Inna is," says Sacha, "selfish".

Anna went back to Switzerland, to her sister, and then to Ukraine. There, she returned to her first profession, marketing, and worked, according to Sacha, "for well-placed politicians". Her troubles will gradually fade away as she seems to fall back into line. Contacted directly to find out more about her current activities, Anna replied that I could come and see "a beautiful exhibition on the history of Femen at the moment in Kiev", but evaded any questions about her personal situation.

In Paris, life has to be organized. Sacha and Oxana are not completely alone. Of course, they cannot accompany the others when they go to lunch in the neighborhood bistros but, from time to time, members or sympathizers do errands for them. Especially Joseph. And especially spaghetti.

Every day feeds the pain...

Oxana and Sacha love the neighborhood. They fight religion, not the believers, at least as long as they don't attack women. They like the ethnic diversity they discover, unlike Inna who does not appreciate it at all. Safia Lebdi remembers, "When I found the Lavoir for Femen, Inna told me she didn't want to be in this neighborhood of Arabs, she asked that we find something for her in the nice parts of Paris."

In this summer of 2013 that is coming to an end, Oxana and Sacha are struggling. Inna sometimes makes them look good, sometimes not, depending on whether witnesses, and especially journalists, are present or not. But they think they see a kind of normalization of relations. After a few weeks, they even manage to think that the episode of the "crisis" via Skype (see chapter 29) was a stroke of madness, something unreal, and that everything will return to normal. That they will now be Femen in Paris. Forever.

Sacha and Oxana tell themselves that the best way to integrate is to keep a low profile and observe the world at work at the Lavoir moderne. This period of "learning" comes at a good time: Sacha is tired and Oxana is still suffering from her two broken wrists (see chapter 28). They try to talk, to make new friends with Pauline, Marguerite or Sarah. Oxana finds a listening ear in Apolline, the daughter of Hervé Breuil, Safia Lebdi's friend who runs the Lavoir. When the young artist from Khmelnytskyï is in trouble, she can count on Apolline. Sacha gets closer to Dimitri, the Russian journalist who was kidnapped with her and Oxana in July in Kiev. An order from the *New York Times* allowed her to rent a room in the Strasbourg-Saint-Denis district, then a studio in Montmartre; Sacha soon took refuge in his home, exhausted by the atmosphere of the Lavoir.

To communicate with their comrades, Sasha and Oxana improve their English at the speed of sound. They try to blend in with the landscape, but they have to move carefully, because the ground is mined.

One day, it was a few weeks after we arrived, Marguerite came to see me and asked me why I was staying here if I was going to leave Femen," Oxana recalls. I was surprised, but I understood that Inna had spread the word that Sacha and I would soon be leaving the movement. Later, we also discovered, through indiscretions or provocations by Marguerite or Pauline, that she was telling people that what we said we had experienced in Ukraine was a lie in order to obtain refugee status. One morning, while she was drinking coffee and I wasn't, Pauline told me that we were mythomaniacs, that we had invented all that to get refugee status, like Inna.

Sasha has no doubt: "Inna also spread this information among her network of journalist friends." No one will obviously publish anything to deny the persecution of Oxana and Sacha in Ukraine during 2012 and 2013 - the factual elements showing the relentlessness of the Ukrainian and Russian powers against them are notorious, and Inna's jealousy is obvious - but, for fear of falling out with Inna, and of course with Caroline Fourest, support will be sorely lacking for Oxana and Sacha...

The evening is not the worst time of the day. Oxana lives in a corner of the second floor, which she soon paints. Her claw gives her den the patina of an artist's studio. She

Every day feeds the pain...

loves her "corner". "And then, in Ukraine, we were used to the hard. The activists in France have always slept in good beds! Sasha goes more and more often to Dimitri's house.

In Paris, the pace of actions is slower than in Ukraine, where awareness-raising marches were almost daily. "Here, we discuss for a long time and at the end Inna takes a decision", says Sacha. They are adapting. But they think that the pace should be increased and they say so. One day, Sacha proposes an action against the Fashion Week which starts. Marguerite and Pauline replied, "Not good enough". Sacha turns to Inna... who looks away.

Inna avoids direct confrontation. She stands back. She has sent her French soldiers to the front against Sacha and Oxana, she can drape herself in a coat of referee of inelegance to observe the killing and pretend not to join it.

When I asked her to comment on the arrival of Sacha and Oxana, Inna deflected the question: "It was not a problem between me and them, it was a problem between the activists of Femen France on the one hand and Sacha and Oxana on the other. Then she insisted on the cultural differences: "Things are different between Ukraine and France, Sacha and Oxana had a hard time understanding it, I was in the middle, I was sad for them, I even felt betrayed, but it was the activists who opposed them, not me."

In front of this tirade, I precisely remember thinking: "When you have a good nerve, it is enough, almost everything is allowed[174]..."

---

174. Bardamu's reflection in Louis-Ferdinand Céline's *Voyage au bout de la nuit.*

For Alain Margot, to whom Oxana often confided by phone or during the Swiss director's visits, Oxana and Sacha, on the contrary, made every effort to adapt, "in their own interest, but also because it was in the interest of Femen and they have always had an acute political awareness of that. Femen above all, and of course before individual interests."

In practical terms, they are trying to maintain Femen's radicalism and prevent its commercial or sectarian drift. Oxana, who made several trips back and forth between Kiev and Paris between Inna's arrival in August 2012 and her own exile in August 2013, is in the best position to judge Femen's media-commercial evolution. "For example, these collective training sessions where the girls scream and fight hand to hand, it was organized for the photographers and the press, we never did that, Femen was not a barracks, well before Inna."

They gradually understand that they are facing a wall of hostility that good will and political sense will not be able to break down, because it is cemented with hatred and bad faith.

On a daily basis, the bullying is often nasty. The girls of Femen France systematically turn their backs on them. Some of them, like Elvire, seem saddened and sometimes talk to them, but no one dares to go against Inna's wishes. Sacha and Oxana are kept away from meetings, decisions, lunches... The examples multiply: "Faces that turn away, interrupted conversations, conciliations behind our backs... I should have understood more quickly, Sacha regrets, but we were still in denial."

Every day feeds the pain...

And the language barrier doesn't help: "It's unbelievable how much it hurts to understand that people are making fun of you or visibly denigrating you, without understanding what they are saying, it's humiliating and it feels like a prison," says Oxana.

At the same time, the two friends had to manage their arrival in France, apply for refugee status, find an address, learn French, and scrape together a few pennies... not only without help, but in the midst of an adversity that was increasingly less concealed.

A perverse relationship that preludes a betrayal, where villainy touches enough to hurt, but not enough to be reproached, where a lowered look, a refused smile, a missed gesture will be enough to fertilize two years of depression. In the violent solitudes of the teenage classes, we almost die of this every day. Sacha and Oxana too.

A dinner at Caroline's

> "Revolution is not a gala dinner; it is not done
> like a literary work, a drawing or an embroidery;
> it cannot be accomplished with as much elegance,
> tranquility and delicacy, or with as much
> gentleness, friendliness, courtesy, restraint
> and generosity of soul."
> Mao Zedong, *The Little Red Book*, 1966.

Paris, March 10, 2016

"We didn't want to believe it. It was so disgusting that we were in denial[175]."

I met Sacha and Oxana for lunch in a bistro in Montmartre where we now have our habits.

They do not eat anything, as usual.

They tell and I listen, as usual.

---

175. Unless otherwise noted, quotes are from interviews conducted by the author between November 2009 and September 2016.

The action takes place on September 20, 2013, in the heart of the Marais, in the bourgeois apartment owned by Caroline Fourest, with its magnificent parquet floor ruined by Inna and its heels[176] even more pointed than the point of Hungary.

It is Sacha who speaks. Almost three years later, her voice is still unsure and her eyes droop as she looks back on that night: "The most sickening night of my life."

It all starts with an invitation to dinner. Caroline is the one who's hosting. Sacha and Oxana have known her for over a year. The year before, they were present at the recording of her program[177] devoted to Femen, on France Inter. For half an hour, Caroline interviewed Anna, but they all understood that it was Inna who caught the journalist's eye. When Inna arrived in Paris, everyone thought it was normal for Caroline to get close to the movement. Normal and beneficial. Her network, among journalists and politicians, is useful. The two friends know her role and the contacts she has made to welcome Inna. Caroline has a long arm. Sacha and Oxana believe that this arm is at the service of Femen, without discrimination. "I thought she was a sincere person", Sacha concludes.

Oxana is more suspicious by nature: "From the beginning, I was suspicious of her. I don't really like girls who smile all the time."

Oxana does not smile all the time.

---

176. *Inna, op. cit.*
177. *Ils changent le monde,* broadcast on August 24, 2012 on France Inter.

At the Lavoir moderne, the Parisian journalist is always there. She takes part in the meetings, takes part in the decisions... She has an opinion on everything and gives it. In *Inna,* she devotes several pages to her highly indispensable role inside and outside the movement. It emerges, in substance, that she is a kind of feminist friend, a political advisor in charge of the promotion of the movement, but also of the definition of its French political line, of the rapprochement with Arab feminism, of the relations with the administration and of the appeasement of the internal conflicts...

Caroline is indispensable. As usual.

Indispensable to Inna. Mostly.

"When we arrive at Caroline's house, Inna is not there whereas we thought she would be with us, it was planned like that. Her absence intrigues Oxana and Sacha. They ask if she is coming. Caroline explains that Inna had to cancel at the last minute for a reason they don't understand. "She had an enigmatic air", according to Sacha, "a liar's air", according to Oxana. In short, the "Ukrainians" are wondering.

Since their arrival in France, they have been more than uncomfortable with Inna. They are still reeling from her rage when they announced their arrival in Paris (see Chapter 29). At that moment, and for the first time, the leader of Femen France made it clear that she did not want them there at any price. "Inna told us that she would oppose us, that she would make the worst problems for us..."

While she beats them cold most of the time, except if journalists are present, Inna redoubles her complicity with Caroline, who pays her in return for as many little things

A dinner at Caroline's

that annoy Oxana but not Sacha. Especially, confides the blonde from Khmelnytskyï: "We could see that she was looking for something else than a simple friendship or militant relationship, and we knew Inna well. Well... not yet so well."

Caroline Fourest helped Inna to settle in France, to obtain a status and papers in an unbeatable time (see chapter 34). She mobilized her network to encourage the establishment in France of a revolutionary feminist movement in every sense of the word. And as the help given to Inna was a political gesture for a persecuted activist, Caroline will naturally have the same gesture for two other even more important and persecuted activists...

"No," says Caroline, "I can't help you get refugee status, nor can I help you settle in France."

Does she not have the contacts she used to have?

"Yes, but they can't act for you, and then most importantly, Inna had done something serious, she was wanted, you, it's not the same."

The kidnapping, the violence, the charge of terrorism following the "discovery" of weapons at the Femen headquarters, the race to take refuge in the French embassy... it's not the same? Did Inna deserve her refugee passport more?

She spoke in English, we had trouble," says Oxana, "but we understood right away. I stayed with my fork in the air, and yet I was hungry and it was good."

Caroline's smiles and her calm tone add to the cruelty of her remarks. The polemicist tries to coat her speech, to make the pill pass.

The two friends know that Caroline Fourest has connections in high places. Inna, the first, told Sacha many times that "Caroline does what she wants in France". Galia Ackerman also told them that Caroline Fourest had "a lot of influence". And Caroline boasts about it enough herself on blogs, TV shows, in magazines, books, meetings and dinners...

The dinner, in fact. There are Italian salads, from a "wonderful caterer next to the Picasso museum", says Caroline smiling at Oxana.

It dried us up when she told us coldly that she would do nothing for us," explains Sacha, "we didn't expect privileges, but support. "Yes, that's right," Oxana continues, "we were confident, we thought we would get political asylum in France because we simply deserved it, but this was different... we understood that she was against us."

Last year at this time, after Inna's escape, Caroline's contacts had already told her that "only Inna could be taken in"; at least that's what the journalist had told them, advising them to "return to Ukraine[178] " and to come back "from time to time" to support Inna in France. But the situation has changed. After what Oxana, Sacha and Anna have just experienced, after having been harassed, kidnapped, beaten, raped, pursued, threatened, persecuted and tortured for a year, Caroline still tells them that Inna deserves political refugee status more than they do?

---

178. They are in Paris, mid-September 2012, at the request of Safia Lebdi, to try to smooth out the emerging conflict between Safia and Inna (see Chapter 35).

For Sacha, "the situation was serious when Inna left but, sincerely, she could have stayed. We, there, were going to die for real if we had to go back to Ukraine, so hearing that, it was horrible."

But Caroline insists, changes her mind. Inna is settled here now. The organization belongs to her ("I can't believe it, the organization I founded belongs to her!" Sacha belches when they leave). Inna is made uncomfortable by their presence...

"She said that we were confusing the issue, that journalists would no longer understand who is doing what and that it would be the death of Femen", remembers Oxana.

How can Inna feel that she is competing? She has no rights over Femen! Sacha and Oxana do not question her legitimacy, but they too are legitimate, and they were there before...

"We even said that, for clarity, she could take the title of leader of Femen France if she wants, who cares."

"Caroline was embarrassed, because she could see that we were right, even with our crappy English."

But she insists, she promised Inna, the two friends are sure of it now: "She was in command service for Inna."

Safia Lebdi, to whom I will report this account of the dinner, makes a contrary analysis: "It is Fourest who saws the branches to be able to manipulate Inna quietly."

Is Caroline manipulating Inna?

Is Inna manipulating Caroline?

In both cases, the victims are called Oxana Shachko and Sacha Shevchenko, and they are playing for their lives.

The cheeses arrive. Oxana and Sacha have never seen so many. Caroline cites Spain, Germany, Brazil where Femen is emerging (see chapter 37), the need to diversify... in the interest of Femen and feminism, obviously.

"But we don't have a penny, we've had a terrible year, Femen is in France because we've put it there. Inna did not found Femen or even Femen France."

Caroline understands, she is gentle: "I have confidence in you, you will succeed anywhere." But relentless: "You can't stay, you'd have everyone against you."

This time the threat is clear.

Also present at the dinner was Fiammetta Venner, the official companion of Caroline Fourest - about whom the journalist says in her book[179] that she is so understanding that she accepts his love for Inna and his rare but necessary desires for adventure, without questioning their relationship. The girls know her: "She didn't talk much, she smiled all the time and approved of everything Caroline said."

And what Caroline is saying now is that not only will she not do anything to help them, but they have little chance of getting refugee status.

"She told us that it was not the right time for that in France, that we were wary of foreigners."

"Yet Inna...", Sacha risks...

"Didn't you understand that Inna is not the same?", Oxana cuts her off in Ukrainian.

---

179. *Inna, op. cit.*

Yes, they did. The two friends understood. They promise each other to tell Inna about it the next day. They will do it. Inna will swear that she knew nothing about it.

Sacha and Oxana are convinced that it is Inna who is behind the staging and organization of this dinner. She does not attend because she has made Caroline her gunsel. "In the hope that we would believe Caroline's lies better than hers." Given the circumstances, if Inna tells her future ex-friends that they have little chance of obtaining refugee status and staying in France, they will suspect that bad feelings are driving her. But if it is Caroline Fourest...

Sacha: "We didn't believe Caroline. We knew that it would be hard, that many people want to come to France, that few files are accepted, but if they don't accept us, then they will never accept anyone in France. Oxana: "And then we had no choice, Ukraine was death."

They raise their heads. And they tell Caroline that they don't believe in it, that they will stay and do the procedures without her help, even if it takes much longer. They don't need her.

Oxana is even more specific: "*Fuck your help!*"

They go out.

Too bad for the strawberries of Plougastel.

Refugee and Refugee Women

"And when the mare Gentle asks the donkey
Benjamin to read him the commandments written
on the wall, he tells her that there is only one left:
'All animals are equal but some will be more
equal than others.'"
George Orwell, *Animal Farm*, 1945.

Paris, February 15, 2016

Sacha and I are looking for a bistro to have lunch in the Halles district. It will be an organic burger. Diet has never been Femen's strong point, but since she's been in Paris, Sacha is a little more careful.

It is cool and Sacha tightens a big mauve scarf around her neck. I point out to her that the cold must seem quite mild when you are used to Ukrainian winters and you don't hesitate to walk around half naked at minus fifteen degrees... She laughs: "In Kiev it's different, the cold, you expect it!

When you are Ukrainian, you think that in Paris there is always the sun[180]!"

Before attacking her organic mayonnaise burger, she agrees to look back on a difficult period in her French history.

"The lady said to me: 'I beg your pardon for yesterday, I talked about it around me, I went to see on the Internet, I understand now...'" The young woman who receives Sacha, this November 12, 2013, is moved behind her Formica counter gnawed by the years, elbows and tears. The scene takes place in the offices of France Terre d'Asile, the association that will help Sacha and Oxana put together the file they will have to present to Ofpra[181] to obtain the grail of the asylum seeker, the status of political refugee.

When a refugee requests political asylum in France, he or she goes through several stages, all of them difficult. The first is border control. Sacha and Oxana entered France with tourist visas. They skipped this step and moved on to the second one: going to a reception center for asylum seekers. This is usually where the obstacle course begins. These platforms are in charge of distributing the applicants to different prefectures according to the reception and/or accommodation capacities. They also offer a single meeting, on the association's premises, which brings together the asylum seeker, a representative of the prefecture and another from the OFII[182].

---

180. Unless otherwise noted, quotes are from interviews conducted by the author between November 2009 and September 2016.

181. French Office for the Protection of Refugees and Stateless Persons.

182. French Office of Immigration and Integration.

It was during an interview prior to this important meeting that Sacha was presented with an apology by a young employee of FranceTerre d'Asile. The reason? "The day before, I had come to explain why I was applying for political refugee status and I had told everything that had happened to me..." The Terre d'Asile employee stubbornly refused to believe that the young woman in her twenties sitting in front of her had been arrested more than a hundred times, that she had been beaten, imprisoned, abducted by the Russian, Ukrainian and Belarusian secret services, that she was prosecuted for crimes in Ukraine and Russia, that she had been expelled from Tunisia[183] and that, with her sweet eyes and her Slavic virgin smile, she was able to establish in the second a hit-parade of the comparative brutality of ten European police forces! "I remember her saying all the time: 'It's too much, it's way too much, you don't have to make it up!" Sacha doesn't understand, her English is weak, her French non-existent, the tone rises, the employee firmly dismisses her with a, "Come back when you've found a less abracadabra story!"

"Abracadabrante, that's one of the first words in the French language I learned!" said Sacha as he finished his Coke fries.

The next day, Sacha came back and the lady at the Formica counter asked her forgiveness: "She was almost

---

183. In early June 2013, Sacha traveled to Tunisia to support Amina Tyler. On the subject, see in particular: "Femen Tunisia: Aleksandra Shevchenko expelled...", Afrik.com, 5 June 2013.

crying, she told me: 'I spoke with my husband, he knew your story, and we looked it up on the Internet, I understand what you have endured, I will show you how it works and I am sure that at the end of the day you will have political refugee status. If anyone deserves it, it's you.'"

In the end, Sacha was granted refugee status. Oxana too.

"For me," Oxana will tell me while eating pancakes in Montparnasse one day in April 2016, "it was even harder because I am very bad with papers, I never know where they are."

Today, the two friends are both holders of political refugee passports, a document that grants them residency in France and the right to travel anywhere in the world... except Ukraine. Oxana has not seen her parents for three years. Sacha is more fortunate, she meets her mother from time to time in Poland or Hungary, each of them making a little way...

In the end, it will be eleven months of waiting (from August 2013 to July 2014) for Sacha, and sixteen months (from December 2013 to April 2015) for Oxana, between the filing of the complete file and the obtaining of the refugee passport. Not to mention the queues, the humiliations, the backtracking. "When you queue at France Terre d'Asile, you have to arrive at dawn, if you are not in the first fifteen, you have to come back the next day." And the check-ins at the prefecture - "there, it's better, they take thirty in one go" - and the interrogations at Ofpra, and the ban on travel... Sacha does not see his parents for a year, Oxana, for her part, will even be prevented from crossing the Italian border while she was going as a guest to the Naples festival, where Alain Margot's film *I Am Femen* was being presented.

The Swiss director remembers: "I had arrived in Naples by a different train and, in retrospect, I say to myself that I should have picked her up in France, with two of us, maybe we would not have been asked for our passports..." The poster of the film announced well the presence, at the Astradoc 2015, festival of "Journey in the cinema of the real", of Alain Margot, director, accompanied by Oxana Shachko, "artist and founder of the Femen movement". Only Alain will be present.

At the Gare de Lyon, on the morning of the departure, Oxana is nevertheless happy. She discovered that she was going to travel in first class for the first time in her life. "In Geneva, policemen came on board and maybe they thought I didn't have the style to travel in first class!" "Your papers, ma'am, please." Oxana produces the only document in her possession: a certificate from Ofpra that allows her to reside in France while awaiting the final decision on her reception, but prohibits her from traveling outside France. She tries to explain: she has already been to Switzerland and Belgium this year... " Well, you didn't have any. Well, you didn't have the right." She calls Alain who tries to explain to the police who is this deserving woman, heroine of a film, he offers to come and get her, to fax an accreditation of the festival... Nothing to do. Oxana is taken off the train. She will wait two hours on the cold platform in Geneva for a train from Italy that will take her back to

Paris with a ticket paid for by the Ministry of the Interior. In Naples, the film will be a huge success. Oxana will be applauded to the skies.

The episode takes place on April 9, 2015, a few days before Oxana officially received her refugee passport - a document that would obviously have allowed her to travel to Italy - and two years to the day after Inna was granted political refugee status on April 9, 2013.

For Galia Ackerman, who regularly deals with Chechen refugees, "this is a pretty normal delay, unfortunately, and even fast for Sacha, twelve to fifteen months is a minimum".

In 2013, Inna was also faced with the anguish of obtaining, or not, political refugee status.

It went better.

Inna filed an application with the prefecture on February 19, 2013 and received her passport on April 9 of the same year.

Forty-nine days.

Forty-nine days during which she did not have to clock in once. Forty-nine days against three hundred and thirty for Sacha and more than four hundred and eighty for Oxana. A delay which suggests that Inna has benefited from a special treatment.

This delay is confirmed by Inna herself who, upon receipt of the precious sesame, cannot help but tweet a mockery to the fachosphere that has been targeting her for a while: she displays the document stamped with the initials "European Union - French Republic" and this comment: *"After a long struggle, I've got my passport! Very proud it's written French Republic. Have a nice day, fascists*[184].

The tweet was immediately deleted - did Caroline Fourest intervene urgently to tell Inna that it was not wise to leave this kind of information lying around on a social network? But the damage is done. Jacques Bompard, unregistered deputy of Vaucluse, saw it and will make it the theme of a question[185] in the National Assembly, January 19, 2014, which essentially questions the government on the advisability of issuing a passport to "a leader of the movement who had fled Ukraine, her country of origin, following the truncation of the crucifix erected in memory of the victims of the NKVD, to avoid prosecution." The right-wing deputy also asks whether "Christianophobia has become official government policy, issuing a national passport to an activist whose anti-Christian messages are no secret[186]?"

The answer is that "the person in question has been recognized as a refugee by the French Office for the Protection of Refugees and Stateless Persons (Ofpra). The Office's decisions on international protection are taken independently under the jurisdictional control of the National Court of Asylum, on the sole basis of the Geneva Convention of 28 July 1951 relating to the status of refugees and Article L. 712-1 of the Code on the Entry and Stay of Foreigners

---

184. "After a long struggle, I got my passport! Very proud that it is marked French Republic. Have a nice day fachos."

185. Question #47614.

186. See in particular on the subject: "The imaginary naturalization of Inna...", Solène Cordier, *Le Monde*, January 9, 2014.

and the Right of Asylum (CESEDA) relating to subsidiary protection, and after an individual examination of the asylum application. No other administrative or political authority interferes in this decision-making process. Recognition of international protection gives the right to travel outside France. This is the reason why, in application of article 28 of the Geneva Convention, the prefecture did not issue the applicant with a French passport, but with a travel document entitled "refugee travel document".

No priority then?

Forty-nine days.

In fact, Ofpra specifies that "the deadlines can be shortened in the context of a priority procedure[187] ".

The Ofpra website, the website of the National Assembly, but also the websites of various refugee aid associations define precisely the conditions for triggering an emergency procedure. But it is a negative procedure that is used when it is presumed that the applicant is a fraudster, when he has used a false name, lied during preliminary interviews, etc. It is also used when the applicant is a refugee. It is also used when the applicant comes from a so-called "safe" country, meaning democratic enough that political persecution is unlikely. In February 2013, when Inna submitted her application, Ukraine was still on Ofpra's list of safe countries. Would we have used a procedure usually used when we want to expel the applicant more quickly to receive Inna more quickly? No, because this procedure provides for

---

187. Ofpra's activity report for the year 2013.

an expulsion period of ninety-six hours to a maximum of fifteen days.

In her book[188], Caroline Fourest confides that in September 2012, she organized a meeting between Inna and François Zimeray, then ambassador for human rights, who expected to discover "a feminist *pasionaria*, enthusiastic but slightly baroque[189]", and instead left "bluffed by this brilliant and structured activist" and said he was "ready to help[190]".

François Zimeray would thus be the "help" from which Inna would have benefited? The interested party, today French ambassador in Denmark, remembers nothing or almost nothing...: "I followed this movement like all the movements that fight against patriarchy in the world, because I consider that this oppression is a danger as well for the woman as for the man, I was thus very favorable. I was contacted by Caroline Fourest, but I don't remember the exact circumstances." He still concedes that "it was Caroline Fourest who took care of all this with the Interior."

With the Interior?

Galia Ackerman agrees: "If there was a boost, it came from someone high up! The human rights delegate is not in a position to shorten the time it takes to obtain refugee status from a minimum of fifteen months to forty-nine days."

Is Caroline Fourest confessing, by writing that she went through François Zimeray, a little help to hide a big plunge?

---

188. *Inna, op. cit.*
189. *Ibid.*
190. *Ibid.*

It would be clever but at the very least abusive, especially considering the moralistic ethics defended by the journalist all day long... She also mentions her "contacts at the Ministry of the Interior" who "assure her that Inna's request is examined with the greatest benevolence[191]". In what capacity does she intervene? In the name of what? And to whom is she speaking? Galia doesn't say: "I don't know, I just know that I am trying to help obtain this status for a Chechen woman in danger and that it is impossible to shorten these delays.

Joseph Paris has an idea: "We can only make assumptions, but it is clear that Caroline Fourest has a relationship that goes beyond the framework of a working relationship with Manuel Valls, for example." The Manuel Valls who calls the prefect to get Caroline out of the salad basket following the scuffles with the Civitas fundamentalists (see chapter 24).

To question n° 47614 asked by Jacques Bompard in the National Assembly, it was thus answered that the decision concerning the reception of Inna had "been taken by Ofpra in complete independence"... Ofpra, placed, at its creation in 1952, under the authority of the Quai d'Orsay, managed from 2007 by the Council of State; before passing, by decree of November 25, 2010, under the joint authority of the Ministry of the Interior[192].

The Ministry of the Interior, Place Beauvau, whose host, at the time of the facts, is Manuel Valls.

Forty-nine days...

---

191. *Ibid.*
192. Ofpra's statutes: www.ofpra.gouv.fr.

Thinking about exile...

> "This fierce and ridiculous game,
> When should it end?
> For what your cruel mouth
> Scatter in the air,
> Murderous monster, that's my brain,
> My blood and my flesh."
> Charles Baudelaire, *Les Fleurs du mal*,
> "Love and the skull", 1857.

Paris, March 25, 2016

Sacha lowers his eyes and blows: "I told you already, the biggest mistake is to have left Inna alone in Paris for a year, but we couldn't come[193]..."

Why? What's stopping Sasha, Anna and Oxana from taking refuge in Paris with Inna? What prevents Sacha,

---

193. Unless otherwise noted, quotes are from interviews conducted by the author between November 2009 and September 2016.

Anna and Oxana from taking refuge in Paris at the same time as Inna?

"A lie, according to Joseph Paris, the most serious lie of Caroline Fourest."

A lie is more than plausible, on behalf of Inna, if not at her express request.

"By this lie," Joseph asserts, "she endangered the lives of Sacha and Oxana, she could not ignore it."

It is mid-September 2012. Inna has just taken refuge in Paris. A few days after her installation at the Lavoir moderne, a meeting, attended by Joseph, Inna, and Safia among others, is held on the second floor, in "Inna's room". Sacha and Oxana are also there, at Safia's request. The objective is to bring back peace between Safia and Inna after the first frictions, and to consolidate the political line. But the subject of the possible immediate evacuation of the other leading members of Femen to Paris is raised. Joseph breaks his usual silence: "I'm in favor of it, Sacha and Oxana must come and settle down too, right now, afterwards it might be too late." Inna, with a lot of diplomacy, temporizes on the theme "the movement must not be cut off from Ukraine". But if the heads of Femen emigrate, Femen dies in the East. The argument carries. Moreover, Anna does not want to leave Ukraine.

As a precautionary measure and to prevent any possible future emergency, Safia Lebdi informs, by e-mail to the Quai d'Orsay, the delegate for human rights François Zimeray. She refers to the presence of the Femen in France, reminds him of their precarious and dangerous situation in Ukraine and the great risks they face there; she gives him a summary of the political situation of the girls. François Zimeray replied, within hours, according to Joseph and Safia, that "given the situation, political asylum will be possible for the four threatened girls", namely Inna, but also Sacha, Oxana and Anna. Today, four years later, François Zimeray no longer remembers: "I won't tell you anything about it, because my memories are hazy. However, he remembers with the precision of a watchmaker the circumstances of the attack[194] in Copenhagen that he suffered with Inna. Fortunately, Safia Lebdi's memories are less selective: "In my mind, there is not even a subject, I asked for a welcome for all four, Anna, Inna, Sacha and Oxana."

At the end of September 2012, Safia Lebdi distanced herself from Femen France, which she had founded, because of deep dissensions with Inna and Caroline over the functioning and political line of the movement. Caroline, according to Joseph Paris, "immediately announced that she was taking over the asylum file, because she knew François Zimeray well, and thought she could facilitate the procedure. Safia Lebdi now has regrets about this "handover": "The situation was so tense, especially because of Caroline who absolutely

---

194. On February 14, 2015, an Islamist terrorist attack occurred during a public conference organized, in tribute to the victims of *Charlie Hebdo*, at the Krudttonden cultural center on the theme "Art and blasphemy". François Zimeray participates in the company of Inna Shevchenko, artists and Danish politicians. It is the artist Lars Vilks, author of the caricatures of Mohammed published in August 2007 in a Danish newspaper, who is targeted. He escaped the shootings. On the other hand, the director Finn Norgaard was killed and three policemen were injured.

Thinking about exile...

wanted to control the movement, that I threw in the towel. The courageous fighter withdraws before the violence of the blows: "I understood that there was nothing more to do. Caroline had Inna under her thumb.

At the end of September, even though Safia Lebdi's "departure-eviction" was not yet official, Caroline Fourest was already "alone on board with Inna. A few days later, she shared her disappointment with Sacha and Oxana: "She told us that only Inna could obtain political refugee status, not us, as France refused to accept four Ukrainian refugees at once.

End of the story about the number of welcomes and the distribution of roles: at the beginning of October 2012, the two friends must return to Ukraine for a year of hell.

In August 2013, exhausted by the suffering, the arrests, the torture, the prosecution for terrorism, Sacha herself writes, at the insistence of Joseph Paris, to the delegate for human rights, François Zimeray. She confided in him their despair, briefly recounted the kidnapping, the violence, the murdered little dog... and of course reiterated her request for political asylum for herself, Anna and Oxana. François Zimeray replied to Sacha, "within half an hour", that political asylum was entirely possible and that all they had to do was make an official request, "as he had already said the previous year". François Zimeray therefore "held", as early as 2012, an agreement for four receptions, and not just one as Caroline Fourest had said.

In September 2013, and after Caroline Fourest's refusal to help Sacha and Oxana obtain refugee status (see

Chapter 33), it is necessary to "shield the asylum application." Fortunately, there are videos. Joseph Paris says: "At the end of July, when the Ukrainian police and the Russian secret service hid weapons in the room and organized a fake search, Sacha called me with his iPad. I asked him to make some very short videos and to send them to me immediately so that I could secure them." Sacha then shot a series of five or six ten- to twenty-second videos and sent them, almost live, to Joseph.

In Paris, Joseph edits the videos and makes them available on his website. He also called journalists from *Libération*, who immediately posted the films on the newspaper's website. These images show faces damaged by the torture suffered in Odessa (see chapter 28) and the search of the Femen's office in Kiev. These documents will be very useful, he rightly thinks, in establishing the proof of their persecution in their country of origin.

But François Zimeray is preparing for new duties, he has just been appointed French ambassador in Copenhagen. He has been replaced as delegate for human rights by Patrizianna Sparacino-Thiellay, who is taking charge of the file.

The position of "ambassador for human rights in charge of the international dimension of the Shoah, spoliations and the duty to remember" was created in 2000 at the initiative of Hubert Védrine, then Minister of Foreign Affairs. Its mission is to maintain the memory of the Shoah and to detect situations throughout the world where France will be able to live up to its reputation as a country of human rights. In her small office on the first floor of the Quai d'Orsay, where she works surrounded by two collaborators, Patrizianna Sparacino-Thiellay explained to me that "it is a mission that takes on even more importance today when human rights activists are under increasing pressure. The ambassador exercises her function all over the world, from critical situations that are transmitted to her by the embassies or that she knows personally during her numerous trips.

Before being appointed to this position, Patrizianna Sparacino-Thiellay worked in the office of the Minister of Women's Rights, Najat Vallaud-Belkacem, and is particularly sensitive to the issue of "women's rights, which are regressing in so many countries.

In September 2013, she remembers receiving Sacha and Oxana: "When the file was sent to me by Zimeray, I immediately declared myself available to meet with them and refer them to the appropriate Ofpra services."

Patrizianna Sparacino-Thiellay is an efficient and benevolent woman who will support, legally and without any form of nepotism, Oxana and Sacha's request for asylum.

In summary, and according to the testimony of Joseph Paris, which he confirmed to me in writing: "At the end of 2012, Caroline Fourest had an agreement in principle from François Zimeray to launch the procedures for welcoming Inna, Sacha, Oxana and Anna. But she told the group that this agreement in principle only concerned Inna; this closed the debate on the possible installation, from September 2012, in Paris, of the whole movement. Oxana and Sacha then return to Ukraine where they will almost succumb to the violence of the government and the Russian secret services. It is clearly a question of endangering the lives of Sacha and Oxana, by openly lying to them about the possibility of obtaining political asylum in France."

What remains is why? Why would the journalist have taken the responsibility of hiding François Zimeray's agreement in principle to a quadruple welcome as early as the end of 2012? Why does she still refuse to help Sacha and Oxana a year later (see chapter 33)? For the love of Inna? This is the most obvious explanation and we understand, when reading her book-confession, that she is ready to push her commitment far for her new conquest.

Love explains everything. It is well known.

Except for Joseph Paris.

"This is not the only reason. Femen was undoubtedly a political opportunity for Caroline Fourest, a way to build feminist legitimacy after several failures with other movements, notably Osez le féminisme."

Joseph goes further and develops a very personal theory based on his experience inside Femen, the shooting of his film *Naked War*, his knowledge of all the actors and the proximity of Caroline Fourest to Manuel Valls. "First, I understood from the beginning the meaning of her actions, she was dividing to make Inna rule. To Sacha, she said to be wary of me, that I was a kind of Viktor - as if Sacha could be afraid of Viktor! - Or that I was not a feminist, while at the same time she asked me to provide her with my images for her film.

But above all, Joseph continues, "she had to make sure that Femen would remain a nice pop movement as it was then presented in the media.

Is he suggesting that she was the "eye of the palace" within the movement? But which palace? Nothing less than those of the Republic, according to Joseph, who does not hesitate to assert that she "was unofficially rolling for the Ministry of the Interior and was unofficial adviser to Manuel Valls for a long time.

The takeover of Femen, in this hypothesis, represented a triple win: to control the "excesses" of the movement, to serve his political convictions and to achieve his personal ends with Inna.

While there is evidence and testimony of Caroline Fourest's lie about the possibility of welcoming the four refugees instead of Inna alone in 2012, Joseph's thesis about a possible double game of the journalist with the Ministry of the Interior or other French services is more difficult to support. The proximity to the minister in place is clear, the intervention of Manuel Valls' ministry in obtaining refugee status for Inna as well... Inna's own distrust, which keeps her new "friend" away from important decisions such as the action at Notre-Dame that will trigger the anger of Manuel Valls, among others, is also an element of the perverse game being played between the two women, who seem to be manipulating each other... Here again, Safia Lebdi offers a personal reading: "Caroline is neither a secret agent nor an independent journalist. One could say that she is a 'state agent' that institutional networks activate to serve certain battles, at certain times." Caroline Fourest is a divisive personality: "That too is useful to institutions, Caroline divides and power needs division. Her networks are just as effective under the left as under the right.

I re-read *Inna* by Caroline Fourest. The journalist confides her fear of seeing Femen fall into armed terrorism - a heresy for those who know anything about the movement - and fantasizes about her possible role in preventing this drift: "I say nothing. Not in front of Oxana, the eye of Kiev. If I want to avoid the worst, the group must not distrust me to the point of forbidding Inna to see me. I don't rule it out[195]."

Not sure that Oxana is the most worrying "eye" of this adventure...

---

195. *Inna, op. cit.*

I Am Femen, by Alain Margot

"You don't have to be manly all the time! Like you
go to a restaurant and you don't have the money
to pay, well, she pays!
- And like you're not a moron?
- No, it's normal!
- I'm hot, I'm a serious feminist actually!
- You're mostly a serious wanker yeah!"
Dialogue Gringe Orelsan,
Programme *Bloqués* Canal+, 15 October 2015.

La Chaux-de-Fonds, January 15, 2016

I meet Oxana and Alain in La Chaux-de-Fonds. The small
town of watchmakers has nurtured a perfidious critic of the
modern world. Alain Margot is a genius jack-of-all-trades.
Journalist, director, provocateur... he became known to the
Swiss media in the 1980s through the program *Le Grand
Raid*, inspired by a mythical program broadcast on Antenne

2 in the 1970s and 1980s: *La Course autour du monde (The Race Around the World)*, which sent young French-speaking candidates to the four corners of the planet. They had to deliver images of each stage of their journey. Equipped with super-8 Beaulieu cameras, they managed to send a film and editing instructions by plane each week.

In France, the program, created by Jacques Antoine and presented by Roger Bourgeon, was broadcast every Sunday and attracted a very large audience, even if the ratings were still difficult to measure. The mythical vintage of *La Course autour du monde* will remain forever the 1977-1978 season which revealed, in decreasing order of final ranking, Didier Régnier, who will become a host of adventure programs, Jérôme Bony, future great reporter, and Philippe de Dieuleveult, irreducible Breton daredevil who will disappear in conditions still not well elucidated during an expedition on the Congo River for the cult program *La Chasse au trésor*, of which he became the host[196]. Alain shares with Philippe de Dieuleveult the taste for adventure, but also that of humor: he stages himself, during comical sequences, in the films he sends to testify of his trip, under the mysterious name of Rackham le Gum. With the same offbeat humor and, according to his friends, "completely

---

196. Author of a legendary autobiography (*J'ai du ciel bleu dans mon passeport*, Grasset, 1984), Philippe de Dieuleveult planned to raft down a section of the river that was considered impassable. On the basis of serious elements, the magazine *XXI* revived in 2008, in the article "Les crocodiles du Zaïre", the thesis of the assassination by the secret police of the dictator Mobutu. In addition, the French Ministry of Foreign Affairs, then headed by Roland Dumas, was accused of having covered up the affair.

destructive", Alain set up a totally crazy punk place in the heart of the very conservative town of La Chaux-de-Fonds, which is still very successful today. The Haunted House is a festive space with a surreal decor that mixes, on three floors pierced by back doors, unexpected bars and mysterious corners, thousands of various hangings, hundreds of recovered mannequins, collections of untraceable erotic books, light shows in ghost train mode, English armchairs and beer crates... A place that expresses Alain's taste for rebellion and that led him to become interested in the Femen movement.

I met Alain in 2011. He came to Ukraine to make a report for TSR[197]. He discovered Oxana, Inna and the others, whom I had already known for two years. Together we will follow the girls' journey in pursuit of "Greg Dickhead" (see chapter 15). Our first contact is chilly. Reporters hate to work on the same story at the same time. For me, this is the worst option: I'll have to do my story with a TV crew next to me. Even if it is reduced - Alain is alone with a journalist from TSR - there will be sound recordings, passages in front of my lens, staging to be redone... It looks bad and I know, when we shake hands, that we think the same thing and that it can be summed up in three words: "Fuck, fuck! I blame the Femen girls a little. Each of us obviously imagined that we would be alone on this report that would take us to the four corners of Ukraine for more than two weeks.

---

197. Télévision suisse romande.

In the end, we will not only be able to support each other, but we will help each other and lay the foundation for a friendship.

As with me, the passion of the girls will act on Alain, triggering the desire to go further than a simple report for Swiss TV. He will come back many times: "I understood that these girls had a fervor that I wanted to tell[198]. Alain looks for financing, thinks of the TSR, but the conditions are draconian, and he will do as usual: "With three bits of string!" Until a Bernese producer came along: "Then the real work could begin, I was even able to bring the girls to Switzerland on budget." Without preconceived ideas, Alain shoots as much as possible, filming each of the girls. Like me, he notes Inna's taste for the camera, Sacha's shyness, Anna's mystery and Oxana's anger. "I thought it would be Sasha who would emerge as the central character of the film, but Oxana is mind-blowing in her presence on camera." The film, released in April 2014, tells the story of Femen through the life and eyes of Oxana. *I Am Femen* will be nominated in many festivals and awarded at the festival "Visions du réel" in Nyon. It is a great film, nothing like the one directed by Kitty Green and presented at the Venice Film Festival in 2013, nor the racy documentary made the following year by Nadia El Fani and Caroline Fourest.

Nothing was easy though. First of all, the filming: "The police prevented us from working several times, the means

---

198. Unless otherwise noted, quotes are from interviews conducted by the author between November 2009 and September 2016.

were lacking, the weather is hard in Ukraine, the witnesses didn't speak much..." Only Oxana's mother expresses herself really unabashedly in the film: "It's true that nothing is ever done for us women in Ukraine, so if I agree with her, I'm not going to say anything. Only Oxana's mother expresses herself without any complexes in the film: "It's true that nothing is ever done for us women in Ukraine, so if I don't share all their actions, I support them morally[199]. *I Am Femen* takes a deeply sincere look at the humanity and simplicity of young girls inhabited by the passion for equality, by the hatred of injustice. Oxana is portrayed with tenderness. Her status as an artist in the group allows the others to leave her in charge of making the disguises, costumes, and masks that will be used for the Femen performances. She willingly lends herself to this. Oxana also talks about her doubts as a young girl, when she thought of entering a monastery, more in search of the absolute than of God: "In Ukraine, at that age, you believe in God and that's all. But anyway, I did not ask myself these questions, it was the time that attracted me, the time for meditation, philosophy, art, finally I believed[200]..." Her mother is touching when she talks about her opposition to the entry of her daughter into the orders: "I was so opposed... It is true that one must be a believer in Ukraine, but from there to devote his life[201]." The sweet mother is so afraid

---

199. *I Am Femen*, testimony of Oxana's mother.
200. *I Am Femen*, Oxana's testimony.
201. *I Am Femen*, testimony of Oxana's mother.

I Am Femen, by Alain Margot

of the "vocation" of her daughter that her investment in a group of feminist revolutionaries will appear to her almost as a relief!

The film is a success. But this success could have been, should have been greater. Alain and Oxana regret it for Femen, for feminism.

In La Chaux-de-Fonds, where Alain prepares a raclette for us, Oxana pouts. She boils inside, but lets Alain explain to me what was missing from the film's promotion: "Inna's presence, simply, she embodies the movement today and she should have supported the release of a film that gives a nice and even glorious image of it!"

So what happened? Why did Inna successively refuse the invitations of the festivals of Aix, Naples, Nyon? Why did she hide behind vague pretexts each time?

"She would give me lame excuses," Alain explains, "like, 'I can't leave Paris for more than two days' or 'I have an appointment with some new activists.' And even 'I'm sick.'"

Oxana explodes: "*She is a bitch!*" Then develops: "She never came because she was not at the center of the film, she could not stand that I was the central character." Alain moderates: "We didn't ask her much but it's paradoxical, she refuses to endorse a film that supports Femen, we can think that it's an ego problem, that's clear." For the Nyon festival, where *I Am Femen* will win the Jury Prize, Inna claims that she cannot leave France even though she has been in possession of her refugee passport for more than a year (see Chapter 34). Moreover, when she answers no to Alain on the phone, she is ten kilometers from Nyon, in Geneva, where she signs Caroline Fourest's book[202]. The next day, she agreed to give an interview, still in Switzerland, to the daily newspaper *Le Temps*[203].

Oxana continues: "I came to all the promotion meetings, Sacha came often. It was difficult for us because we didn't have our refugee papers yet. Oxana even had to turn back on the road to Italy (see chapter 34).

A few weeks later, on a terrace in Montmartre, I ask Inna about her lack of investment in promoting a film that clearly supports the cause of the movement. I look at her, she smiles. I bet with myself on the content of her answer: "I don't understand why Alain says that, I would have come with pleasure, it's just that nobody invited me..."

I win my bet.

---

202. Archives of the Geneva Book Fair.
203. "Femen, sexy and angry," Marie-Pierre Genecand, *Le Temps*, May 11, 2014.

It takes a book!

> "You think one lie is as good as another, but you're wrong. I can invent anything, I can fool people, I can make up all sorts of mystifications, I can make all sorts of jokes, but I don't feel like a liar; these lies, if you want to call them lies, that's me as I am; with these lies I'm not hiding anything, with these lies I'm actually telling the truth.
> Milan Kundera, *Risibles Amours*, Gallimard.

Paris, April 15, 2016

"I hesitated before receiving you because I am disappointed with the evolution of Femen, and especially that of Inna, I must tell you[204]."

I have an appointment with Galia Ackerman, in her Parisian apartment, in the heart of this vertical 13th

---

204. Unless otherwise noted, quotes are from interviews conducted by the author between November 2009 and September 2016.

arrondissement, which hesitates between the suburbs of Beijing and Kiev. I know Galia for her books on Chernobyl, and in particular the last one[205], which is magnificent, and which brings to life the intertwined destinies of "the small fauna of Chernobyl", as she likes to call the ten thousand or so inhabitants, former employees, peasants, the elderly or simply miserable people left behind, who still live in the vicinity of the power plant. I also know her for her unforgettable translations of the books of the 2015 Nobel Prize winner, Svetlana Alexievitch, who owes it to Galia to have succeeded in breaking into the Western European publishing scene in the early 2000s. "I just found a publisher for her," says Galia, modestly forgetting that it took her months and many rejections.

Galia wrote *Femen*, the first book published on the movement. But she specifies: "I would not have accepted a book *about* Femen, it was a book *by* Femen, to which I lent my pen."

A book is needed.

To establish the movement in France.

To be part of history.

To tell the story of the movement.

To make a date.

Because we are in France.

It takes a book to answer the question, "Where the hell are these blonde kids who want to change the world from?"

---

205. *Crossing Chernobyl*, First Parallel, 2016.

It is the Calmann-Lévy publishing house that takes the piece: "I called Mireille Paolini, she agreed immediately", explains Safia Lebdi today.

Having been around Femen a lot, I know the logistical difficulties that naturally arise from the elastic-relativistic conception that Inna, Sacha, Oxana and Anna have of notions as un-revolutionary as precision, punctuality, concordance... Moreover, Galia herself admits her skepticism before starting the book. She is a serious journalist and a recognized author. She is interested in the Femen... from afar.

But, contacted by the publisher, she considers the job offer. And if her initial doubts are quickly swept away by the enthusiasm and sincerity of the girls' commitment, the decision to accept the writing of the book is a little painful. She did not share all of the Femen's convictions and suspected a lack of intellectual distance on the subject of feminism - she had worked extensively on the genesis, the history of the currents, the sociology of feminism and humanism in general.

Galia's work includes many meetings with the three founders of Femen and also with Inna. In the end, she will talk more with Inna than with the others. An imbalance that the writer justifies by the difficulty of meeting the three founders, whereas Inna is very accessible. One is in Paris, the others in Kiev. One is looking for the light, the others for the progress of feminism. Galia has to work fast, and Inna is always available. "That's how my first doubts were born, I understood that Inna was mostly concerned with her personal destiny.

With Sacha, Anna and Oxana, she has shorter interviews, when they are in Paris. And clarifications are made by email. "But nothing is simple, they are always late with their answers. Despite everything, she quickly gets an idea about the level of involvement of the girls: "When you come from a small lost town in Western Ukraine, you are not prepared for feminism, it requires a real training and commitment." And her consideration grows.

Femen is not, I understand from the beginning of our conversation, the book that makes Galia the most proud. But during the three months it takes to write it, and afterwards, Galia becomes friends with Sacha and Oxana, and learns to distrust Inna. "I think, beyond her very personality, that she is taking the movement in the wrong direction." Galia believes, like Joseph Paris, that Femen has become a conformist movement, whose revolt is now part of a formal framework that no longer bothers anyone; even if she does not go so far as to consider, like the director of *Naked War*, that Femen is "following in the footsteps of the government". For her - even if she specifies that she speaks from "a very secular position" - the movement has notably gone astray in its opposition to Islam: "All the discourse on the criticism of Islam and the veil is done in any way, perhaps we should start by talking with these women instead of constantly being in the show business.

This is the trap, for Galia, since the beginning: the bluster: "Femen was born as a revolt that uses the codes of modern communication, but this necessarily implies an escalation as soon as the media gets bored, and they get bored quickly. The trap closes when an action must necessarily be stronger than the previous one... According to Galia, the solution is in the refusal - at least momentarily - of publicity. Doing again, but without letting people know. "It is wrong to say that we did not do anything because we did not make ourselves known. More in-depth but less media-oriented actions will have an impact on the people concerned, through meetings or direct contacts..." The press will probably not talk about the Femen who go to lecture in schools, but the students will remember them forever. Don't bet everything on the show but work on the substance? "That's it, otherwise it's natural that the press will lose interest in the movement, or it will be dragged into a spiral of stupid sensationalism." The physical, judicial or administrative limits will naturally constrain the movement, which will then have to choose between, on the one hand, illegality, trials, prison and, on the other, disinterest, oblivion. This is a view shared by Elvire Duvelle-Charles, one of the first recruits of Femen France (see chapter 38).

But what could have kept Galia away from Inna?" Obviously her behavior with Sasha and Oxana, it was an attempt to drive them away."

Galia understands as soon as Oxana and Sacha arrive in France that cohabitation will be impossible: "Inna behaves like a dictator and, if she can impose herself on any newly-arrived Frenchwoman, she has no natural authority over Sacha or Oxana, who have founded the movement, run more risks and endured more bullying than herself.

It takes a book!

And then, during the interviews, Galia quickly realized that "Inna doesn't have the verve to develop the movement, she just wants to use it for her own benefit. Does this explain why the birth of Femen International was a failure? "It needed structures, assemblies, rules, as for every branched NGO. This is not the case, so it could not work."

In this regard, the successive affairs of Femen Brazil and Femen Belgium speak for themselves. Sara Winter was chosen by Inna to lead Femen Brazil, even though her involvement and even her balance are questionable: a prostitute at 17, she founded a probisexual and anti-Christian movement before joining Femen and then... moving on to pro-abortion activism. She then accused the Femen, in a book[206] completely delirious, of having forced her to prostitute herself and to use drugs. Wasn't there a more serious leader in the Brazilian feminist market?

In Belgium, the case is even more symptomatic of the "Inna-style" management denounced by Galia Ackerman. Margo Fruitier is the leader of a dozen courageous activists who led a "topless jihad" action in front of the Brussels mosque on April 4, 2013, before attacking the car of the Tunisian Prime Minister visiting Brussels on June 25. In a statement to *La Libre Belgique*, September 11, 2013, without questioning the ideology of the movement, Margo denounces "the way this group operates internationally,

---

206. *Vadia nao! sete vezes que fui traida pelo feminismo*, "Not Bitch! Seven times betrayed by feminism," 2015. Not published in France.

everything being dictated by a few people"... Clearly: she accuses Inna of being authoritarian, intransigent and obtuse.

Inna and democracy...

A few months later, Femen France activists, speaking on condition of anonymity, confided to Le *Nouvel Obs*[207] : "Inna is a guru that no one criticizes", or: "One day, I dared to state my disagreement about an action. In front of everyone, Inna told me coldly: 'You, you don't come to the preparations anymore'", or again: "At the beginning, all the girls agreed that we should create spaces for discussion, especially on the veil. The actions were voted by a show of hands. Then Inna blew the whistle on the end of the game, by making me understand curtly that the ideological lines of the movement were already fixed. After that, no one said a word.

Finally, the actions at Notre-Dame and the Mosque of Paris displeased Galia. "France is the only country where secularism is a value. Churches don't have power here, and these attacks have done Femen a disservice by driving away people who could have supported the movement."

But it's too late to write all that... " In fact, it wasn't until the afterword of the English edition that I distanced myself a bit from what I write in the French version. It was their book more than mine."

In this famous afterword, Galia wonders: "Maybe they were given bad advice..." Is she targeting Caroline Fourest?

---

207. "Femen : une dérive sectaire ?", Céline Cabourg and Marie Vaton, *Le Nouvel Obs*, March 9, 2014.

It takes a book!

Is she targeting Caroline Fourest? "No, she was against the action at Notre Dame, but on Islam, yes, she takes it wrong."

Sacha and Oxana have kept relations with Galia, who helps them when she can, because they are "beautiful souls". Inna has cut her ties.

On the cover of the book, there is a beautiful photo of Inna taken by my colleague Guillaume Herbaut, for which he won a second prize at the World Press in 2012.

But this was not the initial choice of the publisher," Oxana objects. Initially, Calmann-Lévy wanted a group shot, with the four of us." The four major figures of the movement. Several possible dates of shooting are even proposed but, explains Oxana with his French essentialist, "Inna still confuses.

The reason for this change of program is as simple as a few emails and phone calls. Nicolas Trautmann remembers very well. At the time, he was a freelance graphic designer and was contacted by the publisher Mireille Paolini to organize a photo shoot with the Femen for the cover photo: "I had chosen a studio and a photographer, I was waiting for the publisher's OK and a date. Instead, a phone call from Inna to Mireille Paolini arrived on November 5 to explain that the girls were in Ukraine and that they were not free for a group photo. Nicolas is therefore asked to make proposals for a cover based on archive photos: "I select three as a priority: 1/ a photo where the four appear; 2/ a photo of Sacha alone; 3/ a photo of Oxana alone...". A choice that does not suit Inna at all. On November 7, she returned to the charge by e-mail: *"Hello Mireille, so we discuss with Anna and girls about the cover [...]. We want on the cover of our book picture of the World Press Photo [...]. Here is our decision*[208].

Nicolas would discover the truth by chance, contacting Oxana the following year for photos: "She explained to me that they were wisely waiting for a call from the editor to come to the photo appointment but that Inna told them that the editor had changed her mind."

Inna confuses...

Not so sure, according to Safia Lebdi: "Finally, that Inna is a troublemaker, the facts are there, but my feeling is that it is Caroline Fourest who is behind this maneuver." To support her thesis, Safia relies on a factual argument and a personal judgment.

The factual argument: "There were indiscretions, I knew that it was Caroline who wrote the whole "confession" part of Inna, which was then given to Galia Ackerman. And since Caroline was furious with me and wanted to use Inna to control Femen, she made her say some slanderous things about me that would not pass the stage of corrections, it was still me who facilitated the book project, it was ballsy."

And the personal judgment? "Pffff, that's Fourest all over!"

---

208. "Hi Mireille, so we discussed the cover with Anna and the girls [...]. We want on the cover of our book the World Press Photo [...]. That's our decision."

Elvire towards the future

"I have confidence in the human species, confidence that it does not always justify. I have
opinions about our species. When I was young
I wanted to do prehistory to try to reconstruct the
species to which I belong, to find its origins and
follow it, step by step. Human beings have good
sides, but I am very wary of the bad ones."
Germaine Tillion, Interview with Jean Lacouture,
France Culture, 1997.

Paris, March 2016

"Honestly, it's a bit of a drag! But you have to do it, it's
important[209]."
Elvire Duvelle-Charles is 28 years old. She has been a
Femen since Inna arrived in France at the end of 2012.

---

209. Unless otherwise noted, quotes are from interviews conducted by the author
between November 2009 and September 2016.

She found her way, her fight: "I was interested in many other associations, it was Femen that suited me, for its mode of action."

The task in question is the chore of answering all the requests of the students who work on the Femen movement. And as is often the case since the world is a world and chores are chores, this one falls to the latest arrivals: "It's not a punishment or even an obligation, it's a job for those who are not yet used to talking to the press or working on actions. Since the movement took root in France, the interest of young people and especially students has never waned. The Femen are among the most popular subjects of the TPE[210] in the baccalaureate. Girls, but also boys, choose the movement founded by the Ukrainian blondes as a subject of study. What motivates them? "Obviously the novelty and the style of the movement, but also the history, the claims, the feminism..." In June, they have to answer more than a hundred requests from students, so it's a tannoy. But for Elvire, there is no question of evading it: "It is essential, our message must go through them. As a result, blogs and tumblers dedicated to Femen are flourishing on the Web, as satisfied students often publish their work online and on social networks. A deep mode of communication that irrigates the connected youth, even in its most difficult to access components.

Elvire is deeply feminist. She has never read Simone de Beauvoir or Elisabeth Badinter, yet she says in the schools

---

210. Supervised personal work (TPE), school research projects in groups of 2 to 4 students.

that "it's okay if you don't want to have children, there is no such thing as maternal instinct".

When she arrives in a high school - "you only go there if you're invited, of course" - she always finds the first place of contact with exclusion: "It's at school that they spread the idea that women are weaker than men, I tell them that no, it's simply not true." If equality is a legal fact, the reality is quite different, so it is necessary to give examples, to talk to students about wages, authority, physical strength and even gender...

She does not hesitate to use the social codes of the students: do the high school girls adhere to the glamorized *girl power* of Beyoncé? "No problem, we talk to them about that and we try to make them evolve towards a stronger, more serious, more profound message..." Has she seen the religious fact occupy more and more space in schools? "Yes, it's undeniable, so we talk to them about equality, freedom..."

We also talk to them about the "rape culture". And Elvire, here again, goes on their ground by creating a parodic and feminist duet with her friend Sarah Constantin to hijack a sexist song by the rapper Orelsan (*Saint-Valentin*[211], where we hear lyrics like "but shut your mouth or I'll marry you") which was making the rounds in the playground. The new text with offensive humor that they declaim on the music of the rapper gives pop cultural weapons to the girls: "I

---

211. *Saint-Valentin* is the first song that made Orelsan known thanks to social networks and YouTube. It launched his career in 2007.

tell you nicely, I'm not here to make sentiment / I'm here to cut your ten centimeters [...] / But shut your mouth or you're going to get jacqueline-savage... " The level is low? Certainly. But Elvire understood that, to prevent the return of the war of the sexes in schools, "because the girls will always be the victims", it is necessary to fight on all the grounds, even the most muddy. Especially since at the end of the clip[212], successful, of the two interpreters, the video recalls the terrifying figures related to the "rape culture" in France. Elvire explained herself on this performance in a press release: "It is by learning the release of the rapper Orelsan prosecuted for his violent texts towards women that CLIT, parodic and feminist duo, was born. In France, sexism seems to have a very special legal status: it is called freedom of expression. So Orelsan would have nothing to reproach himself for, since it's not him who calls for raping women, but his character. But wait, if you replace "woman" by "Black", "Arab" or "Jew", that's called incitement to hatred, isn't it? Would sexism be less serious than racism? Is being discriminated against because of one's sex less serious than being discriminated against because of one's skin color? This parody of *Valentine's Day* by Orelsan, where "clit" replaces "cock", is meant to be a mirror of the sexist remarks we hear daily in rap lyrics, whether those of Booba, Kaaris, Seth Gueko or Vald, to name but a few. Let's stop with this excuse that supports

---

212. *CLIT - Valentine's Day* Elvire Duvelle-Charles and Sarah Constantin, March 2016. Viewable on YouTube.

texts that promote rape culture and misogyny under the pretext that rap is a violent means of expression. Rappers who accumulate millions of views on YouTube have a responsibility to their fans, they are part of pop culture. In France, a woman is raped every seven minutes and more than a hundred women die every year from the blows of their spouse. Nearly a third of 18-24 year olds believe that women can get pleasure from being forced into sex. So, isn't it time to change things[213]?"

Last year, there were also many questions about secularism, the attacks, religion... Elvire explained relentlessly the freedom of expression, public space, private sphere, religion... A deeply republican speech that is dear to her heart: "After *Charlie* it was hard," she says lowering her eyes, "we knew them well, I have a lot of trouble talking about it."

Elvire is a convinced militant. She has been involved in all of Femen France's major actions: the Manif pour tous, Notre-Dame (see chapter 24), with different reactions in public opinion, and also in the political class. The young assistant director notes the difference in treatment between the Notre-Dame action, seen as an outrage by Catholics when "Notre-Dame is frankly a tourist place," and the homophobic discourse of Civitas when the fundamentalist association organized a large collective prayer in front of the National Assembly: "During the gay marriage, the Church invited itself into the street, we were the street inviting itself into the Church," she says with a smile. More seriously, she

213. Press Release, March 8, 2016.

wonders: "Why do Sarkozy or Valls accept dialogue with the religious and not with the feminists?"

Elvire wants to embody the future of Femen. Far right, religion, minorities, civil rights, feminism... She believes in the intersectionality of struggles. "We want to interfere with everything!" And Elvire especially thinks that feminist movements must work together... A convergence that is not really in Femen's habits: "But that is also changing, last year we did a three-day "camp" with the MLF, we discovered many points of convergence." This year, the experience was repeated at the time of the Femen "congress", with delegations arriving from the different countries where the movement is present; the place was kept secret because of the risk of attack.

The movement has changed in recent months. Inna is still there to give the impulse, and especially ideas, "for example the hanging for Rohani, the antifascist vaccines[214] of Hénin-Beaumont... that comes from Inna". Elvire is unaware that these ideas come mainly from Ukraine, a long time ago... That they come from Sacha, Oxana and Anna, who invented them and used them in many demonstrations before Inna transposed them to France.

Elvire sees that the movement has "democratized" in a way. The newspapers sometimes refer to her as the

---

214. On May 25, 2014, French activists gather outside the Jean-Jacques Rousseau school in Hénin-Beaumont where FN leader Marine Le Pen is scheduled to vote. Stripped naked, they hold large syringes supposedly injecting an anti-fascist vaccine. They shouted slogans such as: "The FN in quarantine" and "Who has not had his vaccine?

"vice-president of Femen France". She recognizes that this was not always the case, but says that "Inna has evolved, she realized that she could not do everything alone, at first she wanted to control everything, but then she understood that she had to trust certain people". Elvire is careful with her words when she talks about Inna. She has been seeing her for four years, but, in the best interest of the movement, she does not say more.

Elvire is atheist but comes from a family of believers, of Haitian origin. She is not opposed to the idea of Femen welcoming believers, but still... " It's a bit of a stretch because all churches are sexist, backward, misogynistic and backward. It's a bit borderline because all churches are sexist, backward, misogynistic and behind on so many issues." She says that debate is possible when you share "a base of beliefs."

Elvire thinks that the movement must go towards less actions but well thought and spectacular, and more presence on the field of education. She has understood the strength of topless actions and never has any trouble getting naked, "because, obviously, Femen nudity is not the seductive nudity of magazines, it is on the contrary an armor".

She remembers the beginnings, the arrival of Sacha and Oxana. She regrets that they did not stay. She thinks that the future of Femen is to have a structure, offices, employees: "We must also expand horizontally, on the territory.

On the other hand, Elvire is convinced that, if the future of Femen is indeed political, it is not "in" politics. There is no question of presenting candidates for elections, as this

Elvire towards the future

would be contrary to the values of the movement. Is Inna thinking about it? "No, I don't think so. When I ask her directly the question, the next day, Inna will have a half-smile and will answer that "nobody knows the future."

Before Femen, Elvire was doing an internship as a director in the first French commercial television: "I was only with macho men, I was touching racism, I was crying every night, but nobody ever knew.

Her job was to watch images on TV all day and select the most impressive ones for a zapping: "That's how I came across images of Femen actions."

Elvire loved it: "To say the least, it spoke to me right away." Engaged.

When she arrived four years ago, she remembers that Inna didn't take her very seriously, but since Femen needed soldiers... "In fact, she thought I was going to stay three days and I'm still here! In fact, she thought I was going to stay three days and I'm still here!"

Elvire is a good girl.

The scandal paper

> "It often seems to me," she said in reply,
> "that men hardly put into practice the good
> feelings they so willingly parade."
> Leo Tolstoy, *Anna Karenina*, 1877.

On September 14, 2014, an article by Quentin Girard appeared in *Libération* entitled "Femen, combien de divisions?" Quentin knows the movement well, following it for *Libé* since it moved to France. He has developed a cordial, even friendly relationship with Inna. He knows the others less well, but he has already met Sacha and Oxana, notably in Ukraine.

The title "Femen, combien de divisions?" announces both a count of Femen's forces, but also, in true *Libé* style, an account of the movement's internal divisions.

He uses a questionable dialectical method, developing his entire comparative presentation of the divisions within Femen on the basis of equality of treatment, birth and importance of the French and Ukrainian movements. However, these premises are irrelevant. We are in the summer of 2014, Femen has existed in France for barely two years while it germinated in Ukraine more than eight years ago. Its principles, its genesis, its legitimacy, its notoriety proceed from Ukraine and not from France. Sacha, Oxana and Anna founded the movement and made it exist, not Pauline, Marguerite or Sarah… even if they animated the French movement.

In short, he compares the incomparable, but with impartiality.

Sacha and Oxana have a short-lived ally, Josephine Witt[215], the German who spent time in prison with Pauline and Marguerite in Tunisia, at the time of the action in support of Amina. She will leave Femen shortly after this interview. She is sincere and motivated, but she felt betrayed: "When we came back from Tunisia, after being released, Inna welcomed us very coldly. She reproached us for having apologized, Pauline and Marguerite started to cry in front of everyone. I didn't know Inna yet, but I understood right away that I had to get away from her[216].

Josephine Witt, one of the most involved characters in the Joseph Paris film *Naked War*, will leave the movement very affected. She will be back in the spotlight a few months later, in April 2015, when she will jump on Mario Draghi's desk, sending napkins and documents flying, covering the

---

215. Independent activist since breaking with Femen in 2014.
216. *Naked War, op. cit.*

boss of the European Central Bank (ECB) with confetti and ridicule. Not one to shy away from anything, Inna will try, on Twitter[217], to recuperate some of the media prestige of the action... Not a chance, the Femen leader will collect 9 retweets and 6 likes!

After their return from captivity, Pauline and Marguerite will regain, by dint of sycophancy, the favors of Queen Inna. Marguerite has now left the movement.

The article lists the grievances of the one against the other. The French say they are legitimate, the two Ukrainians say they are Femen. Between the two, Inna does not speak or hardly speaks at all, she adopts her favorite attitude: watching the dogs she let loose devour the designated prey while pretending not to have started anything and deploring the excesses of the war.

The hostility, which led, after the publication of the article, to the exclusion of Oxana and her physical expulsion from the squat in Clichy, had been going on for months. From the beginning, Inna rejected her friends and used her Femen France troops to eliminate them politically and in the media, spreading the rumor that Oxana and Sacha were in transit or that they would soon leave the movement (see chapter 32). A year later, she delivered the coup de grâce.

Among the members of Femen France, only Elvire will show any form of fairness, even paying tribute to the courage of the founders. In an interview[218] given to *Menly*

---

217. https://twitter.com/femeninna/status/588800402520420353.
218. "Nudity is our armor," *Menly*, February 22, 2013.

The scandal paper

magazine shortly after Sasha and Oxana's arrival in France, she answers the question: "What are the differences between Femen France and the collective in Ukraine?" "None," says the young assistant director, "except for the language. We operate according to the same manifesto[219]. Obviously, the course of action is simpler here than in Ukraine where Femen are easily arrested by the police. *On the other hand,* Pauline or Marguerite will not cease, from September 2013 and the arrival of the founders, to spread the message that they are no less legitimate.

Following the publication of the *Libé* article, Oxana was taken to task by the French women - Sacha already shared Dimitri's studio in Montmartre. The girls reproached her for asserting her difference, for saying that she was Femen Ukraine and not Femen France, for saying, along with Sacha, that the squat, like the Lavoir moderne before it, had become a meeting place for journalists, photographers, stylists... In short, a new trendy place in Paris. Nothing to do with the vocation and raison d'être of Femen. In the heart of the interview, Sacha also expresses his disagreement with certain actions.

Quentin Girard has transcribed Oxana's and Sacha's words without watering them down: one can hardly blame him. But the article refuses to consider the power of the forces at work, because if the Ukrainian movement is much better founded, it is very weakened. It does not play on its own ground. It is under-represented. It lost in betrayals,

---

219. *Femen Manifesto*, Utopia, 2015.

denials and low blows its living forces. Its two representatives speak in a still mediocre English, the others speak their mother tongue which is also that of the interviewer.

Oxana and Sacha are alone and at the end of their tether.

The others are numerous and at the top.

The match is unequal, not to say lost in advance.

Quentin Girard can't ignore it: he makes Teddy Riner fight against Amandine Buchard, and says that the match is honest because the Olympic champion of the more than 100 kg respected the rules to massacre the departmental champion of the Creuse in the category less than 48 kg.

And if the reading of the paper really shows the depth and the seriousness of the Ukrainian women in front of a certain frivolity of the French women... The result will be to increase tenfold the fury of Pauline, Marguerite and consorts.

Does the journalist know that he is signing the exclusion of the two founders, who are not strong enough to resist the French organization, which now has a written pretext to unleash the curse? Perhaps not.

Oxana recounts: "The very morning of the publication of the interview, I receive a text message from Marguerite telling me to come to the squat to get my things. As I didn't obey the orders, I didn't come until the next day, and I discovered my things thrown out of the squat, in bulk, all my things[220]." A few weeks earlier, the fire department had advised the group of some firefighting equipment, including

---

220. Unless otherwise noted, quotes are from interviews conducted by the author between November 2009 and September 2016.

The scandal paper

an axe. It was this weapon that was used to break down the door of Oxana's room!

For their part, the girls of Femen France establish their legitimacy by the mere fact that they are presented as "the other part", the second branch of the Femen alternative. The prize goes to Pauline: "We too have legitimacy, we have gone as far, or even further than them. Pauline was arrested and imprisoned in Tunisia. It was a brutal experience during which she proved to be brave, even if Inna later spat on her excuses. For the rest, never has the situation in France been comparable to the situation in Ukraine where Sacha and Oxana risked their lives every day between October 2012 and August 2013, where they were imprisoned, abducted, tortured, raped... Where they may only owe their lives to a peacekeeper who releases them when he is not sure he has the right to do so (see Chapter 28). This denial of reality is made more credible by the fact that the story of Sacha, Oxana and the others has been very little documented in the media, whereas the Femen in France are very present.

This is all part of the semantics imposed by Inna and Caroline Fourest. It's all about "de-ukrainizing" Femen. This interview is the last step of the process. Inna adds: "Anna is very attached to the Ukraine, to what is happening there, she does not speak English, she had a hard time getting on the Femen International train. Sasha and Oxana, on the other hand, have decided to take a step back.

Quentin Girard knows very well that Sacha and Oxana have not decided to step back at all. They tell him so, but he does not deny Inna's words.

In January 2014, Marie Vaton and Céline Cabourg had been the first, for the *Nouvel Obs*[221], to question the drifts of the movement. Their article, one of the best written on this period, had already caused some trouble for Sacha and Oxana, accused of having contacted the magazine behind the backs of others.

When she collects her belongings from the squat, Oxana is a refugee persecuted by foreign secret services, she has no papers, no home and no money, and finds herself evicted from her home by activists who claim to base their political action on the fight against all forms of exclusion.

A few months later, when the police arrived at the Femen premises as part of the protection operation following the attacks on *Charlie Hebdo* and the Hyper Cacher, they evacuated Marguerite and Pauline in order to protect them. Neither of them will say that, in the remote wing of the dilapidated building where she found refuge after her exclusion, Oxana is there. "It's disgusting, it's pure hatred," she says on the verge of tears. When they came back the next week, the police told me they asked how many people lived there, and they said no one lived in that wing."

The curtain falls on the last act of the story of the two friends of Khmelnytskyï inside the movement they created.

In early March 2016, an article by Marguerite Stern appeared on *L'Obs - Le Plus.* Marguerite is a French Femen activist of the first hour. She fell in love with a Sudanese refugee in the "jungle" of Calais; this is what she tells in

---

221. "Femen: a sectarian drift?", art. cited.

The scandal paper

her paper. She describes with humanity the inhuman journey that candidates for political asylum must face. In 2014, when Sacha and Oxana were living this hell, Marguerite was participating, in the service of Inna, in their exclusion. In September 2014, Marguerite herself, in Oxana's words, "threw a political refugee in danger onto the street"...

Oxana has not participated in an action since the celebration of Ukraine's independence at the Trocadero on August 24, 2014.

Sacha last saw Inna on June 11, 2014 at the Biografilm festival in Bologna for the presentation of Kitty Green's film, "Her gaze weighed on me like a death sentence."

The beautiful souls of Femen enter a long night.

Oxana takes off!

"Once the chaos has passed, reason is revived and
the balance with perception is regained.
We see less intensely, but we remember
having seen.
I intend to stay awake, attentive to the slightest
sign of beauty.
This beauty that saves me, giving me back
the lightness."
Catherine Meurisse, *La Légèreté*, Dargaud, 2016.

Paris, May 20, 2016

"What's *Télérama*?"

Oxana is not very familiar with the media canons of French culture and she has trouble understanding why Azad seems so worried.

The reason is simple: the art critic of *Télérama* is in the room.

"That's her over there in front of *Christ with a hard-on*!" the curator explains with deference and excitement.

Azad mounted Oxana's solo exhibition at the Mansart Gallery, where the girl had already shown two small paintings *a tempera* in April 2016. As planned. But he tore his hair out: "We opened at 11 o'clock this morning, at 9 o'clock Oxana was still working." The young woman gives her best in a hurry. Azad understands this, but it stresses him out. Oxana was also worried. This is not her first exhibition, these are not her first works. But it is an important moment: "First personal exhibition in Paris in a famous gallery", she says in a French that improves day by day.

At 11 am, the press reception was attended by few journalists. But at the evening cocktail, there is a crowd. There is Lucie, the gallery's commercial director, and Azad, the curator, who say that it looks good. There is Katherina, a Russian artist who has been living in France for ten years and who knows Oxana and likes her very much. There is a painter from a nearby gallery who says that it will take Oxana ten years to get there because "that's how it is"... There are collectors who ask about prices. There are some curious people who make round eyes at the blasphemous icons. There are other journalists. There is Alain Margot, who walks his camera in the street, around the works, between groups of champagne drinkers who trample a nice floor of tommettes as one finds in the private mansions of the Marais.

Above all, there are twenty-three icons hanging on the white walls of a pretty rectangular room. From each work emanate both gentleness and violence. Sweetness first, the suave and golden one of the first Italian Renaissance, a Giotto yellow, a Cimabue-like composition. Violence then, in the details, here a severed head, there an androgynous body... Irony finally, as these saints smokers and drinkers, and blasphemy of course, Christ in erection, lustful saints, virgins in burqa, riders of the Apocalypse...

Oxana has paint in her veins. In the squat of Clichy or in the theater of the Lavoir, she created a real universe based on colors, disorder and soft violence.

Oxana has neither the networks nor the codes to break into the often hermetic world of contemporary art, "but I believe that talent, when it is of this level, cannot escape its destiny for long[222] ", confides Azad.

The icon is a tradition of the Orthodox Church, an art developed in Turkey, Russia or Cyprus. Ukraine has had one of the most beautiful iconographic traditions since the [11th] century, inherited from the Russian princes and the Mongol domination, who allowed a religious culture to develop in Kiev and in the large cities of eastern and southern Ukraine. Many archaeological sites, even today, bring to light in Podolia and Volynia icons of great classical beauty directly evoking the ancestors of Orthodox icons: the hot wax portraits known as "Fayum", named after the Egyptian desert where they were found, and which often date from the first century of the Catholic calendar. Through the Roman

---

222. Unless otherwise noted, quotes are from interviews conducted by the author between November 2009 and September 2016.

Oxana takes off!

Empire, the monks of Mount Athos and Byzantium, these techniques arrived in Kiev and especially in Lvov, the artistic capital of Ukraine, at the beginning of the second millennium. At the beginning of the third millennium, Oxana will be inspired, in particular for her artistic work, by the collection of stories *Partekiron of the Kiev caves*, where the stages of the arrival in Ukraine of the techniques of the icon, but also of the fresco and the mosaic are dissected.

I watch the *Télérama* journalist from the corner of my eye, like everyone else. Impossible to know if she likes it. Oxana is a little surprised to see us worried about the opinion of this elegant and discreet little lady.

I am convinced that nothing brutal can happen to Oxana as her work combines technical quality, fundamental argument and graphic harmony.

Between the small icons, as if to pay a paradoxical homage to the magnificence of religious art, a few sentences chosen from the Apocalypse and dripping with black blood say the taste of death that, for the artist, any transcendental belief organized around the adoration of masters and the submission of men, and especially women, carries: "I saw a pale horse appear. He who rode it was called Death, and Hell followed him, the power was given to them on the fourth part of the earth, to make men die by the sword, the famine, the mortality and by the wild beasts of the earth[223]..."

Sacha arrives. She doesn't like crowds much anymore and, as usual when she is not half naked, she is shy. Sasha

---

223. Revelation of Saint John, Chap. 6, verse 8.

was familiar with Oxana's early works, before the fire that largely destroyed them in her friend's parents' house. Here she discovers many new ones. She finds that "the precision of the line and the drawing is the same in the drawings of 2008 and in the works exhibited". Has Oxana not progressed? "No, it is that her talent is innate, she has worked a lot on the meaning, on the finesse, on the humor, but the technical quality, it is something almost supernatural... " A gift from elsewhere... " As if a god wanted to say to him: "You see that I exist!" " Sacha laughed. Oxana too. And it is a good surprise. In the middle of this bobo fauna, I was afraid that Oxana would have difficulty finding her place. And it is exactly the opposite! She shines. She answers to everyone, and even often in French. She explains, she details, she even receives compliments without putting anyone down... Oxana is simply happy as I have never seen her.

I leave her with a bright smile... a little too early to witness the sensational arrival of Caroline Fourest.

Oxana says, "She said she didn't have much time but was so happy, she kept repeating my name loudly - Oxana, Oxana!"

Then the journalist admired the exhibition, said it was beautiful and turned to the press officer to announce that she was going to talk about it on her blog and that it would be a great publicity for Oxana.

Sacha is still there. She welcomes him without a word and without a smile: "She left right away." Sacha will never forgive. Neither will Oxana, but tonight she is elsewhere.

Oxana takes off!

A few days later, Sabrina Silamo wrote a magnificent article in *Télérama*[224], expressing the depth of Oxana's humanity and talent.

We won't read anything on Caroline Fourest's blog. But on May 14, she will "strongly recommend" to the friends of her Facebook page "to go to the Mansart gallery where Oxana Shachko is exhibiting her paintings for the first time in Paris".

And on the guestbook that the gallery puts at the disposal of the visitors, one will find, with regard to the past sufferings and the inflicted violence, the most moved of the comments: " *I love you, I want to make love with you*[225]. Signed Caroline Fourest.

224. "Oksana Shachko, a Femen in the midst of a crisis of faith," Sabrina Silamo, *Télérama*, May 14, 2016.

225. "I love you, I want to make love with you."

Epilogue

> "But the truth remains first and foremost
> a story of the future that serves to project itself.
> It is a basis for building and not repairing.
> There is the incurable and there is the intrinsic
> dimension of truth, that of building."
> Cynthia Fleury,
> *Les Irremplaçables*, Gallimard, 2015.

**Paris, esplanade du Trocadero,
June 23, 2016**

"What is life after Femen?"

Between a shrink who tells her to do sports, a French class and reading a report on an expected and failed Femen action against the National Front, Sacha wonders... "There is no doubt that there is life after Femen, but I don't want to live it. No doubt there is a life after Femen, but I don't want to live it, Femen is me, it's us[226]", she says, pointing to her friend Oxana.

Sacha and Oxana are a little moved. They are coming back to the Trocadero, where they have done several performances; moved especially because they are going back in time... This morning, they painted on their bodies and it had not happened for more than two years: "But it's as if it was yesterday", says Oxana. In Montmartre, in Sacha's little room, the young artist wove the wreaths, chose the colors. They smiled when Oxana confessed that she had already repeated these gestures several times, alone in front of a mirror, "when things were not going so well".

As for me, I went back a few years, to Kiev in the back room of the Cupid, to Zaporoje in a cellar, to Odessa in the corner of a door... and I photographed the same attentive and slipped gestures. Then we headed to the Esplanade by metro. It's the state of emergency. There are soldiers patrolling. Sacha and Oxana are wearing light, closed jackets and, in a plastic bag from Auchan, two wreaths of flowers. I see them concentrated. They point out to me without hesitation four or five onlookers, "policemen in civilian clothes, no doubt".

We have to make the cover photo of the book.

For Oxana, as for Sacha, Femen is dead, or to be reinvented. The artist has sometimes had a harder time than her friend to get out of the hostile nights that populated 2015

---

226. Unless otherwise noted, quotes are from interviews conducted by the author between November 2009 and September 2016.

and still 2016. Sacha has flirted with oblivion, Oxana with the end. It's time to believe again.

Inna's war was the most violent, but it was Anna's felony, the other betrayal, that hurt Oxana the most: "Inna, I didn't really love her, we didn't grow up together, but Anna, we were sisters."

Contacts with Ukraine, Anna and Viktor are definitely broken.

With Inna.

Would a reconciliation ever be possible? Of course nothing will ever be possible," answers Oxana, "Inna waged a cowardly war on us, she launched her henchmen against us, she manipulated the press, lied, cheated... and finally she left us for dead at the side of the road."

Neither time nor space can repair these wounds.

Sacha agrees, but adds: "What is important is Femen, and by becoming complacent and media-friendly, the movement has lost its way, which is why we must continue to fight."

Would the pain have been less severe if the movement had followed a route more in line with his ideal? Sacha raises his head... " But I don't want to consider this question, because nobody had the right to keep me away from Femen, nobody!"

Sacha's path is first of all that of a truth scorned, mocked, trampled on in the name of superficiality, laziness... Sacha says that being able to shout this truth will already do her "more good than all the sport in the world", after having been gagged for so long. A question of survival.

But then, is there a continuation to this path?

Anyone who gets close to them knows that these two women are unstoppable. Whatever their next battle, they will fight it with courage and passion. Sacha would like to write, she has ideas. Oxana will become a great artist. She was afraid of her first Parisian exhibition. She will be afraid of the second one, but a little less...

For Oxana, "it may be necessary to find a way to militate". Hyperactive, the artist of the decimated band is of all the fights. As soon as something moves in Paris, she points her nose... She marched for the climate at the time of the Cop 21, she stayed up all night in République in May... From her squat, she follows the movements in Spain, the United States and Italy. She adds, "At the same time, since Femen is no longer Femen, everything has to be reinvented, maybe we have to start over."

Sacha is more concretely focused on feminism. Within the movement, her struggle has always been one of immediacy: challenging a law, attacking the manifestations of patriarchy, the symbols.

But their ideals are common: to change the world and give women an equal place in it.

No more and no less.

But forever.

I mount the 200mm and walk away. I want to take the photo with a telephoto lens to get a squashed perspective on the Eiffel Tower in the background. Associate Paris with Oxana and Sasha. Japanese tourists are watching us. Everyone has understood that they are Femen. We have to be quick. No question of being caught!

Sasha and Oxana climb up the parapet, slip on their jackets and put on their crowns.

Hands on the hips, legs stretched, torsos bulging, no smile. They are there, stronger than ever, these two beautiful souls.

On their breasts is written their life:

"Femen".

Afterword by Sacha Shevchenko

> Could it be that we believe men are less sensitive
> to the painting of our sorrows than to the image of
> our charms, and would we promise ourselves even
> more ease in seducing them than in touching them?
> Denis Diderot, *The Nun*

This quote from the French writer and philosopher whose writings prepared minds for the great French Revolution accurately describes the essence of our tactics in the struggle we have waged to spread feminism in a patriarchal world. However, it seems to me that I can in no way apply it to the author of this book. Indeed, Olivier Goujon, a man, not only sought to meet us but also wanted to listen to us. It is also significant that this reporter, a specialist in Femen, was a French citizen whose life and actions testify to a real attachment to the motto of the Republic: "Liberté, Égalité, Fraternité". This motto is also at the heart of my struggle. I would like to express my deep gratitude to Olivier for his firm determination to seek and tell the truth, for his irreducible will to help us reclaim our share of truth in the face of History, for his ability to fight in the name of the present to restore the past.

In writing this book, he has not relied on superficial reporting in the wake of the successive scandals caused by our successful actions. Instead, he conscientiously explores how the Femen movement has transformed itself over the course of its history. He analyzes, dissects and does not neglect the internal relations between the former sisters in arms, now separated. To the people who parasitize our ideas, we can now oppose something written: our history, to Oxana and to myself, the history of Femen.

Seven years ago in Kiev, Olivier met a wild Amazon, fragile in appearance but with a strong spirit, entirely devoted to her only goal: to rekindle the flame of the world women's revolution. I was ready to fight against patriarchy at the cost of sacrificing my life, not to mention my family, friends and loved ones. I was burning with enthusiasm, because I knew I was on the right side of history, and through my voice millions of oppressed women could express themselves.

There is little mention in this book of the state of depression in which I found myself, when I saw the author again almost a year ago, at the beginning of 2016. The one he had in front of him then was like a little girl, broken by the betrayal of her sisters in arms, and who only wanted one thing more: to run away and hide, far from her own heroic past. Far from herself.

Is there a life after Femen? That's the question I've been asking myself for over three long years. And I still haven't found an answer that isn't deadly scary. I, who felt like a true Pallas Athena, at the forefront of the global feminist movement, was suddenly exiled from my native country, and, what is truly awful, removed from my organization by the treachery of my sisters in arms. The people who were most dear to me cowardly banished me from the movement that I created and which was the very meaning and expression of my life. So I took refuge in a philosophy of escape from reality and suddenly I became a frightened woman, in constant doubt, to whom the very idea of a conversation about feminism only brought pain and disappointment.

Femen is over for me. The innovative ideas and forms that Oxana and I developed, which were the result of hard and scrupulous work, are gone. My model has turned into a Frankenstein's monster. Inna and her small circle of fanatics have decided that Femen is a franchise, a business that can be used as a career. They mutilated this movement that was a complete body, depriving it of its essence: solidarity and camaraderie. In doing so, they were no longer sisters, but despicable rivals creating a disgraceful parody of our organization, without soul or intelligence.

I can no longer, I don't want to be part of this gathering of "freaks" that empties the revolutionary movement of all its strength and potential.

I am a perfectionist who suffers deeply for the fate of women, and that is why I have always refused to exchange the fame that Femen gave us, the realization of a great idea, for a comfortable personal success.

With *Histoire d'une trahison,* we understand how, by relying on our feelings, our emotions and our inflexible will, we were able to implement the feminist ideology in a system dominated by a patriarchal and capitalist world-view. How we were able to embody, ourselves, this idea that has become primordial for me, formulated, admittedly quickly, by Victor Hugo that "the naked woman is the armed woman[227] ".

I thank Olivier who believed in me and in my fight.

I thank him because he wanted to show the creation, evolution and death of a great idea.

Translated from the Russian by Léonide Aslanoff

---

227. *The man who laughs,* Victor Hugo.

Acknowledgements

To Oxana Shachko and Sacha Shevchenko, who have overcome their pain to tell their story.

To Jean-Charles Gérard who trusted me.

To Delphine Mozin-Santucci, who made this book a book.

To Galia Ackermann, Safia Lebdi, Alain Margot, Joseph Paris, who did not hesitate.

To my daughter Aurélie and my wife Laura for their unfailing support.

Table

Best sellers Max Milo Editions

Hitler's banker, Jean-François Bouchard

Confessions of a forger, Éric Piedoie Le Tiec

The Koran and the flesh, Ludovic-Mohamed Zahed

Governing by fake news, Jacques Baud

Governing by chaos, Collectif

A political history of food, Paul Ariès

Mad in U.S.A.: The ravages of the "American model",
Michel Desmurget

Mondial soccer club geopolitics, Kévin Veyssière

Putin: Game master?, Jacques Braud

Treatise on the three impostors: Moses, Jesus, Muhammad,
The Spirit of Spinoza

TV Lobotomy, Michel Desmurget